KEEPING THEIR MARBLES

Tiffany Jenkins is an author, academic, broadcaster, and consultant on cultural policy. Her writing credits include the *Independent*, the *Art Newspaper*, the *Guardian*, the *Scotsman* (for which she was a weekly columnist on social and cultural issues), and the *Spectator*. She is an Honorary Fellow in the Department of Art History at the University of Edinburgh; a former visiting fellow in the Department of Law at the London School of Economics and Political Science, and was previously director of the Arts and Society Programme at the Institute of Ideas. She completed her PhD in Sociology at the University of Kent and divides her time between London and Edinburgh.

She has advised a number of organisations on cultural policy, including Trinity College, Dublin; English Heritage; the British Council; the Norwegian government; the University of Oslo; Norwegian Theatres and Orchestras; and the National Touring Network for Performing Arts, Norway.

PRAISE FOR *KEEPING THEIR MARBLES*

A *Catholic Herald* Book of the Year 2016

'The dubious means by which museum collections were gathered has fuelled the demands for treasures to be repatriated. Surely they ought to be returned? No, says Tiffany Jenkins, and she marshals a powerful case.'

—Robbie Millen, *The Times*

'Tiffany Jenkins applies her considerable experience of cultural policy to construct an excellent survey . . . Her level-headed and balanced book . . . is a valuable contribution to the international debate, and will enrich audiences and scholars for a long time to come.'

—Mark Fisher, *The Spectator*

'Jenkins's book provides a welcome introduction to some of the questions facing museums today.'

—William St Clair, *Literary Review*

'Clear, informed, and well-referenced . . . Specialists, and anyone with an interest in contemporary culture, can equally enjoy and learn from this calm, balanced, and respectful review, in a field distinguished more by polemic than wisdom.'

—Mike Pitts, *British Archaeology*

'Jenkins skillfully critiques the manifold issues that beleaguer museums today.'

—David Lowenthal, *Evening Standard*

'This book is both a lucid account of how the great world museums came by their treasures and a robust argument as to why (human remains such as bones aside) they should keep them.'

—Michael Prodger, *RA Magazine*

'Jenkins does an excellent job of portraying the extreme reactions elicited by repatriation conversations.'

—David Hurst Thomas, *Nature*

'Brilliant and fascinating'

—James Delingpole, *The Spectator*

'Jenkins exhibits an unfashionable determination to eloquently argue that what we have, we hold.'

—Marina Vaizey, *Art Newspaper*

'[Jenkins] has much of interest to say about the development of museums and their changing ideology.'

—Peter Jones, *BBC History Magazine*

'Elegantly lines up the arguments and provides careful, balanced, and well-considered responses.'

—Adrian Spooner, *Classics for All*

'[An] eloquent defence of museums . . . A well-researched and thought-provoking take on a very complex and controversial subject.'

—Lucia Marchini, *Minerva*

KEEPING THEIR MARBLES

How the Treasures of the Past Ended Up in
Museums ... and Why They Should Stay There

TIFFANY JENKINS

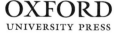

OXFORD

UNIVERSITY PRESS

Great Clarendon Street, Oxford, OX2 6DP,
United Kingdom

Oxford University Press is a department of the University of Oxford.
It furthers the University's objective of excellence in research, scholarship,
and education by publishing worldwide. Oxford is a registered trade mark of
Oxford University Press in the UK and in certain other countries

© Tiffany Jenkins 2016

The moral rights of the author have been asserted

First published 2016
First published in paperback 2018

Published in the United States of America by Oxford University Press
198 Madison Avenue, New York, NY 10016, United States of America

British Library Cataloguing in Publication Data
Data available

Library of Congress Cataloging in Publication Data
Data available

ISBN 978–0–19–965759–9 (Hbk.)
ISBN 978–0–19–881718–5 (Pbk.)

Printed and bound by CPI Group (UK) Ltd, Croydon, CR0 4YY

INTRODUCTION TO THE
PAPERBACK EDITION

In early 2016, a row broke out over the fate of a brass cockerel that had stood in a student dining hall in Jesus College, Cambridge, for about eighty-six years. Known as the Okukor, it is one of almost 1,000 Benin Bronzes, so termed even though many are made from brass, taken from Benin City, present-day Nigeria, during a punitive expedition by the British in 1897. The Okukor had perched among the young scholars as they ate their meals in the college since 1930, when it was bequeathed by George William Neville, a member of the Benin Expedition, whose son had attended the college. It was adopted as a symbol of Jesus because three cockerels' heads appear on the college crest.

At a meeting of the Jesus College Student Union in March 2016, the Benin Bronze Appreciation Committee passed a motion which supported the repatriation of the Okukor to Nigeria. In a dense eleven-page document, the students argued for 'returning [the artefact] to its place of origin.' Sending it back to the 'community from which it was stolen,' they said, was 'just'. They wanted to return the cockerel to make amends for the 'sins' of British imperialism. They continued: 'the contemporary political culture surrounding colonialism and social justice, combined with the University's global agenda, offers a perfect opportunity for the College to benefit from this gesture.'[1] Cambridge University agreed that the statue should be taken down from the hall and the possibility of return considered. A university spokesperson said: 'Jesus College acknowledges the contribution made by the students in raising the important but complex question of the rightful location of its Benin bronze, in response to which it has permanently removed the Okukor from its hall.' It pledged to work with university authorities and museum professionals to 'discuss and determine the best future for the Okukor, including the question of repatriation.'[2]

On her blog, the racial equalities officer at Jesus College cheered this decision: 'It's nice to see Jesus setting a precedent and taking steps in the right direction to weed out the colonial legacies that exist in bits of the university. We still have a lot of work to do . . . but how exciting and momentous and revolutionary is this?!'[3] Joanna Williams, a lecturer in higher education at the University of Kent, took a different view in the *Daily Mail*, declaring that it was a 'cowardly' move on behalf of the university and that 'students have declared war on the past and this is another example of how students are using history as a morality play to express their own moral superiority in the present.'[4]

The case of the cockerel is one of three controversies that erupted in the months surrounding the publication of *Keeping Their Marbles*, and which illustrate the themes I discuss in the book; indeed, my reservations about the politics of repatriation. These three cases reveal the dynamics that propel claims for repatriation, which are internal to western institutions as well as external to them; the limits of trying to repair the past through the movement of artefacts; and the divisive and censorious consequences of the idea that one culture has a greater right than others to own objects and to decide their future.

Take the dynamics of repatriation. The demand for the return of the cockerel came, not from people in Nigeria, though Nigeria has long appealed for the return of bronzes, if not the Okukor, but from students *within* Cambridge University. What I suggest in the following pages is complicated: the inclination to repatriate objects, or at least grant a sympathetic ear to the possibility, often comes from within museums and the academy—in this case, students at one of the oldest and most important universities in the world. This pattern of events is also what happened in the second controversy, which was set alight one month before that of the cockerel.

High up on a building on the main road in the city of Oxford, above the entrance to Oriel College, stands—for now—a small statue of Cecil John Rhodes, the Victorian imperialist who shaped Britain's empire in Africa and who, in 1887, told the House of Assembly in Cape Town that 'The native is to be treated as a child and denied the franchise.'[5] In February 2016, students at Oriel College, led by a South African Rhodes Scholar, Ntokozo Qwabe, kicked-started what became known as the 'Rhodes Must Fall' campaign, arguing that the statue of Rhodes should be removed. Rhodes had studied at Oriel, intermittently, between 1873 and 1881, and bequeathed £100,000 to the college in his will. It is this money that funded the students who wanted his statue removed.

The campaign had its origins at the University of Cape Town in South Africa, where Rhodes built his fortune and power before his death in 1902 and where there was a statue honouring his legacy. In March 2015, activist Chumani Maxwele smeared excrement on the statue, triggering further protests by activists who complained that the statue had 'great symbolic power' which glorified someone 'who exploited black labour and stole land from indigenous people' and should be taken down.[6] In a short space of time they were successful: one month after the protests began, the university authorities removed the statue. The campaign then spread like wildfire to America and Europe where different groups, especially on university campuses, argued that statues that included Jefferson Davis, the Confederacy's president, and Thomas Jefferson, the American president, be toppled.

In one respect, it is hard to get all that excited either way about a small statue of a Victorian imperialist. There are lots of monuments to old white men all over the world, men whose influence and often names have been forgotten, and whose time has passed. Unlike many of the contested artefacts in museums, they are unremarkable; neither pretty to look at nor unique evidence of past peoples' ways of living. We might not even notice their absence: I grew up in Oxford and, despite walking past the college often, only noticed the statue of Rhodes once the campaign drew it to my attention. In one way then, it does not matter what happens to a bit of old statuary that is barely identifiable from the street. But in another, this controversy is important because of the claims that are made for removing old pieces of stone: primarily, that it is a necessary part of decolonization, which is an idea that bears similarities to the arguments for repatriation. What warrants scrutiny are the claims made for what taking down statues can achieve.

Decolonization, which took place in the second half of the twentieth century, was driven by the great social movements that swept through Africa and Asia and forcefully challenged the might of European rule. They grew out over the insistence that people of Africa and Asia could and should run their own lives and be free from the domination of Europe, challenging Rhodes' argument that they were to be treated like children, or worse. To compare this major transformation which came out of many years of hard struggle to what might be brought about through the removal of a statue is to elide two very different movements and achievements. And in so doing, there is a danger that it diminishes the earlier battles and even the meaning of 'decolonization'.

It is true that the toppling statues was at the heart of significant political and social change in the past. During the Protestant Reformation, Catholic statues were defaced and destroyed; during the French revolution, statues of monarchs and their art were demolished; in post-independence India, statues of Viceroys and British monarchs were taken down and neutered by placing them in Delhi's Coronation Park. But in all these cases the toppling of statues came as part of a great social upheaval or in the midst of great change when the old oppressive regime also was removed. The 'Rhodes Must Fall' campaign formed a long time after decolonization, and—not insignificantly—in a time of political *in*action, where removing statues appears to stand in for social change. As the writer and author of *The Meaning of Race*, Kenan Malik, observed in an article on *Aljazeera*: 'Once upon a time, student activists used to demand that capitalism must fall, or that apartheid must be crushed, or that colonialism must be swept away. Now, it seems, they just want to take down statues.'[7] This is one of the limits to such campaigns and, indeed, repatriation: that it stands in for social change, that it does little to advance material and political equality, and that objects are expected to do more work than they can achieve.

The third controversy that broke out as *Keeping Their Marbles* was published was a series of fractious arguments about the rights and wrongs of cultural appropriation, which is when someone adopts parts of a culture that is considered not their own. The debate over cultural appropriation bears similarities to the arguments over who owns culture, discussed in Chapter 6, and shows the chilling consequences of the idea that only one culture owns culture.

In June 2017, the sculptor Sam Durant's piece *Scaffold*, which was lauded when shown in the Netherlands, Scotland, and Germany, was dismantled after protests erupted when it was displayed in the sculpture park of the Walker Art Center, in Minneapolis.

Scaffold is a powerful artwork about the death penalty: the steel and wood sculpture is a composite of the representations of seven gallows that were used in US state-sanctioned executions by hanging between 1859 and 2006. One recalls the largest mass execution in US history, when, in Mankato, Minnesota, in 1862, thirty-eight Dakota men were executed under orders from President Lincoln following the U.S.–Dakota War; another, the gallows used to put to death four Lincoln Conspirators, in Washington D.C. in 1865, including the first woman to be executed by the federal government.

When it was shown in Europe, *Scaffold* was praised by Amnesty International as a way to talk about capital punishment. It was crucial that it was exhibited in the US—the only remaining Western democracy to still have the death penalty: one of the structures referenced in the piece is the scaffold used just over a decade ago to hang Saddam Hussein. And thirteen people between January 2016 and July of the same year were executed in the US by lethal injection: six white men, six black men, and one Latino male.

You might expect, then, that *Scaffold* would provoke anger about state executions. Instead, outrage exploded over the ethnicity of the artist, for Sam Durant is white. The indigenous Dakota community took exception to the representation of the Mankato gallows in the sculpture. Indigenous activists protested that Mr. Durant was appropriating their history about which he had no right to comment and that the placement of the piece in an art park trivialized the event. After a meeting with the Dakota tribal elders, a decision was made to take down the sculpture and burn the wood in a ceremony, though they have since suspended this pending further consultation.

Fighting racism and injustice used to be about people coming together from different ethnicities to demand equality. It used to be about creating a colour-blind society and limiting state power. But in this instance neither was achieved: instead, race dictated an act of creation, or its dissembling, and state power went unquestioned.

It is one of many similar controversies. Earlier in the same year, New York's Whitney Museum selected for its Biennial Exhibition Dana Schutz's painting of the body of Emmett Till, a 14-year-old African-American murdered in 1955 by two white men in Mississippi. The artist Hannah Black organized a petition to have the work removed and destroyed, as she objected to a white painter responding to Black suffering.

What we have here is problematic, for political activism and for art. To argue that an artist should not create an artwork because of their race will chill not only creativity but relationships between people; it rehabilitates the language of racial purity and suggests that unity and commonality between people of different ethnicities is unattainable. Artists need to be free to explore all ideas and all history, held to account for their work, certainly, but for its quality—not their identity. To argue otherwise is to limit an important empathetic act: thinking about another time and another place, and about how things could be different for people who may not be like you, is the basis for much of art, and indeed politics.

Whitney Museum defended its decision to show the artwork. But Sam Durant and the Walker Art Centre did not. As part of the agreement with the elders, Durant pledged never to recreate *Scaffold* and to transfer to the Dakota tribe his intellectual property rights to the work. Walker director Olga Viso, issued an apologetic statement: 'We are deeply, deeply sorry and pledge to be better stewards of our relationship with communities going forward.'[8] Here is a case of an institution bowing quickly to claims over rightful ownership based on both race and historic wrongs, bringing me back to my first point: in a number of cases institutions themselves appear to find it difficult to argue for the universality of knowledge and creation, and are not able to challenge segregationist ideas or calls for censorship. It is this uncertainty and insecurity *within* institutions that is as much a threat to the pursuit of knowledge and the free play of the imagination as any claim made on them from campaign groups external to them.

Tiffany Jenkins,
Edinburgh, July 2017

ACKNOWLEDGEMENTS

This book is the result of many years of thinking about museums and cultural artefacts. I am lucky to have had plenty of opportunities to discuss my thoughts with colleagues and students. I have in mind Tatiana Flessas, Tom Freudenheim, Eva Silvén, Richard Williams, David Lowenthal, Amy Clarke, Felicity Bodenstein Howard Williams, Annie Malama, and Duncan Sayer. I have also been able to work through related questions at length with Jonathan Williams, Ian Jenkins, Karl-Erik Norrman, Lesley Fitton, Hannah Boulton, and Karl Magnusson, all of whom gave their time—and criticism—generously. Jonathan Conlin's feedback on a draft was especially helpful. Jennie Bristow gave invaluable editorial advice.

A number of organizations and projects granted me space to test out my arguments, I wish to highlight and thank the project European National Museums—Presenting Cases of Heritage Conflicts in Europe; and Durham University Archaeology Society. Some of the necessary travel was made possible by a grant from the Society of Authors, for which I am grateful. Matthew Cotton helped me finish the project. Andrew Gordon saw the possibility. Iain put up with my constant preoccupation and obsessive musings.

CONTENTS

LIST OF ILLUSTRATIONS

Introduction

>─┼─◆>─•O•─<◆─┼─<

For more than three centuries, museums have acquired treasures of the past so that visitors to the British Museum in London, the Louvre in Paris, and the Metropolitan Museum of Art in New York, to name but a few, can wonder at the ingenuity and creativity of humanity. As well as exhibiting these objects to hundreds of thousands of visitors every year, scholars research the collections, exploring how artefacts were made, what they were used for, and what they have meant to people, opening our eyes to past lives and furthering our knowledge of human civilizations.

Today, however, the right of museums to hold and display their collections, and their reasons for doing so, are under question. Objects are often said to 'belong' to a particular people, rather than all people. Attention is increasingly focused on how the artefacts came to be in the possession of the institution, rather than on what they can tell us about a culture. Collections are as often condemned as 'loot', 'plunder', 'pillage', or 'booty', as they are lauded as interesting, revealing, or beautiful. The underlying implication is that museums are not the proper place for such artefacts, that these institutions may even do more harm than good. Indeed, museums have been placed under such scrutiny that I fear for their future.

In recent decades, various countries, individuals, and groups have requested the repatriation—the return—of artefacts they consider theirs. The Elgin Marbles,[1] exhibited in the British Museum for over 200 years, are a prominent example and the focus of a campaign for repatriation that has won considerable support. These ancient marble sculptures, including some of the most remarkable pieces of ancient Greek art in existence, were once an integral part of the Parthenon in Athens, built as a temple dedicated to the Greek goddess Athena which had stood on the Acropolis in the Greek capital for close to 2,500 years. Around half of the sculptures were removed at the turn of the nineteenth century, with permission from the then rulers, the Ottoman Empire, by the agents of the British ambassador to Constantinople, Lord Thomas Elgin. Elgin's agents took 200 tons' worth, by picking parts off the floor and hacking parts off the Parthenon, before shipping them to Britain, aided by the Royal Navy, where they ended up in the British Museum as the centrepiece of one of the greatest collections in the world.[2]

Few doubt the legal right of the British Museum to keep the Elgin Marbles. Many, however, openly and vocally dispute the moral right. Although Elgin argued that he rescued the Marbles, removing them from the site and transporting them to London was controversial, and their arrival triggered intense debate. Some considered it an act of vandalism.

> Dull is the eye that will not weep to see
> Thy walls defac'd, thy mouldering shrines remov'd
> By British hands, which it had best behov'd
> To guard those relics ne'er to be restor'd

decried Lord Byron in his poem *Childe Harold's Pilgrimage*.[3]

Campaigners want the Marbles to be returned to Greece so they can be displayed in the Acropolis Museum, situated about a mile from the original site, and which holds much of what is left from the Parthenon. The Elgin Marbles are 'theirs', it is said; they are 'Greek'. One argument contends that reuniting the Marbles with the rest of the sculptures would greatly benefit our understanding and appreciation of their original form.

The British Museum, as you might expect, wants to keep them, justifying the retention on the basis that they have preserved and protected the Marbles for centuries, and that in the context of their encyclopaedic collection—which holds objects from multiple civilizations across time, including artefacts from Persia, Rome, Mesopotamia, India, and Turkey—visitors can understand the relationship of the ancient Greek culture to the wider world.

The Elgin Marbles have become a cause célèbre, top of a long list of artefacts that people want returned to their country of origin. Another set of objects—about 900 sculptures and plaques—that have become the focus of campaigns are the Benin Bronzes, held variously in the British Museum, the Ethnological Museum in Berlin, the Ethnology Museum in Vienna, the National Museum Lagos in Nigeria, the National Museum of Scotland, and the Art Institute of Chicago. Their story of removal is not as morally ambiguous as that of the Elgin Marbles: the Benin Bronzes were taken by the British army as they razed the Kingdom of Benin to the ground.

Benin had been at the centre of a medieval African kingdom, founded in the tenth century in what is now Southern Nigeria, which flourished between the fourteenth and seventeenth centuries. The Benin Bronzes— magnificent dark red, copper alloy sculptures and plaques—were made during this period. Elegant, narrative works, they provide an insight into a sophisticated culture. Their arrival in Britain is said to have stimulated the 'discovery' and appreciation of African art. But the story of their acquisition is not quite so civilized.

Towards the end of the nineteenth century, Oba Ovonramwen—the king of Benin—was involved in a territory and trade dispute with Britain. Germany, Britain, France, and Belgium were competing to carve up the African continent. The Oba in Benin had a monopoly over trade, partly due to its strategically advantageous location in the middle of north–south and east–west trade routes and because it was close to the sea. The

British had their eye on this territory. British powers decided that the Oba had to go when he would not bend to their will, and the Benin Bronzes were caught up in this battle: they were removed by the army as they destroyed Benin City. Troops burned down the palace and took its riches during a massacre, with the British using the newly manufactured Maxim machine guns. The sculptures and plaques were taken deliberately to sell in order to recoup the military expenses of the campaign. The Foreign and Commonwealth Office sold them off and they ended up in museums, and bought by collectors.

In 2012 the collector and New York banker Robert Owen Lehman bequeathed to the Boston Museum of Fine Art thirty-four rare West African works of art, bought in the 1950s and 1970s, thirty-two of which are from the Kingdom of Benin and form the basis of a new public gallery. There was a cry of protest. Yusuf Abdallah Usman, director general of the National Commission for Museums and Monuments in Nigeria, issued an emotional plea for their return:

> Without mincing words, these artworks are heirlooms of the great people of the Benin Kingdom and Nigeria generally. They form part of the history of the people. The gap created by this senseless exploitation is causing our people untold anguish, discomfort and disillusionment.[4]

Yusuf Abdallah Usman did not achieve what he so desired. The Boston Museum opened its gallery devoted to the Bronzes.

Elsewhere, Turkey has requested that the Victorian and Albert Museum (V&A) in London send back the marble carving of a child's head, removed from a sarcophagus in Anatolia by the archaeologist Sir Charles Wilson in the late nineteenth century, and has refused exhibition loans to multiple museums until many other demands for the return of antiquity are met. Questions have been raised about the acquisition of the Nefertiti bust, now in the Neues Museum in Berlin, discovered by a team of German archaeologists in Amarna, Egypt, in 1912; the Rosetta

Stone, now in the British Museum; as well as the 2,060-year-old Dendera Zodiac relief, blasted from the ceiling of the Hathor temple by the French in the early nineteenth century (now in the Louvre in Paris). The Chinese are searching for the objects taken from the Summer Palace in Beijing during the Opium Wars, plundered by the British and French armies before they burnt the palace to the ground, and which were subsequently scattered in institutions including the V&A, the Museum of Fine Arts in Boston, and the Army Museum in Paris. The list of objects that people want to be given back is long, and frequently updated with new requests—or returns.

There are legitimate reasons why some feel that the treasures in museums belong to them. These objects were created by people in particular moments and places, and they speak to people about those important times past. They are often beautiful and/or intriguing. Additionally, many of these objects in museums were taken under circumstances that are now generally perceived as dubious. The acquisition of artefacts from cultures that include ancient Egypt, Greece, the Middle East, Africa, and China took place during a period of Western dominance. Imperial ambitions and rivalry, especially with and between Britain and France, fuelled the extensive excavation of faraway ancient lands for monuments and sculptures. Armies and diplomats hauled them back to Europe, creating well-stocked collections as a consequence. Little attention was paid, then, to the idea that objects found in foreign lands might not belong to the European explorers, invaders, and travellers who took them; that the people of the countries might want to keep the treasures for themselves. Many argue that it is now time to make amends for such acts, to repair the wrongs of the past.

The requests for repatriation appear to be having some effect. In certain cases, the flow of artefacts into museums is starting to be reversed. In the late 1990s, Glasgow City Council returned a Ghost Dance Shirt—a sacred piece of clothing—to the Lakota people of South Dakota. A totem pole from a Native American tribe, donated to a museum in Sweden in the 1920s, was sent back to the Haisla people. At the end of the 2013, the US-based charity the Annenberg Foundation bought twenty-four sacred Native American masks at a controversial Paris auction in order to send them back to the Hopi and Apache tribes. In the summer of July 2012, Berlin returned the Boğazköy Sphinx, dated from around 1600 BC and found at the Hittite capital of Hattusa in 1915, to Turkey. One year earlier, the Metropolitan Museum of Art in New York sent back relics from Tutankhamen's tomb to Egypt. In 2011 and 2012, Yale University returned to Peru artefacts found at Machu Picchu by the explorer Hiram Bingham—said to be the inspiration for the Indiana Jones character. In 2013, a wealthy French businessman returned two bronze animal heads to China that had been looted by French and British troops in the nineteenth century. In 2014, the Denver Museum of Nature and Science repatriated thirty memorial totems to the National Museums of Kenya. That same year, Mark Walker, the great-grandson of Captain Herbert Walker (a principal figure in the British expedition in Benin), returned two bronzes—a so-called 'bird of prophecy', known as an Oro bird, and a bell used to invoke ancestors—taken by his great-grandfather, to Nigeria.[5]

Peru asked for the return of a collection of elaborately embroidered textiles, discovered by tomb raiders in the early twentieth century, after they were exhibited in the show—*A Stolen World*—at the Museum of World Culture in Gothenburg, Sweden, in September 2008–2009. The repatriation request was successful. An ancient shroud and four other textiles were returned in 2014. It is intended that another eighty-five textiles are sent back by 2021.

Although the British Museum refuses to part with the Elgin Marbles, the museum has agreed to the 'permanent loan' of parts of the Lewis Chessman collection to Lews Castle, in the town of Stornoway, Scotland, and has repatriated human remains—vital research material—to Aboriginal communities in Australia. Indeed, thousands of human remains have been repatriated from museums in America, Australasia, Canada, and Europe.

In 2011, the Natural History Museum returned 138 bones of men and women to the Torres Strait Islands, located between Australia and Papua New Guinea. In 2012, the Montreal Museum of Fine Arts returned a tattooed head—a Toi Moko—to Te Papa Tongarewa, a museum in New Zealand. The same year, a Swedish museum announced intentions to repatriate three human skulls, collected in the nineteenth century, to Polynesia. The curator of the University of Uppsala's Gustavianum Museum, Anne Ingvarsson-Sundström, told the *Uppsala Nya Tidning* newspaper that the institution 'wants to make things right'.[6] In the United States and Australasia, repatriation is now the norm—it is unusual if human remains stay in the institutions that collected and preserved them.

This book has three aims. First, I chart how museums were formed and how they acquired their artefacts. Many of those who I have labelled 'repatriation sceptics' in their defence of the museum and its retention of objects tend to underplay the more questionable acts by means of which objects were seized; and while I too can be described as a repatriation sceptic, I do not wish to shy away from discussing this past. Understanding it is vital in order to appreciate that the museum is historically constituted: it is not an institution that is always the same but one that is shaped by the social context in which it is situated. And it is crucial that we address the question of how to deal with pasts that are, in the present day, often uncomfortable.

The second aim of this book is to explore the influences that have contributed to the rise and dominance of the repatriation controversy, and the character of the contemporary demands. The rights and wrongs of plundering artefacts have been the subject of debate for centuries, but there have been changes in the arguments advanced. More countries, groups, and individuals have agitated for the return of 'their' artefacts since the late 1980s than did in the past. The objects that they want returned were taken centuries ago. Yet the cries for return escalate. And there are a number of developments accompanying the claims of 'It's ours!' that warrant scrutiny. The primary arguments for repatriation are now made with shifting and expanding rationales: because one culture owns its own culture; because of the way the artefacts were acquired— with force, under duress, or during the Age of Imperialism; and because they have been ripped out of their original context where, it is said, they belong. Returning artefacts is said to heal the wounds of the past, to provide a kind of therapy to the descendants of those violated, and to restore the objects to their rightful place. Great claims are made for what repatriation can do and what the movement of cultural artefacts can achieve.

The shifts in the prominence of the problem, and the expansion of reasons for return, prompt a number of questions. Why does the ownership of ancient artefacts stimulate such passion today? Can repatriation succeed in making good historical wrongs? Why are we turning to museums and objects to stimulate such outcomes? *Keeping Their Marbles* situates this ongoing controversy in its historical and social context to explore why conflicts over the ownership of artefacts are on the rise. Although cultural treasures have always been the focus of dispute, the increase in claims over artefacts in the twenty-first century, and the character of these claims, stems less from ancient wrongs and more from contemporary political, social, and cultural shifts.

We live, it has been argued,[7] in a period of social and political defeatism, in which the search for a better future has been cast aside. In this context, the past has become a surrogate area for struggle, with different groups competing to show their wounds of historical conflict. As economic and social solutions to society's problems have fallen away from the political agenda, the cultural sphere has developed into a sphere of activism for groups seeking change. These social changes have helped to transform museums into key sites of cultural and political battles.

'Representation is a political act. Sponsorship is a political act. Curation is a political act. Working in a museum is a political act,'[8] argues Michael Ames, the anthropologist and museum director. Culture has become perceived as the solution to many problems, with emphasis increasingly placed on the role of education, art, and music in promoting certain values and cohering communities. As a consequence, the museum has been encouraged in pursuit of a new mission, in relation to the perceived good it can do for society and a widening of expectations of the social role it can play.

The museums holding the contested artefacts, on the whole, prefer to keep them. However, despite a firm historical resistance to such demands, there have been substantial concessions in recent times. Certain authorities have become increasingly reluctant to mobilize the important scientific and moral arguments for retaining objects of historic significance in collections. They tend not to tackle the arguments for repatriation robustly. They appear to find it hard to justify, in particular, retaining artefacts acquired under colonialism.

My central observation is that our great museums as institutions are struggling to find their place in the new millennium, and that this is an important contributing factor in why they have become the object of scrutiny, and defensive in response. Social changes and intellectual currents have contributed to challenging the foundational purpose of the museum: to extend our knowledge of past people and their lives. Since the latter half of the twentieth century, museums have faced a crisis of conscience and confidence, as an array of social and intellectual shifts—including the ideas of postmodernism and postcolonialism, which question the possibility of knowledge and common understanding—have become mainstream. With the influence of these trends, the institution has become a focus of a relentless critique, castigated for historical wrongs and current social ills.

One of the most important arguments in this book is that the argument over who owns culture is not simply a battle between curators inside the institution pitched against outsiders who claim ownership, which is how it is conventionally portrayed. At times, the loudest and most important voices raising questions about the role of the museum and agitating for repatriation are academics and senior managers within these institutions. There is a push for repatriation from *within* the institution, as well as the pull from outside.

The third aim of this book is to restate the role of the museum and to reassess what we should expect of objects. Museum collections are more than merely the sum of their exhibits: they have played an important role in the expansion of our understanding of history, the specificity and the interaction of different cultures. The arguments made for repatriation—as well as those for retention—undermine this role.

There is literature proposing a variety of ways in going forward, especially within the field of law, but my aim is different: to understand how we got here.[9] The important first step required in this debate is to unpick the influences on the current state of affairs. What you will read here, then, is more analysis and argument than case studies or policy recommendations; and resolving individual cases is not my intention. Nonetheless, the expert on art and cultural property law, John Henry Merryman, proposed an approach to the question of where artefacts should be that I endorse as a good starting point. Merryman suggests that a 'triad of regulatory imperatives' be invoked. This comes down to holding certain priorities when thinking about where artefacts belong: 'preservation, truth, and access'.[10] Ultimately, this means working out where the artefacts belong on the basis of what is best for the artefacts, scholars, and the public: where the artefact is best preserved, displayed, and understood. These questions are helpful in thinking about the fate of artefacts, much more so than assertions about what the object will do for us today—but we are a long way from this starting point. My aim, by the end of the book, is that we are closer to understanding why.

To do this, we need to go back to the beginning of the story. Part I traces the formation of the great museums and their collections over the last three centuries. Part II then explores why museums have become the target for repatriation claims in recent decades, engaging with the arguments on both sides of the debate.

PART I

1

Great Explorers and Curious Collectors

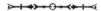

In a quiet corner of the British Museum, one artefact commands the attention of the room. It looks like a Roman helmet fit for a punk rocker—a hat made from orange, yellow, and black feathers, with a dramatic Mohican-style crest (see Figure 1). It is a *mahiole*, ceremonial headgear made 200 years ago for the Ali'i, the chieftain class of the island of Hawaii. All of a chief's garments were regarded as *tapu*—having a divine power—but the helmet was especially sacred and the feathers highly valued.

On the other side of the world in Wellington, New Zealand, in the museum Te Papa Tongarewa, there is a similar helmet as well as a cape with a crescent design that echoes the shape of the *mahiole*. The Hawaiian word for crescent—*hoaka*—means to 'frighten away', but also splendour or glory. And it is glorious. The vivid red plumage is from the honeycreeper bird, the black and yellow down from honeyeaters.[1]

These two helmets and the cape now on different sides of the world are thought to have been collected on a series of voyages during the Age of Exploration, on journeys that would change forever our understanding of the Pacific and its people, captained by the British explorer James Cook. In all, his crews returned from three pioneering voyages with an estimated sixteen *mahioles*, now distributed across museums in Europe and

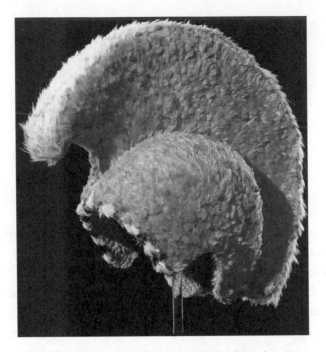

Figure 1. Hawaiian feather helmet, Polynesia, eighteenth century. Possibly collected on the third voyage of Captain Cook (1776–80). © The Trustees of the British Museum.

Australasia.[2] The Captain, however, did not. He was killed and did not leave Hawaii alive.

The travellers were central protagonists in the Age of Exploration. From the fifteenth century until the early seventeenth, Europeans, beginning with the Portuguese and Spanish, set sail to explore the unknown world, searching for trading partners, better routes, and goods. It was risky to travel into uncharted waters, dangerous to go to places that could not be found on any map. It was impossible to anticipate what they would find, and the friendliness or hostility of the people they could encounter. Life on board ship was hazardous—although Cook would help to eliminate scurvy (which killed thousands of maritime explorers) by introducing a regime of cleanliness, ventilation, and a better diet, other diseases, accidents, and illnesses would continue to threaten both crew and passengers.

Enlightenment thinking fuelled their plans. Between the sixteenth and eighteenth centuries, Europe underwent major intellectual and social transformations that laid the foundations of the modern world. The received wisdom of the ancients was challenged by the role of reason. The English philosopher Francis Bacon declared, on the cusp of the new era, 'Men have been kept back, as by a kind of enchantment from progress in the sciences by reverence for antiquity, by the authority of men accounted great in philosophy, and then by general consent.'[3] Bacon argued that knowledge had to come from observation and reasoning. Scholars moved away from the study of ancient texts to the examination of nature; where once they consulted old books, they would soon try to find out for themselves—with their own eyes—how the world worked.

ENDEAVOUR

The voyages transformed a speculative view of the Pacific into an understanding based on observation. James Cook and the naturalists, artists, and scholars who went with him, drew the first systematic maps of the islands, conducted the first comprehensive surveys of the geological structures they saw, and gathered extensive knowledge of the flora and fauna of the area. The first (1768–71) was a combined Royal Navy and Royal Society trip to the South Pacific on HMS *Endeavour*. Ninety-four people were aboard when it set sail. The trip took almost three years, during which one-third of the passengers would die.

The primary objective was to monitor the transit of the planet Venus across the Sun, in order to calculate the size of the solar system, and thereby to aid the travels of the British navy. There had been major developments in the science of navigation, and improvements in astronomy had made a difference to their knowledge of the planet: navigators now understood latitude and the shape of the Earth. A second motive was to search for the unknown Great Southern Continent to the south and west of Tahiti. Terra Australis Incognita—Latin for 'the unknown land of the south'—was a hypothetical continent with roots in a notion held by the philosopher Aristotle, which appears on European maps from the fifteenth to the eighteenth century.

Cook explored the New Zealand coast and parts of Australia with the help of the Tahitian navigator Tupaia and the English botanist Sir Joseph Banks. Tupaia was originally from the island of Ra'iatea in the Pacific Islands, and boarded the ship at Tahiti. He had extensive knowledge of the area, helped to introduce the crew to other islanders, and was especially helpful with the Maori. Tupaia made a number of drawings, one of which shows a naval officer in the act of exchanging what looks like a piece of material for a lobster with a man from New Zealand (see Figure 2). Joseph Banks may have been this naval officer, for he wrote of such a sketch and exchange taking place at Tolaga Bay:

> Tupaia the Indian who came with me from Otaheite Learnd to draw in a way not Quite unintelligible[.] The genius for Caricature which all wild people Possess Led him to Caricature me & he drew me with a nail in my hand delivering it to an Indian who sold me a Lobster but with my other hand I had a firm fist on the Lobster determined not to Quit the nail till I had Livery and Seizin of the article purchased.[4]

Tupaia and his son Tayeto were casualties of the adventure—both died on board suffering from scurvy. Tupaia's drawings were brought back by Banks and are now in the British Library, although they are still formally attributed to Banks, 'The Artist of the Chief Mourner', as he was originally assumed to be the artist.

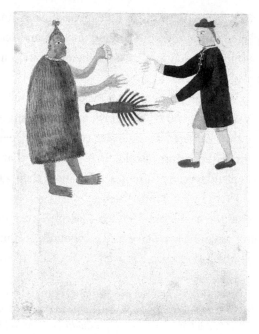

Figure 2. A Maori bartering a crayfish with an English naval officer.
Image taken from *Drawings Illustrative of Captain Cook's First Voyage, 1768–1771*.
By Artist of the Chief Mourner 1769.
© The British Library Board.

Joseph Banks was wealthy and well connected. A patron of science, he had a passion for natural history, subsequently became president of the Royal Society, and contributed to establishing Kew Gardens. Banks equipped the *Endeavour* with the natural history components out of his own finances by donating £10,000—compared to £4,000 from King George III. Also on board was the Swedish naturalist Daniel Solander, a former student of the natural scientist Carl Linnaeus, whose pioneering classification system allowed for clear descriptions of plants, animals, and minerals. Solander had started as an assistant librarian at the British Museum before his travels. Later, he became Keeper of the Natural History Department. Back in Britain, after their voyage, these men would form an informal network of influential thinkers and collectors who would play a pivotal role in emerging research and scientific institutions, establishing London as a base for the exploration and study of natural history.

They were the first Europeans to reach the east of Australia, landing on a harbour they originally named 'Stingray', but later changed to Botany Bay. On shore they gathered an extensive collection of 'natural curiosities': objects from the natural world. It is estimated that the voyage accrued 30,000 plant specimens, representing more than 3,600 species, of which around 1,400 were new to science.[5]

Many surprises were in store for them. Joseph Banks describes the startling sight of an animal 'as large as a greyhound, of a mouse colour and very swift', which they soon discovered was called a kangaroo:

> in *gathering plants* to-day I *had* the *good fortune* to *see* the *beast so much talked* of, *though but imperfectly; he* was not *only like* a *greyhound* in *size* and *running, but had* a *tail* as *long* as *any greyhound's*; what to *liken him* to I *could not* tell.[6]

The sight of the animal threw them into confusion—it was the first time they had seen a mammal that gestates in a pouch. Scottish Quaker and official artist Sydney Parkinson captured the greyhound-like beast in a sketch. Parkinson made a large number of detailed drawings before he died on the voyage—twenty-one large bound volumes are now in the Natural History Museum in London. Banks took back to Britain a couple of the kangaroos, gifting them to John Hunter, the founder of scientific surgery, whose collection of specimens and preparations would form the basis of the Hunterian Museum at the Royal College of Surgeons in London in 1799.

Banks had the rest of the material he collected sent to his home at 14 New Burlington Street, London, which became a well-visited research centre with an unrivalled collection of specimens and books. Edward

Jenner, who went on to pioneer the smallpox vaccination, helped Banks to organize this material, which was studied and became type specimens for genera and species. 'His house is a perfect museum', extolled the parson-naturalist Gilbert White, after a visit in 1772, and 'every room contains an inestimable treasure':[7]

> I passed almost a whole day here in the utmost astonishment, could scarce credit my senses, had I not been an eye-witness of this immense magazine of curiosities, I could not have thought it possible for him to have made a twentieth part of the collection.[8]

Gilbert White elaborated on the contents of two of the three large rooms:

> first the Armoury; this Room contains all the warlike instruments, mechanical instruments, and utensils of every kind, made use of by the Indians in the south Seas, from Terra del Fuego to the Indian Ocean...The second room contains the different habits and ornaments of the several Indian nations they discovered, together with the raw materials of which they are manufactured...Here is likewise a large collection of insects; several fine specimens of the bread and other fruits preserved in spirits; together with a compleat *hortus siccus* [herbarium] of all the plans collected in the course of the Voyage.[9]

And, in the third room,

> an almost numberless collection of animals; quadrupeds, birds, fish, amphibia, reptiles, insects, and vermes...Add to these the choicest collections of drawings in natural history that perhaps ever enriched any cabinet public or private;—987 plants drawn & coloured by Parkinson; and 1300 or 1400 more drawn with each of them a flower, a leaf, and a portion of the stalk, coloured by the same hand; besides a number of other drawings of animals, birds, fish, etc. And what is more extraordinary still, all the new genera and species contained in this vast collection are accurately described, the descriptions fairly transcribed and fit to be put to the press.[10]

The collections from the travels had a significant impact upon scholarship in natural history. Botany and zoology were then in embryonic form, and their efforts were to add to the cataloguing of nature. They remain essential reference material for the study of the natural history of the area.

When, in 1777, Banks moved house, he gave his ethnographic collection to the British Museum, of which he was a trustee for forty-two years. Writing to the Dutch plant physiologist Jan Ingenhousz, Banks apologized:

> I am sorry that Mr. Jacquin is so angrey that I have not yet fulfilld my Promise of sending him arms & curiosities from the South Sea the reason I have not yet done it is that in order to give preference to the British Museum who engagd to fit up a room for the sole purpose of receiving such things I long ago sent all mine down there consisting of several Cart Loads.[11]

Banks followed those in the Admiralty, including Samuel Wallis and George Carteret, in donating collections. Their combined efforts were the starting point for the South Sea Room, which was set up in 1775 to receive material from Cook's travels, and opened in August 1781. 'The Museum is going to be enriched with a complete and most superb collection of all the natural as well as the artificial curiosities which have been found in the expedition to the South Seas,' enthused the principal librarian (then the head of the museum) Matthew Maty, noting that the Admiralty were 'insistent' that they were to be displayed 'in a distinguished place as a monument of these national exertions of British munificence and industry'.[12]

Precedent set, sea captains would send their collections either to Joseph Banks or straight to the British Museum. Later, Banks gave the museum 'numerous animals, most of them in spirits' from the Cook voyages.[13] Other ethnographic items went to friends such as Lord Sandwich who, in turn, donated them to Trinity College, Cambridge. Christ Church, Banks's college at Oxford, received a number, as did Johann Friedrich Blumenbach, an anthropologist at Göttingen University. The Scottish surgeon and anatomist John Hunter ended up with a great deal more than merely the kangaroos, receiving a large part of the zoological collections. When Joseph Banks died in 1820, the original building for the British Museum—Montagu House—had been outgrown by the collections. His great herbarium and natural history specimens were transferred to the new building in 1827, together with his library, which is now in the British Library.

Plants, insects, and birds were brought back for personal profit or as gifts for patrons, as well as for scientific research. Dealers had showrooms devoted to their display. Auction houses, including Christie's and Sotheby's, sold them to private collectors for small fortunes. The Duchess of Portland, Margaret Cavendish Bentinck, was one such buyer. She was a great collector, one of the richest women in the Britain of her time, who built on her father's acquisitions (mainly coins and medals, and the collection of Greek marbles—the Arundel Collection—all of which she inherited) with her own tremendous collection of natural curiosities. Conchology (the study of shells) came to be her specialism. Indeed, this period saw a rise in interest in shells, accompanied by a fall in interest in collecting medals. The duchess built one of the largest and most admired assemblage of shells in Europe, branching out into insects, birds, and minerals. She helped finance a number of major expeditions, including Captain Cook's first voyage. In addition to supporting Cook, she employed sailors, naturalists, and travellers to bring objects of interest back to her. Many were enlisted to further her acquisitions. Horace Walpole, the Whig politician and man of letters who knew the duchess well, recounted:

> My evening yesterday was employed, how wisely do you think? in what grave occupation? in bawding for the Duchess of Portland, to procure her a scarlet spider from Admiral Boscawen. I had just seen her collection, which is indeed magnificent[14]

The provenance of objects in the catalogue of the duchess's collection, when later sold, tells a story of the extensive interest of British exploration in this period. Her shells came from the West Indies, New Zealand, Tahiti, Hawaii, Madagascar, Sierra Leone, and Norway.[15]

The Duchess of Portland lived in Bulstrode Hall in Buckinghamshire, a mansion which came to be referred to 'The Hive' in court circles, because it was a hub of extensive research carried out by a team of botanists, entomologists, and ornithologists. Among them were Daniel Solander, the Revd John Lightfoot—a founder member of the Linnean Society, a forum for the study of natural history, who was her chaplain and librarian—and Mary Delany, a close friend, who became a regular guest. In a letter, Delany described Bulstrode Hall as dominated by the spirit of intellectual inquiry with the specimens rapidly taking over all of the physical space. The breakfast room

> is now the repository of sieves, pans, platters, and filled with all the productions of that nature ... spread on tables, windows, chairs, which with books of all kinds, (opened in their useful places), make an agreeable confusion; sometimes, notwithstanding twelve chairs and a couch, it is indeed a little difficult to find a seat![16]

Delany was interested in the natural sciences. Her exquisitely accurate paper-cut flowers, collages, and needlework are now in the Enlightenment Gallery of the British Museum.

Jean-Jacques Rousseau, the political philosopher who was at that time in exile from France and Switzerland, was another visitor. He was also a botanist. Over a ten-year period from 1766, Rousseau and the Duchess of Portland exchanged letters. But although he respected her knowledge and shared her passion, collecting specimens and seeds for her herbaria, their exchanges ended after she sent him the *Herbarium Amboinense* by Georg Rumpf: a work about Asian flora. Rousseau returned it because he preferred indigenous and local plants to those that were foreign. Critical of exotic botany and of the European appropriation of naturalia from outside Europe, Rousseau believed that it deformed nature, and represented a sorry case of free nature being made subordinate to man.[17]

Upon the death of the duchess in 1785, her substantial collection was parcelled into 4,000 lots and sold at a massive auction lasting thirty-eight days. Major agents from all over Europe attended. As he introduced the sale that broke up the collection, John Lightfoot, her curator and chaplain, mourned the duchess along with Daniel Solander, who had died shortly beforehand:

> all the Three Kingdoms of Nature, the Animal, Vegetable, and Fossil, were comprehended in her researches. In all of these she took infinite Pleasure and Delight but in none of them is her Cabinet more richly stored than in . . . Conchology . . . It was the Intention of the enlightened possessor to have had every unknown Species described and published to the World; but it pleased God to cut short the Design, not only by the Death of the ingenious Naturalist employed by her for that Purpose; but in a short Time afterwards, to the great and irreparable Loss of Science, by her own also.[18]

RESOLUTION

The naturalist Johann Reinhold Forster and his son Georg, who would become a central figure in the German Enlightenment, but was then aged only 17, accompanied Cook on his second voyage (1772–5) on board the *Resolution*. The trip was again tasked with searching for evidence of the Terra Australis Incognita. They failed to find it and finally proved it did not exist, changing the assumptions of many, ending a reliance on ancient philosophers for this theory, and redrawing the map of the world based on what they had seen. (Antarctica would be discovered fifty years later.) The explorers returned to Europe with a wealth of botanical and zoological findings as well as artificial curiosities: odd and interesting man-made objects that they exchanged or bartered, or that were gifts from native peoples. Much of the crew had bought material to sell, hoping to make some extra money, to the annoyance of senior members who then purchased the material themselves at exorbitant prices. Johann Reinhold Forster was one who complained:

> Today a Saylor offered me 6 Shells to sale, all of which were not quite compleat, & he asked half a Gallon brandy for them... This shews however what these people think to get for their Curiosities when them come home, & how difficult it must be for a Man like me, sent out on purpose by Government to collect Natural Curiosities, to get these things from the Natives in the Isles, as every Sailor whatsoever buys vast Quantities of Shells, birds, fish, etc. so that the things get dearer & scarcer than one would believe... [19]

When the *Resolution* docked back at Woolwich, prominent figures flocked to see her and her wares. Daniel Solander, who had travelled on the first voyage, joined a party of John Montagu, Earl of Sandwich and First Lord of the Admiralty, and other grandees who sailed down the Thames to the shipyards. Between the many ceremonies and general festivities Solander went to examine the cargo, reporting back to Joseph Banks:

> Mr Clarke shew'd us some of his drawings of Birds, made by a midshipsman, not bad, which I believe he intends for you... Forster had on board the following livestock: a Springe Bock from the Cape, a Surikate, two Eagles, & several small Birds all from the Cape. I believe he intends them for the Queen. [20]

Solander described weird and wonderful objects, including gruesome human heads, one from New Zealand. 'Pickersgill made the Ladies sick, by shewing them the New Zealand head, of which 2 or 3 slices were broiled and eat on board the Ship.' Far from being repelled, Solander reserved it for the Scottish anatomist William Hunter: 'It is preserved in spirits; and I propose to get it for Hunter who goes down with me tomorrow on purpose, when we expect the Ship will be in Deptford.'[21] William Hunter was an anatomist and brother to John. William Hunter's collection, with the ethnographic artefacts from the

Cook Pacific voyages, found their way into the University of Glasgow's Hunterian Museum and Art Gallery.

Then, the natural sciences dominated the intellectual landscape. Ethnography and anthropology did not formally exist. Spears, tools, robes, and ceremonial objects were not considered museum pieces as they are now, and when the *Resolution* returned, those seeking to buy items from the haul were disgruntled with what was on offer. 'When I came on board was never more Disapointed,' a John White grumbled:

> as I saw but one baskett of shells and not a Single bird—Instruments of warr and dresses of the Natives seem'd the only cargo they had brought not an Insect, or animal could I find Except one Starved Monkey.[22]

One multi-pronged fishing spear from Botany Bay is in the Museum of Archaeology and Anthropology in Cambridge, which holds some 10 per cent of the 2,000 objects yielded by Cook's voyages. A carved bark shield, thought to have been collected on the same occasion, is in the British Museum and resembles one reported in the journals of Joseph Banks:

> Defensive weapons we saw only in Sting-Rays [Botany] bay and there only a single instance—a man who attempted to oppose our Landing came down to the Beach with a shield of an oblong shape about 3 feet long and 1¼ broad made of the bark of a tree; this he left behind when he ran away and we found upon taking it up that it plainly had been pierced through with a single pointed lance near the centre.[23]

Banks's diary entry describes more than the shield. It hints at an unfriendly welcome from some of the native people whose lives were transformed—for better and for worse—by the travellers.

THE FINAL VOYAGE

The third voyage (1776–80) was launched to answer the question of whether any North-West Passage existed, which would have enabled a shorter passage from Europe to the growing markets of Asia. And there was an additional task. During Cook's second voyage, Captain Furneaux of the *Adventure*, one of Cook's fleet commanders, had taken on board a young man of the island of Huahine near Tahiti. Mai, who came to be known as Omai, was a 20-year-old Ra'iatean who became the first Pacific Islander to visit Europe. Upon arriving in Britain he was introduced to society by Joseph Banks and became a sensation in London, meeting the king and queen, and mixing in high social circles.

Omai epitomized the 'Noble Savage', a concept popular in Europe and much popularized in the Romantic theories of the eighteenth and nineteenth centuries, including by Jean-Jacques Rousseau, which debated whether man in his natural state was superior to 'civilized' man. Omai was praised by thinkers who saw in him a natural, noble dignity. He had, according to the novelist Fanny Burney, an 'understanding far superior to the common race of us cultivated gentry'.[24] A well-known and highly valued painting of Omai, by the painter and aesthetician Joshua Reynolds, has Omai grandly depicted in a white toga—the clothing of a Tahitian aristocrat—even though he was an ordinary man.

A few years later it was decided that Omai should return with Cook on his third voyage. Having been treated as a prince in Britain, he was unable to reintegrate back into his home society, where he held no special position. Omai is thought to have died two years after arriving back on the island from a throat infection introduced by Spanish colonizers. His gifts and possessions from Britain had been stolen, his house was destroyed, and the livestock were all dead. Omai's legacy lives on in those still pursuing the romantic ideal as a metaphor for the destruction caused by the traveller's wanderlust.

The expeditions had a great cultural, economic, and political impact on the Southern Pacific region. They marked a new epoch in relations between Europeans and native peoples, whose encounters were documented for the first time. Contact triggered major changes in traditional ways of life. Travellers and natives exchanged a diverse collection of items through barter and gifts. Cook's third trip brought across a 'second Noah's Ark', as described by the surgeon David Samwell who was on board: horses, sheep, goats, and bulls, to help generate farming, 'to the great Astonishment of the New Zealanders, who have never seen horses or Horned Cattle before'.[25] They also equipped the local people with nails and weapons, exchanging them for coconuts and food.

Contact drew the Pacific Islands into the growing network of global trade. By the end of the eighteenth century, they were trading with Americans and Europeans, who in turn had goods from China and the Marquesas Islands, hundreds of miles away. Collecting was not the main point of these travels, but it came to be an important legacy. The historian Jenny Newell turns around the more common stories of how the Europeans accumulated material, to examine how the people of the Pacific collected European artefacts, explaining: 'The passion to acquire exotic objects was mutual.'[26] European materials and goods, such as nails, pins, buttons, and glass beads were distributed as an introduction, to open friendly relations, as well as to secure necessary food, drink, and natural and man-made objects. Newell draws attention to the collecting passion of Kamehameha the Great of Hawaii in the eighteenth century, who bought, took, and bartered all kinds of things from travellers, picking up European brocade rugs, Chinese porcelain dinner sets, English glassware, silverware, and decorated dress uniforms. He is also said to have accompanied his uncle (King Kalani'opu'u) aboard the *Discovery*, witnessing the killing of Captain Cook. In 1889, the Bernice Pauahi Bishop Museum was founded in Hawaii, in honour of Princess Bernice Pauahi Bishop, the last legal heir of the Kamehameha Dynasty. Today at the Bishop Museum, you can see the spectacular feather capes thought to have belonged to Kamehameha the Great, as well as a number of items from the Cook voyages acquired through purchase or donations from various collectors.

A two-way exchange could take place because the islanders were interested in acquiring materials and European goods. The nails from Europe were an improvement on wood for fish hooks. Iron tools, especially the axes, made hard work a little easier. In turn the new tools influenced changes in their society, such as craftwork. The historian Anne D'Alleva shows how the decorative work of Tahitian women, sheets made from a type of bark known as tapa, was altered by the introduction of English scissors, creating new designs.[27]

It took time to establish commonly accepted rules of exchange, barter, and purchase, and there were frequent complaints that islanders stole the travellers' property. And there were negative consequences. The travellers brought with them venereal and other diseases; they were not always welcome and did not always behave peacefully. 'What is more to our shame as civilised Christians, we debauch their morals already too prone to vice,' Cook reflected in his diaries, 'and we introduce them [to] wants and perhaps disease which they never before knew, and which serves only to disturb that happy tranquility which they and their forefathers enjoyed.'[28] Furthermore, the wider context of the travels was the Anglo-French rivalry to establish control of the oceans and to discover new colonies. Although the voyages of discovery were not ostensibly for this purpose, in the long run the encounters with Europeans resulted in evangelization and colonization. Cook had been given *The Secret Instructions*, documents that gave him the authority of the British Crown to take possession of a continent or land in the southern latitudes—evidence of Britain's early interest in Australia. And this is exactly what he did with the Australian coast north of Queensland on Wednesday, 22 August 1770, when he declared the coast a British possession and named it 'New South Wales', as it is still known. Cook's report on his travels would, in time, inform the decision to establish the colony at Botany Bay in 1788, which he had named on this second voyage, even if he did not live to see it.

Captain James Cook was killed on the third voyage, on 14 February 1779. The group had arrived on the island of Hawaii a year earlier, during a festival devoted to the god Lono, in the season of peace. The first outsiders to visit in 500 years, they appear to have been welcomed, and this is when the Hawaiians presented Cook with the chieftain's helmet. According to Lieutenant James King, the chief 'got up & threw in a graceful manner over the Captns Shoulders the Cloak he himself wore, & put a feathered Cap upon his head, & a very handsome fly flap in his hand'.[29] Cook considered this gift as an acknowledgement by one ruler of another. Only the high-ranking would be so honoured with such elaborate garments made out of the prized, highly valued, colourful feathers.

They spent a month taking measurements of latitude and longitude, before leaving to sail north. Four weeks later a storm forced them back to Kealakekua Bay on the island. It was now the season devoted to Ku, the god of war. Incidents broke out between the locals and the travellers, including the theft of a boat from one of Cook's ships. There are conflicting accounts and interpretations of what happened next. Cook is said to have invited a chief on board his ship in order to hold him hostage until the stolen items were returned. It was a strategy that failed, for Cook was stabbed to death in a tussle, and two Marines were also killed. Cook's voyages of discovery ended twelve years after they began, with his brutal and premature death. The Hawaiians burned the Captain's body, and the skull and long bones were presented to the chiefs in a funeral ritual. The remains were given to the crew for a sea burial.

The first European collection of artefacts from the third voyage was formed on their return to Britain, as a consequence of stopping off in May for resupplies, at Kamchatka in the Russian Far East. It was there that the news of Cook's death was conveyed to Europe. The Russian authorities were helpful and Captain Clerke, who was new in command, thus 'gifted a complete assortment of every article'[30] from the islands they had visited in the South Seas, assembled by William Anderson, who had been the surgeon on board the *Resolution* before he died of tuberculosis. What Anderson had gathered together ended up in St Petersburg and in 1780 became part of the Academy of Sciences collection in the Kunstkamera, the cabinet of curiosities on the banks of the Neva, founded by Peter the Great. Parts of Cook's dinner service of Oriental Lowestoft china ended up in Stromness Museum, Orkney—the first stopping point in Britain on the way home.

Captain Cook became a national hero. The Duchess of Portland was one of many who lamented his death, although it would seem that her sadness was somewhat influenced by her anticipation of the impact on her collection, stating that she 'regretted' his loss, when she heard the news, for 'he had made me many promises to collect shells for me poor Man! all those hopes are vanish'd'.[31]

In the preface to *A Voyage to the Pacific Ocean*—the official account of the third voyage, written anonymously by a fellow naval officer—Cook's commitment to science is praised, along with his friendly nature:

> The death of this eminent and valuable man was a loss to mankind in general; and particularly to be deplored by every nation that respects useful accomplishments, that honours science, and loves the benevolent and amiable affections of the heart.
>
> For, actuated always by the most attentive care and tender compassion for the savages in general, this excellent man was ever assiduously endeavouring, by kind treatment, to dissipate their fears, and court their friendship; overlooking their thefts and treacheries.[32]

References to the 'savages' sounds questionable to our modern ears, but this was common at the time, and was not based on the racialized concept that later developed. Savagery was seen as a stage in the development of human society: Europeans had also been savages once, but they had become civilized, as the 'savages' would too.

OBJECTS FROM THE COOK VOYAGES
IN MUSEUMS TODAY

Over 250 years later, objects from the Cook voyages are dispersed throughout most major museums in Europe, as well as institutions in North America, Australia, and New Zealand. This is partly down to accident. Eighteenth-century collections of objects were brought together in a haphazard fashion. Only through developments in the academic disciplines, and with changes in the way the world was understood, would these objects become part of museum collections with devoted curators and specialists. Early on in the history of the museum the man-made objects from these travels were considered of minor import compared to natural curiosities. Although many were at first donated to the British Museum, Neil Chalmers's study notes a 'certain indifference of tone' in relation to the artificial curiosities in the minutes and the published Museum Synopsis for 1808.[33] In 1815, much of the ethnography was moved to the basement. Given that the basement is a euphemism for a place of little interest and being put out of the way, it is not surprising that some were lost—indeed, it is lucky that any survived at all.

By following the diaries and accounts of the crew, examining paintings of the artists on board as well as the collectors' diaries and museum records, it is possible to trace just over 2,000 artefacts. The anthropologist Adrienne Lois Kaeppler has documented many of the various routes these artefacts took to reach different museums. Today, institutions including the British Museum, Pitt Rivers in Oxford, the National Museum of Scotland, the National Museum of Australia, and Te Papa Tongarewa in New Zealand are researching the collections from the voyages and how they went from the islands, to the boat, to that particular institution.

Artefacts also found their way to the Museum of Ethnology in Vienna, the Natural History Museum in Vienna, and to the National Maritime Museum in Greenwich, London. The Museo di Storia Naturale di Firenze holds the first such collection to be documented in a systematic way, by the Italian zoologist and anthropologist Enrico Hillyer Gignoli, at the end of the nineteenth century. It arrived in Florence when Giovanni Fabrioni—an Italian scientist and director of the Mint in Florence, who knew both Joseph Banks and Felice Fontanta, director of the museum in Florence—bought it from a London-based art dealer in 1779. Much of the material from the second and third voyages went into the museum of Sir Ashton Lever—the Holophusikon, in London, also known as the Leverian Museum. At one stage Lever offered to sell his collection to the British Museum for a very low price, but Joseph Banks, who seems to have disliked Lever, advised them against purchasing it and they passed on the opportunity. The Holophusikon was then sold at auction in 1806. The Museum of Ethnology in Vienna did not pass on the opportunity, ending up with 238 objects purchased at auction.[34] Other items have since crossed back to Australia and New Zealand in the hands of more modern travellers. One helmet and cape presented to Cook are thought to have ended up in the hands of the collector William Bullock, and were then bought by another collector, Charles Winn. In 1912, out of the blue, Winn's grandson, Lord St Oswald, presented his family collection to the Dominion of New Zealand, where they are held in the collection of Te Papa Tongarewa.

Objects from the trip taken by Joseph Banks with Captain Cook provided the starting point for the collection of the University of Göttingen in Germany. Johann Friedrich Blumenbach, a friend of Banks and an influential physician, physiologist, and anthropologist, established the Academic Museum in 1773, as a research and teaching institution. It housed natural, geological, anatomical, and cultural collections, comprising more than 100 pieces, mostly from the South Seas (above all,

Polynesia), as well as much of the Forsters' personal collection. (It was at Göttingen that the terms *Völkerkunde* (ethnology, or anthropology) and *Ethnographie* (ethnography) were first coined, appearing in a publication of 1771 by the historian A. L. Schlözer and his colleague J. C. Gatterer.) Artefacts collected by the Forsters have also been found in Worlitz, Germany, having been given to one of their patrons, Prince Leopold Frederich Franz. The British Museum has a number of items from the voyages, including a delicate hummingbird nest from Rio de Janeiro—one of the few bird specimens to have survived the travels and years. Most of the fragile zoological collections from Cook's voyages have since been lost or have simply deteriorated. The British Museum also holds the august *mahiole* and shields from the voyage.

The reason that these artificial curiosities are so important to us today is because of what happened to the people afterwards. The common objects quickly fell out of use. Iron from the Europeans replaced stone and wooden implements; Pacific Islanders rapidly replaced stone blades with iron in their tools for working with wood. Other new materials such as beads, glass, and metal were adopted for decorations. The later introduction of Christianity by missionaries altered the structure of their institutions and their ceremonial rituals. Collections from these voyages and these times have no trace of the new materials or new ideas. The feathered helmets, capes, wooden objects, and spears, arbitrarily gathered and now displayed in museums, speak to us of the time before any encounter with Europeans. If we are to understand those cultures and how they lived, then their material culture—their objects of everyday use, ritual objects, weapons, and items of adornment—is important research material.

We can study these objects in conjunction with the travellers' journals, which describe the behaviour, appearance, and customs of the native people together with their material culture. George Forster's scholarship from his travels has proven invaluable in this respect. His were the most systematic of the voyagers' collections and observations, and his writings have contributed to the ethnology of the people of Polynesia. George Forster advanced the study of language, creating the first comparative word list that contained dozens of Pacific languages, and proved that they were interrelated. With that insight, he argued that the inhabitants of many islands must have been in contact with each other long before the Europeans arrived. His book *A Voyage Round the World* discusses the social structure, religion, languages, and living conditions of the peoples of the Pacific Islands.

These, however, are the words of the travellers, not the natives; and whilst they are essential they are only one voice in a larger story of what happened. Objects can tell us about life before the explorers. And so we turn to museums today to learn about the past.

As the disciplines of anthropology and archaeology developed a century on from the voyages, artificial curiosities would elicit greater interest, becoming the focus of more systematic study. And as the particular collections grew in size and changed in conjunction with ideas about the role of knowledge and in relation to ideas about the populace, these eclectic assortments of artefacts were over time transformed into ordered museums for the public.

2

The Birth of the Public Museum

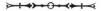

The term 'museum' originates from the Greek word *mouseion*, denoting a temple or place dedicated to the Muses: the nine goddesses of music, poetry, and the liberal arts of classical times. But it was not until the eighteenth century that the museum began to take the form of the institution we know today. Museums emerged from and were part of a revolutionary period in intellectual, political, and social life, during the foundation of early modern Europe. In overlapping stages, over the course of centuries, collections were transformed from private, seemingly eclectic and confused assemblages, into taxonomically ordered and politically purposeful displays for the public.

The study of nature had begun 1,500 years earlier with Aristotle's travels to the island of Lesbos in the mid-340s BC, where the philosopher began classifying botanical specimens and developed an empirical method of enquiry. The approach to understanding the world through classification led to the creation of the Lyceum: a school with a community of scholars and students devoted to the systematic examination of biology and history. Aristotle's Lyceum contained a *mouseion*, and the word came to be connected to scholarship.

One of the most important institutions of classical antiquity was the Mouseion of Alexandria in Hellenistic Alexandria in Egypt, founded by one of Aristotle's students, Demetrius of Phalerum, in the fourth century BC. Here, a community of scholars worked in a room for the study of anatomy and astronomy, as well as in a purpose-built library where intensive editing, cataloguing, and translation took place. It was thought to have contained more than half a million volumes at its height, and was the basis of much of the classical literature that survived the dissolution of Hellenic civilization. According to the Greek historian Plutarch, the library was burned to the ground unintentionally by Julius Caesar and thereafter fell to the Muslim invaders, who translated many classical texts into Arabic and preserved them for posterity.

The Roman Empire also brought extensive acquisition and display of objects, leading to the creation of picture galleries—*pinacotheca*—and the parading of ancient Greek artefacts through the streets as spoils of war before they were put on display in the Forum. During the Middle Ages the Catholic Church maintained great sacred treasuries, and precious objects were kept by royal and aristocratic families throughout Europe. Thus there were many artefacts kept together over time. But there are significant differences between this and the practice that later developed of collecting artefacts in a dedicated physical space for the public. To explore these distinctions, we begin with the emergence of private collecting in the city states of early Renaissance Italy, the backdrop to which would create the conditions for a pivotal stage in the formation of museums.

CABINETS OF CURIOSITIES

References to the Muses proliferated in the fourteenth and fifteenth centuries, whereas during the early Middle Ages they were infrequent.[1] The humanists, whose study of the liberal arts of the classical age stimulated the Renaissance, engaged with ancient thinkers and with the Muses, rather than relying on the interpretation of the medieval and Arab scholars. An antiquarian interest came to accompany their study of the past. They dug up statues from the ground, recovered manuscripts from the monasteries, and studied original texts, all of which needed to be located somewhere. They revived the *musaeum*, which emphasized their ties with the ancients, referring to the mythical setting of the Muses and to the library at Alexandria. A new temporal consciousness developed as scholars started to appreciate that the past was different from the present.

A major expansion in trade influenced the character of the Italian city states, where a rising class of bankers and merchants began to use conspicuous consumption as an expression of their new and important social position. Princes, merchants, bankers, and scholars collected. Mastering a knowledge of the ancients earned them authority, collecting and showing off their riches displayed their curiosity as well as their success.

The first museum is often identified as a private collection in the sixteenth century that belonged to the Medici family, a political dynasty and later a royal house founded on banking wealth and patronage. The family controlled Florence, on and off, for centuries, during which time four Medici men became popes of the Catholic Church. The Medici recognized the value of a physical space that would demonstrate their position and power: the Palazzo Medici, a domineering Renaissance palace, commissioned by Cosimo de' Medici in the 1440s, was where it all began. Within, they continued the medieval tradition of gathering treasures, valuable gems, and coins, all of which were transportable and could be melted down if their value needed to be realized. Cosimo became a passionate collector of antiquities, initially from the local area, bringing together local Etruscan pieces followed by pieces from Rome. Florence subsequently came to be an important repository of items of antiquity, many of which would end up in the Uffizi museum.

Inside the Palazzo Medici, in 1570, a secret *studiolo* was built for Francesco I de' Medici, who became the first Grand Duke of Tuscany and ruler of the Florentine state in 1574, as part of Giorgio Vasari's larger restoration of the Palazzo Vecchio. Francesco's *studiolo* was a room situated adjacent to the *sala grande*, where he would receive state visitors, but it was a small private space—it only measured 26 by 10 feet in size,[2] and no one else was allowed in.

The celebrated humanist Vincenzo Borghini was involved in the decoration of the *studiolo*, arranging it at first by the theme of the four elements (earth, water, wind, and fire) and, to a lesser degree, the four corresponding humours (blood, phlegm, black bile, and yellow bile). Paintings and objects were also organized according to these properties.[3] Though the objects of study were initially kept behind closed doors, it is this *studiolo* that is cited as the first museum.

In uncertain times, this cabinet, in which all of reality in miniature was assembled, was one way a prince could reclaim control—even if only symbolic—over the natural and artificial world. This was a world in transition: an era no longer dominated by religion, but which had not yet fully developed the scientific methods of the following century. The world was understood as animate—'the world is animal' was a common phrase. It was also moralized. Different characteristics, such as warmth, were considered to be better than others, such as cold. And it was organized in terms of correspondences, not causes.[4] Eilean Hooper-Greenhill, in her study of museums and the different epistimological systems that produced them, draws on Michel Foucault's three major periodizing epistemes—the Renaissance, the Classical, and the modern epistemes—to characterize this period as one in which 'interpretation' and 'similitude' were the organizing principles,[5] reflected in the ordering of cabinets. Collecting, which proliferated, functioned to enable the interpretation and reinterpretation of these relationships made manifest in the collections. Things—objects and oddities—were read for their hidden relationship to each other. To know was to understand how the things of the world were the same.

By the end of the sixteenth century, establishing a *musaeum* was common across Europe in courtly circles. They took on different forms and names according to the settings and collections: *pandechion, studiolo, gabinetto, wunderkammer, galleria*, and *kunstkammer*, with varying foci and specialisms. These 'cabinets', which have become known as 'cabinets of curiosities', were initially just that: a room/cabinet full of things—natural and man-made—moving, in time, into a larger devoted space. The craze for collections included gardens: a guidebook describes how, 'in this little theatre, as it were a world in miniature, a spectacle will be made of all the marvels of nature'.[6]

Cabinets of curiosities were intended to demonstrate the diversity and unity of the world. They upheld the Glory of God and man's place within his creation, arranged according to the epistemic idioms of the day, such as 'The Four Elements', 'The Four Continents', or 'The Seven Virtues'. They were an attempt to gather the world under one roof and are best understood, ventures Eilean Hooper-Greenhill, as 'cabinets of the world'.[7] They were an attempt to manage and make sense of the large amount of empirical material from the study and dissemination of ancient texts, as well as the Voyages of Discovery. Major social and political changes, including the Reformation and the religious wars in Europe, had led to a destabilized religious, social, and political order. 'Collecting', historian Paula Findlen posits, 'was one way of maintaining some degree of control over the natural world and taking its measure.'[8]

An important shift came when Francesco dismantled his *studiolo* in 1586, moving many of the objects and art to the Uffizi buildings. This process would start to make the objects public, and was done as a way of shoring up his authority. The historian Giuseppe Olmi explains: 'The need to legitimize the Grand Duke and his dynasty meant that the glorification of the prince, the celebration of his deeds and the power of his family had constantly to be exposed to the eyes of all and to be strongly impressed on the mind of every subject.'[9]

In Europe, cabinets open to a select audience were used to advance the reputation of princes and powerful families. Many were often located next to the main parade rooms. As visitors entered they would walk through or pass by a stunning arrangement of precious and interesting objects.

The use of the collection of Emperor Rudolf II–the Holy Roman Emperor, king of Hungary and Croatia, and archduke of Austria, towards the end of the sixteenth and early seventeenth centuries–is a case in point. A patron of Northern Mannerist art and a devotee of arts and learning, Rudolf II was also interested in alchemy. Rudolf's cabinet was in his castle in Prague, the capital of his empire, and it was legendary. His *Kunstkammer* was stuffed full of the wonders of the age: antiquity, ivories, books, sixty clocks, and 120 astronomical or geometric instruments, globes, antlers, and musical instruments. There was both *naturalia* and *artificialia*, including drawings and paintings by Leonardo da Vinci and Pieter Bruegel the Elder. It was thought that such a collection, believed, as this one, to be complete, could form a microcosm which could be manipulated 'pantographically'. That is, it was thought that the model could influence the real world as well as reflect it. This may seem amusing today, but it is worth bearing in mind for later chapters when we explore the idea that redistributing objects to minority and disenfranchised groups will bring about profound social changes that politicians and social movements have failed to achieve.

The *Kunstkammer* was used to proclaim Rudolf's magnificence at diplomatic functions as a form of *representatio*–'imperial self-representation'.[10] State visitors were shown the collection. Cardinal d'Este from Ferrara describes how, during his visit to Prague, he was taken around Rudolf's 'most recondite and valuable things, and particularly his paintings, marvellous for their quantity and quality. Besides them vases of precious stones of various kinds, statues, and clocks . . . a treasure worthy of him who possesses it.'[11] Rudolph's cabinet was visited by artists, travellers, and other interested parties.

At the start of the seventeenth century there was a clear move away from the Renaissance episteme towards a more scientific approach. During this age, scholars began to look for verifiable knowledge. The old canonical texts of the ancients were seen as no longer holding all the answers, especially to all the new material acquired from the Voyages of Discovery. One renowned cabinet brought together during this period belonged to Ole Worm, a Danish physician and antiquary, who had made major advances in embryology: the wormian bones—small bones in the cranium—are named after him. Ole Worm collected artefacts from the expeditions to the new world and from traders, bringing together natural artefacts: coral, fossils, and animals, including stuffed sharks and the teeth of mammals. Worm's cabinet contained fact and fiction, straddling the premodern and modern period. He proved that the unicorn did not exist, by showing that the horn—or rather, what purported to be a unicorn horn—was in fact the tusk of a narwhal; but he also boasted that he had a Scythian lamb: a fern that was thought to be both a plant and a sheep.

Upon the death of Ole Worm, his collection was transferred to the king of Denmark and Norway, Frederik III, who used it to create his own *Kunstkammer*. A book detailing the contents of his collection was published with a frontispiece featuring a copper plate engraving of the museum (see Figure 3). And at least forty of his objects have survived to this day, including a jawbone of a horse with a tree root attached to it, which is in the Natural History Museum of Denmark. In 2011, the *All Things Strange and Beautiful* exhibition opened at the Geological Museum in Copenhagen, inspired by Worm's collection and containing parts of it.

There were fewer such cabinets in England initially, and nothing comparable to the princely collections on the Continent, but that would change with the early seventeenth-century attempt to Italianize English aristocratic culture, which included the establishment of

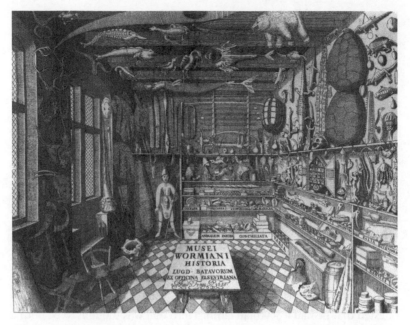

Figure 3. Frontispiece of Ole Worm's cabinet of curiosities from *Museum Wormianum* by
Ole Worm, published 1655 (engraving), Wingendorp, G. (seventeenth century).
Private Collection/© The Bridgeman Art Library.

museums. The private collections formed were initially housed in small
cabinets, but by the end of the century had grown into something like
an early museum, at which stage there were around six institutional
museums, and more than 100 private collections, recorded.[12]

One collection that would become pivotal to museums in England and
beyond was that of John Tradescant the Elder, whose collection became
known as 'The Ark'. John Tradescant the Elder had served as a gardener
to various earls, a duke, and to Charles I and his wife Henrietta Maria of
France. He travelled to France, Russia, the Levant, Algiers, and the Low
Countries, in order to purchase plants for them, and was responsible for
introducing a considerable number of new trees, shrubs, and plants into
England, including the Virginia creeper, the poppy, and apricots. When

on these travels, Tradescant picked up natural history specimens and ethnography. On his return, he displayed them in a 'closet of rarities' in his house in Lambeth, to which gifts from King Charles, as well as others from travellers, were added.

Tradescant was one of a number of men from the lower nobility who were collectors, perhaps in the pursuit of social elevation. But it is also worth bearing in mind that the backdrop to collecting in England in the late seventeenth century was the Civil War, which would halt, temporarily, collecting in the most elite circles.

Upon his death, Tradescant the Elder left his collection to his son Tradescant the Younger, who succeeded his father as head gardener to Charles I and Henrietta Maria and also continued collecting. He opened The Ark to visitors, who had to pay sixpence to see such delights as 'a mermaid's hand' and what purported to be a piece from the True Cross. It became a popular attraction. The headmaster of Rotherham Grammar School praised London as the best place in England for the 'full improvement of children in their education', one reason for which was due to 'the variety of objects which daily present themselves to them, or may easily be seen once a year, by walking to Mr John Tradescants, ... where rarities are kept'.[13]

The catalogue, *Musaeum Tradescantianum*, documented both the collection and the garden, and in 1656 was the first of its kind to be published in Britain. In his introduction, Tradescant the Younger wrote of how

> the enumeration of these Rarities (being more for variety than any one place known in Europe could afford) would be an honour to our Nation, and a benefit to such ingenious persons as would become further enquirers into the various modes of Natures admirable workes, and the curious Imitators thereof.[14]

Here, the private collection took on a transitional character gradually opening to the public, anticipating the use of the institution to the nation and in the service of instruction. Upon his death, Tradescant the Younger bequeathed the entire collection to the antiquarian Elias Ashmole, who in turn left it to Oxford University. It was the basis for the Ashmolean Museum in Oxford, which opened in 1683 as the first museum to have a public status. The earliest example in English of the use of the word 'museum' is recorded in *The Oxford English Dictionary* in 1693, in reference to this institution.[15]

FROM WONDER TO ENLIGHTENMENT

The English philosopher Francis Bacon described a 'huge cabinet' as vital for the learned gentleman—together with a library and a garden—where

> whatsoever the hand of man by exquisite art or engine has made rare in stuff, form or motion; whatsoever singularity, chance, and the shuffle of things hath produced; whatsoever Nature has wrought in things that want life and may be kept; shall be sorted and included.[16]

Bacon proposed the concept of a collection displayed in a gallery. Natural history, in his view, should pursue and record the knowledge of the world for the betterment of mankind. In time, there would come to be many in England who wanted to forge a collection so ordered. The Ashmolean contained not only a collection of artefacts (the Repository), but also a school of natural history, and a chemical laboratory with the aim of advancing the New Philosophy: the observation of data and testing hypotheses through experiments.

The historian Ken Arnold suggests that the early English museums survived the Civil War by being ordered empirical institutions, moving away from book-based learning, transforming into 'scientific institutions of a type—used to establish publicly accessible knowledge'.[17] These collections aimed to divide the world of experience into discrete objects, to discover the essence of things, and to order things accordingly for the public. This was the approach pursued at the Royal Society in

London—one of the most powerful of the London societies, which was founded in 1660—and the method of organization for its 'Repository', where the objects came to be arranged in the vein of a more normative and systematic approach.

Robert Hooke, a natural philosopher and curator of experiments at the Royal Society, suggested:

> The use of such a Collection is not for Divertisement, and Wonder, and Gazing, as 'tis for the most part thought and esteemed, and like Pictures for Children to admire and be pleased with, but for the most serious and diligent study of the most able Proficient in Natural Philosophy.[18]

In 1681, the first catalogue was published, describing each object in detail, trying to define and order them, comparing them to others in different museums, and noting differences. The ambition underlying the Royal Society's Repository—to taxonomize reality as a hierarchical series of differentiated objects—became a dominant approach in the eighteenth century, in England and then in Europe. Scholars began to *separate* where once connections had been made. The collection of the Royal Society was eventually subsumed into the collection of the British Museum, in 1779. You will now also find parts of it in the Natural History Museum in London.

THE BRITISH MUSEUM

> You will scarce guess how I employ my time; chiefly at present in the guardianship of embryos and cockleshells. Sir Hans Sloane is dead, and has made me one of the trustees of his museum, which is to be offered for twenty thousand pounds to the King, the Parliament, the Royal Academies of Petersburg, Berlin, Paris and Madrid. He valued it at fourscore thousand; and so would anybody who loves hippopotamuses, sharks with one ear, and spiders as big as geese! It is a rent-charge to keep the foetuses in spirits![19]

So remarked Horace Walpole in February 1753, as executor of the will of Hans Sloane, the Irish Protestant physician, botanist, and collector. It was Sloane's will that brought about the British Museum, inspired by the passion of one individual for collecting just about everything.

Hans Sloane had served as physician to three sovereigns: Queen Anne, George I, and George II. He succeeded Isaac Newton and preceded Joseph Banks in becoming president of the Royal Society. A voracious collector, both on his travels and by acquiring the curiosities of others, over his lifetime he accumulated more than 71,000 items from nature and man. These items encompassed the representative, odd, and exotic, including 23,000 coins and medals; 50,000 books, prints, and manuscripts; 200 large volumes of dried plant samples; and 1,125 'things relating to the customs of ancient times', all of which he wanted to be preserved intact after his death.[20]

As well as making a fortune out of selling quinine, a treatment for malaria, the talented Sloane was responsible for the invention of hot chocolate. When travelling in Jamaica as the family physician to the Duke of Albemarle and Governor of Jamaica, he sampled chocolate, describing the first taste as 'nauseous, and hard of digestion', which, he thought 'came from the [chocolate's] great oiliness'.[21] On returning to Britain, after a few experiments, he found it tasted better with milk. Today, specimens of the cacao plant—the source of chocolate that Sloane brought back—are in a display case in the Enlightenment Gallery in the British Museum.

Long before there was a British Museum, Sloane's collections were placed on display at his home in Bloomsbury Place, where the composer Handel is said to have visited, enraging Sloane whilst there by placing a buttered muffin on a rare book. The collection was moved to Sloane's Manor House in Chelsea, where a visitor commended what was on show in a poem, painting a picture of a paradise on Earth where it was possible to see all of nature and wonder at God's creations:

If six whole days ye new born world employd
Six might in viewing thine be well enjoyd
Spent as seventh too by heavens command
In wondering at ye great Creators hand
Here all his works in beauty rang'd appear
If theres a paradise on earth tis here
No more the Traveller from pole to pole
Shall search the seas or round the earth shall hurll
Safe from the dangers of the deep may be
And visit nature while he visits thee.[22]

Although he is now celebrated unreservedly as the founder of the British Museum, Hans Sloane did not receive unanimous praise for his collecting efforts. Indeed, over the course of his lifetime, reactions to his collecting practices mirrored the different kinds of esteem in which collecting was held and what it was deemed to be for. At the start of the Restoration, the scholar gentlemen who collected was seen as contributing to the social good. But by the middle of the eighteenth century, he was perceived as self-absorbed. At one stage the sheer number of Sloane's accumulated bits and bobs was considered a manifestation of greed, pride, and self-importance.[23] The poet Edward Young penned a poem in which Sloane is described as 'the foremost Toyman of his Time'. Young portrayed the collector (described as *S in the poem) as someone who was merely drawing together childish objects of little value in an attempt to achieve greater social prominence. Moral values were thought to be under threat by commodities and collectables. In the same stanza of the poem, the Ashmolean is dismissed as a baby house:

But what in oddness can be more Sublime
Than *S—, the foremost *toyman* of his time?
His nice Ambition lies in curious Fancies,
His Daughter's Portion a rich *shell* inhances,
And *Ashmole's* Baby-house, is in his View,
Britannia's golden Mine, a rich *Peru!*[24]

The rising dominance of the scientific approach and interest in natural history was taken as a threat to literary writing, especially because, when acquiring the various pieces, Sloane did not only record every detail about the object, but added a narrative about how the object was obtained. This—it was feared—encroached on England's thriving literary culture. Later, at the end of the century, collecting was seen as a positive way to improve and advance oneself.

Sloane's collection turned out to be central to one of the most important museums ever built. Collectors had started to think about the posterity of their work and the potential for the instruction of others. Sloane wanted to ensure that his collection was not broken up or abandoned. If London turned it down, he proposed to offer the collection to the academies of St Petersburg, Paris, Berlin, and Madrid—in that order—where he held honorary memberships. The collection was first offered to King George II, in exchange for £20,000 to go to Sloane's heirs—a huge sum then, but much less than it was worth (it was valued at £80,000 and Sloane believed it worth more).[25] Sloane made two demands: first, that it be kept together as a collection; and second, that it should be 'visited and seen by all persons desirous of seeing and viewing the same'.[26] The proposal was initially turned down by King George II but it was ultimately accepted. On 7 June 1753, an Act of Parliament established the British Museum as a Trust, which meant it was to be run independently of Parliament, and thereby granted autonomy from government. The deal also included manuscripts purchased from the Earls of Oxford, and the Harleian manuscripts from the Duchess of Portland (which today forms the basis of the British Library's Harley collection). When the museum was established, the library was central: the official title for the director of the museum was, for some time, 'Principal Librarian'.

The British Museum opened on Monday, 25 January 1759, in Montagu House, a seventeenth-century mansion on the site of today's building in

Bloomsbury, London. It had no entrance charge—it was free to visit from the outset. There were three departments: Printed Books; Manuscripts and Medals; and Natural and Artificial Productions. There was no department of antiquities.

The museum was the first public institution with the prefix 'British'. It was probably intended to embody the values of the new state, which had been created in 1707 in a political union between England and Scotland. It was also formed in opposition to the French idea of royalty—in Britain, society was rethinking the place of the monarch, and the relationship between Parliament and the people. 'British' meant belonging neither to the Church nor to a king, but to the citizenry.

A nation was in the process of being imagined. Alongside the evolution of the novel and the newspaper, museums were institutions that came to give a visual form to the ideals of different nation states. Indeed, historians generally attribute the birth of the idea of heritage in the late eighteenth and nineteenth century as in part due to these national contexts.[27] The idea of Britishness was reinforced by the name of the British Museum, but the institution did not explicitly showcase the British nation, nor did British material culture or history figure strongly in the collection for some time. Only in 1866 was the Department for British and Mediaeval Antiquities and Ethnography established, under Augustus Wollaston Franks, its first Keeper. The collecting focus was in stark contrast to a number of national museums that would come to play an explicit role in the promotion of a particular national identity with the rise of the nation state, including the National Museum in Budapest, which played an important role in forging a Magyar identity; the National Museum in Prague, founded in 1818, which promoted Czech interests in the Habsburg Empire; Copenhagen's museum, established in 1807 as part of Denmark's promotion of its own identity; and the Louvre in France, which we turn to later in this chapter. Paula Findlan notes that even in Italy, which was not at that time unified by government or language, 'illuministi, as the Italian philsophers called themselves, presented museums as a primarily instrument through which to effect a more national culture'.[28] Although the British Museum did not present a national narrative, it would develop a story of civilization. The museum would become a surveyor of other cultures, arising from the relationship of Britain to parts of the world through trade, colonization, and imperialism.

At the heart of the British Museum was the developing museum science that classified and ordered the collection taxonomically, for the public. Gowin Knight, the first principal librarian—the head of the museum—drew up the plans a few years before it opened, proposing that

> things relating to Natural History [are to be]... classed in the three general divisions of Fossils, Vegetables and Animals. Of these Fossils are the most simple; and therefore may be properly disposed in the first Rank; next to them the Vegetables and lastly the animal substances. By this arrangement the Spectator will be gradually conducted from the simplest to the most compound, and most perfect of nature's productions. I would therefore, humbly propose that the Fossils may be placed in the first room next to the Saloon; and when they are properly disposed, to begin with the Vegetables where the Fossils end ... In like manner the Vegetables may be succeeded by the Animals and animal substances: and since there is found in Nature a gradual and almost insensible transition from one kind of natural production to another, I would endeavour both in the general and particular arrangement to exemplife [sic] those gradual transitions as much as possible.[29]

When reflecting on this empirical and taxonomic approach, it is worth remembering that this was still an era in which Sloane specified that the collection should be kept together in the aim of understanding nature and thus serve the Creator. He believed that 'nothing tends more to raise our ideas of the power, wisdom, goodness, providence, and other perfections of the Deity ... than the enlargement of our knowledge in the works of nature', and hoped that 'for the promoting of these noble ends, the glory of God, and the good of man, my collection in all its branches may be, if possible kept and preserved together whole'.[30] And Sloane's collection included items such as ground Egyptian mummies' fingers as 'proper for contusions', ground amethyst for drunkenness, and nephrite to be placed against the skin for kidney disease.[31] But whilst he felt that the collection was for God and thus benefited man, the English Parliament made no reference to God as one of the intentions of the collection. English politicians were perhaps understandably more reticent on religious matters after the turmoil of the previous century.

Shifting intellectual and political priorities would change the focus of the institution over time. As the different scholarly disciplines emerged and developed, they became the basis of the organization of museums, forming natural history collections, departments devoted to anthropology, ethnography, archaeology, antiquity, and art. Following the lead of natural history, the reorganization of artistic collections after 1750 reflected the growing thinking throughout Europe that works of art could also be organized along rationalist principles, like plants and animals. Beauty became an ideal, in the mid-eighteenth century, as part of an independent science of aesthetics that would influence the development of art history and the basis for collections organized around their perceived aesthetic value.

Natural history reigned at the British Museum until 1772, when a collection of vases, bought from the collector and diplomat William Hamilton—husband of Emma Hamilton, the mistress of Lord Nelson—signalled a blossoming interest in antiquities. Hamilton would play a key role in the acquisition of antiquities, including the acquisition of the Elgin Marbles, which entered the museum in 1817. The British Museum subsequently lost much of its *naturalia*, which had so fascinated its founders and early contributors, when the Natural History Museum was established in London in 1881, based on the natural history collections from the British Museum.

OPENING UP TO THE PUBLIC

The long process by which palaces and private homes with collections started to open their doors to selected audiences began in Venice in the fourteenth century; it continued in Basle in the fifteenth; and in Rome with the Musei Capitolini in the sixteenth century. Many collections initially tied to royalty became increasingly publicly orientated, such as the Prado Museum in Spain, which King Ferdinand VII opened to visitors in 1819 as the Royal Museum of Paintings and Sculptures, and the Hermitage Museum, founded by Catherine the Great in 1764, which opened to the public in 1852 and demanded full dress—formal wear—until 1866.

This 'public' were well-educated specialists: access to the early private collections was really for artists or scholars. It would take some time for this access to widen, but it did so, gradually. The boundary between public and private altered in the seventeenth century. The second half of the century saw the rise of ideas about the production of scientific knowledge as requiring dissemination and public scrutiny. Then, during the eighteenth century, a more liberal treatment of the public developed together with the idea of civic obligation.

In seventeenth-century Europe, an increasingly engaged and influential public emerged, engaged in dialogue in salons, reading clubs, coffee houses, and in print culture, about music, theatre, and the issues of the day. The emergence of the bourgeois public sphere was possible, in part, due to the rise of the modern nation state and the congruent development of society as an arena distinct from the state; the rise of capitalism and unparalleled economic growth, which in turn led to the growth of literacy, and the widening culture of consumption. The historian John Melton explains that the concept of the public became a 'cultural and political arbiter' that contemporaries referred to as sovereign.[32] In 1747, the art critic La Font de Saint-Yenne called for the establishment of a public in museum in the Louvre on the grounds that 'it is only in the mouths of those firm and equitable men who compose the Public . . . that we find the language of truth'.[33]

The British Museum was, from the beginning, an institution with the public in mind. Hans Sloane had specified that the objects would be held 'for the use of learned and studious men both native and foreign' as a condition of its sale.[34] Indeed, it is due to what was considered most advantageous for the public that the Trustees departed from Sloane's specification that the collections should remain in Chelsea:

> It should hereafter be judged the most beneficial and advantageous for the publick use, to remove the Collection from the Manor house at Chelsea, where the same is now deposited, that it be placed properly in the Cities of London or Westminster or the Suburbs thereof. [35]

And when the museum opened, it was free to enter for

> all persons desirous of seeing and viewing the [collections] . . . that the same may be rendered as useful as possible, as well towards satisfying the desires of the curious, as for the improvement, knowledge and information of all persons.[36]

Any adult could visit, in theory. Groups were taken around on a two-hour tour by the assistant librarian, until 1810 when people were able to wander around on their own. Children were forbidden until 1837.

As London was a trading centre and the largest city in Europe, the visiting public included people from much of Europe. In his will, Sloane referred to visitors from beyond British shores:

> for the Use of learned & studious men, as well natives, as foreigners, in their researches into the several parts of knowledge, yet being a national establishment . . . it may be reasonable, that the advantages accruing from it should be rendered as general as possible.[37]

Visitors from abroad were permitted to look around outside visiting hours. Carl Philip Moritz from Germany visited in 1782 and found the contents to be remarkable: 'you are astonished by the huge collection of treasures—of natural curiosities, antiquities and examples of learning... for sheer bulk, this collection has no equal'. As for the clientele, he was taken aback and impressed by the inclusion of different classes: 'The visitors were of all classes and both sexes, including some of the lowest classes; for, since the Museum is the property of the nation, everyone must be allowed the right of entry.'[38]

Catherine Talbot, a poet and essayist, and member of the Blue Stockings Society, visited the museum just before it opened. 'I was delighted to see Science in this Town so Magnificently & Elegantly lodged,' she wrote, praising 'Valuable Mss, Silent Pictures and Ancient Mummies'.[39] By the early nineteenth century, women were permitted to attend museums more generally; the popular and lively coffee houses were reserved more for men, and the presence of women led to some barbed comments from other visitors. One visitor to the Ashmolean Museum complained that 'even the women are allowed up here for sixpence: they run here and there, grabbing at everything and taking no rebuff from the Sub-Custos'.[40] Anxieties were evident about who else might be in attendance as one gazed upon the specimens. Whilst praising the collection, Catherine Talbot, too, voiced a humorous concern about the impact it may have on the 'wrong' sort of visitor:

> Indeed in another Reverie I looked upon the Books in a different view, & consider'd them (some persons in whose hands I saw them suggested the thought) as a Storehouse of Arms open to every Rebel Hand, a Shelf of Sweetmeats mixed with Poison, set in the reach of tall overgrown Children.[41]

Our idea of public access today is different to that of a time when, despite the absence of entrance charges, there were formal and informal restrictions on who was welcome. Potential visitors had to apply in writing, giving their name, 'condition', and place of residence, as well as the day and hour they wished to visit. They then had to wait to be allocated an approved time. And they had to have clean shoes! Attendance reflected the social divisions in society outside the British Museum, but despite these limitations, during this period it became a place for working men and women, in certain conditions, within certain parameters. And apart from the closure during the two world wars, it has remained open ever since, increasing its audiences from 5,000 per year to 6.7 million in 2014.

REVOLUTION

On 10 August 1792, Revolutionaries stormed the Tuileries Palace in Paris, taking King Louis XVI prisoner. The French Revolution, spreading to countries under French jurisdiction from 1793 to 1814, removed the king and ushered in a new social order. This transformed the nature of museum collections within and beyond France, confirming the evolution of the museum as a key institution of the modern state throughout Europe.

In the decades leading up to the Revolution, the potential for a public collection of the king's art collections had been identified, partly in response to the galleries opening elsewhere in Europe, in cities such as Dresden and Rome, that were adopting an approach to ordering art based on schools and chronology. The French king had one of the largest art collections in Europe, and many felt that it could be put to good use, as well as being better cared for. The Luxembourg Palace opened in 1750 as the first public art gallery in France, subsequent to which designs were drawn up for a larger museum that would contain the bulk of a collection of Old Master paintings. The Louvre Palace, then partially empty, was identified as the perfect setting. It was a respectable and architecturally impressive building that already housed the royal academies. The intention was to build an institution that would reinforce the glory of the king by championing his art to the people of France, and, for some, to show and commission works that would influence public opinion on political matters.

Those challenging the rule of royalty also felt that art could be put to use: in the service of the Revolution. When the monarchy fell, the king's art collection was declared national property. On 19 August, one week after the attack on the Tuileries, an order was issued urging the creation of a museum:

> The National Assembly, recognising the importance of bringing together at the museum the paintings and the other works of art that are at present to be found dispersed in many locations, declares there is an urgency.[42]

The right of the public to ownership of museums was confirmed in legislation. On 30 August 1792, the National Convention (which had succeeded the Assembly) passed a decree that the Louvre Palace was to be designated the Musée Français and was to house the artworks that once belonged to royalty. A bill in November 1792 ordered that all art objects confiscated in the royal households be sent to the museum. They were already building quite a collection—art had been taken from the Church, divesting it of its religious context for a Republican purpose, as well as from émigrés and the royal academies. The royal collection was seized as national property, the intentional confiscation of art taken from the most powerful man in the land, whilst the king sat in jail awaiting his death on the guillotine.

Jean-Marie Roland, the new minister of the interior, was in charge of overseeing the national museum. He explained his aim in a public letter to the painter Jacques-Louis David:

> The museum must demonstrate the nation's great riches ... France must extend its glory through the ages and to all peoples: the national museum will embrace knowledge in all its manifold beauty and will be the admiration of the universe.

Roland desired the museum to be a physical manifestation of what the Revolutionaries were fighting for: 'By embodying these grand ideas, worthy of a free people... the museum... will become among the most powerful illustrations of the French Republic.'[43] The museum was to become a symbol of freedom and the sovereignty of the people, with art taken from the once-powerful elite.

But there was substantial resistance to these plans. Those in senior positions were divided on whether art and artefacts associated with the Ancien Régime (and with religion) should be saved at all. For three years between the attack on the Tuileries in 1792 and the establishment of the Directory in 1795, extensive iconoclasm was difficult to control. Monuments associated with the Ancien Régime were destroyed; paintings and pictures belonging to the royals were piled high and burnt in bonfires. In radical journals, there was opposition to preserving and presenting these artworks because they were seen as tainted by their association with the old order. An article in *Révolutions de Paris* argued against saving the art of the royal family, because it could never be the people's art, and would always express the interests of the king: '[T]he statues of kings in our cities are not the work of the people, but of courtesan ministers.'[44] The author called for the creation of new, progressive work and a public monument. Certain Revolutionaries believed that the physical legacy of the Ancien Régime had to be crushed if its values were also to be eradicated.

There was a struggle over the two plans of action: to save or destroy. The word 'vandalism' was first used in this context, employed by the Catholic priest and abolitionist Abbé Henri Grégoire to draw attention to what he considered to be a very grave problem: French people destroying French art and monuments.[45] Abbé Grégoire argued in favour of rescuing these works, advancing the idea of heritage. Iconoclasm, he suggested, was counter-revolutionary. True liberty was based on education, and monuments of art and science were essential to this project, he said. Grégoire made a link between the preservation of heritage and civilization, an idea that would remain important. Those arguing to save the art and artefacts asserted that the museum would recontextualize their meanings: they would belong to everyone and would no longer be tainted by the king's rule. Art commissions were established and tasked with identifying what was exceptional so that it could be preserved, with artists and scholars appointed to help select the work.

Despite the attempts to preserve the art, certain works close to or marked with feudal, religious, or royal associations were set aside and broken, melted down, or burned. But a great number of the treasures were saved and the Musée Français opened on 10 August 1793. The art historian Andrew McClellan estimates that when the museum opened, three-quarters of the exhibits in the new museum were derived from the royal collections, and the remainder was confiscated Church property. That the property of the great and the good was taken and delivered to the people in such a way was seen as a triumph. According to Abbé Grégoire, those treasures 'which were previously visible to only a privileged few . . . will henceforth afford pleasure to all: statues, paintings, and books are charged with sweat of the people: the property of the people will be returned to them'.[46]

The museum was opened on the same day as the Festival of Unity and Indivisibility of the Republic, which visually dramatized the nation. The festival celebrated the end of the monarchy and the birth of the Republic, just one year after the storming of the Tuileries Palace. The staging of the festival on the same day as the opening of the museum linked these two events. The Musée Français became a symbol of the fall of the old regime and the rise of the new order, embodying the ideal of Liberty, Equality, and Fraternity. All citizens were encouraged to participate and given free access on three days per week; artists and special guests were to visit on the other days. But debates continued to rage. Should work such as Ruben's Medici cycle be on display, when it glorified the monarchy? If art was symbolic, should it not be instructive of the acceptable morality?

And what about religious painting?[47] These questions were resolved by elevating discussions about artistic quality and by arranging them in order of their school and chronology, somewhat neutralizing their political or religious connotations with the discipline of art history.

The establishment of the Musée Français sent a message intended not only for the people of France, but for the political elites beyond the nation's borders. Leaders of other countries were watching, fearful of the influence of the Revolution on their rule. The new order needed to show its civilized qualities, and reassure others that liberation of the people meant more than just the bloody fighting that had taken place and would intensify with the Terror. Although the artwork was torn from the hands of the king before his execution, it was also hoped that art and antiquity could be used to distract attention away from the work of the guillotine.

Museums and galleries modelled on the new museum subsequently sprung up all over Europe. By the end of the nineteenth century, almost every capital and every major city in Europe boasted a public art museum of its own. They were a means of representing and authorizing the new political systems, making visible a new conception of the state and the citizen, with the royal treasures displayed in a public setting.[48] The scholar Felicity Bodenstein outlines that between 1789 and 1870 every important political regime change in France was explicitly tied to a museum project: Napoleon's Louvre (1803), Charles X's new antiquities gallery in the Louvre (1827); King Louis-Philippe's Musée d'Histoire de France at Versailles (1837); and Napoléon III's Musée des Antiquités Nationales (1862).[49] The continual renaming of the Louvre similarly indicates a shift in ideas of ownership and authority, stamped upon one particular museum. The Louvre has been called the Musée Français, Musée Central des Arts, Musée Napoléon (from 1803 to 1804), before finally settling on the Musée du Louvre.

Although many of the artworks in the Louvre originally belonged to the king, there has been no call to restore them to the descendants of the

French royal family, nor to those members of the clergy from whom they were originally seized. But if we were to follow the logic of certain arguments for repatriation, it could be said that the dispossessed royal families were the true owners of many of the exhibits in the Louvre. This is worth recalling in Chapter 8—Atonement: Making Amends for Past Wrongs—which suggests that contemporary sympathies for repatriation are often less about the artefacts and the conditions for removal, and are more an expression of concern for the particular communities who demand their return. Hence certain groups are given a hearing, and others—such as descendants of French royalty—decidedly are not.

THE IMPROVING MUSEUM

In Britain, there was an explicit move to use museums for social and political purposes in relation to the domestic public. After chairing the 1834 Select Committee on Drunkenness, the Sheffield MP and social reformer James Silk Buckingham proposed Bills in order that local committees be permitted to levy rates to establish parks, theatres, and museums and art galleries. The hope was that this would civilize the working classes, and limit their drinking, 'to draw off by innocent pleasurable recreation and instruction, all who can be weaned from habits of drinking'.[50] The Bills were unsuccessful at the time, but they attracted considerable interest and were adopted two decades later.

In the mid- to late nineteenth century, museums were tasked with improving the population. High culture in general—fine art, museums, and music—was thought to transform people's lives, by subduing passions and improving behaviour. Participating in high culture was seen as ennobling. Historian Juliet Steyn explains that the idea was 'to inculcate in the population a higher subjectivity which could transcend nature by offering experiences, feelings and pleasures' that were not part of their ordinary lives.[51] As the critic John Ruskin put it:

> The first function of a Museum—(for a little while I shall speak of Art and Natural History as alike cared for in an ideal one)—is to give example of perfect order and perfect elegance, in the true sense of that test word, to the disorderly and rude populace.[52]

The political class was responding not only to bad behaviour and drunkenness, but also to rising agitation about working and living conditions, and there were loud demands for the widening of the suffrage. The Tory Sir Robert Peel justified the provision of funds for the National Gallery in a speech to Parliament, in part because of the role it would play in calming social unrest: 'In the present times of political excitement, the exacerbation of angry and unsocial feelings might be much softened by the effects which the fine arts had ever produced upon the minds of men.' He trusted that 'the edifice would not only contribute to the cultivation of the arts, but also to the cementing of those bonds of union between the richer and the poorer orders of the State'.[53] Peel's speech, and the plans for the National Gallery, took place soon after the 1832 Reform Act—the first reform of the electoral system—which granted representation to the new cities that had emerged with the Industrial Revolution, rather than to the rotten boroughs with small populations that had been used to gain unrepresentative influence.

Peel hoped that museums and galleries would help to dampen down such agitation and protest, but they achieved no such thing. The political elite found that viewing a Raphael did not prevent people from taking to the streets in protest. Feelings were not much softened by viewing the artefacts and the sculptures. Working men and then women went on to demand the suffrage and better working and living conditions. But great museums were built.

THE MUSEUM AGE

Inspired by the museums in Europe, a period of museum-building in North America took place during the nineteenth and early twentieth centuries. The Smithsonian Institution in Washington was just one such museum, founded in 1846 from a bequest from James Smithson, a British scientist who had never even visited America. Smithson advised in his will that if he died without an heir the estate should go to the new nation to help create an 'Establishment for the increase & diffusion of Knowledge among men'.[54] The very idea of a new nation and all that it promised was enough for him to pledge considerable financial support.

Many American museums in this period emerged out of an ideal of self-governance, a belief that a people with a sense of duty and the public good might create institutions in the public interest that could one day rival or even exceed the museums of Europe. But these evolved along a different model, without much—if any—government support. Many were supported by private individuals rather than the state, and those involved in business found that it improved their reputations. That museums were built in the aftermath of the American Civil War in the late 1870s was no coincidence: these, too, were seen as playing a role in educating and reconstructing American society—a way to improve taste and the welfare of the public.

The Metropolitan Museum of Art in New York was founded in 1870, pledging to play a role in 'encouraging and developing the study of the fine arts, and the application of arts to manufacture and practical life, of advancing the general knowledge of kindred subjects and, to that end, of furnishing popular instruction'.[55] The aim of the Met's founders was not only to found a museum in New York, but also to inspire similar institutions. And so it did: the American Museum of Natural History, the Field Museum of Natural History, and the Philadelphia Museum of Art followed soon after.

The American ichthyologist (fish specialist) George Brown Goode, who ran both the fish research programme of the US Fish Commission and the Smithsonian Institution, shared his views on museums in his influential *Principles of Museum Administration* (1895). In his paper 'Museums and Good Citizenship' (1894), Goode argued that exhibitions could 'minister to the mental and moral welfare' of the masses and contribute to rebuilding the national state. Museums should be 'passionless reformers' committed to 'the continuance of modern civilisation'.[56]

This aim of civilizing the populace has come to haunt museums. As we will see, in recent times museums have been castigated by academics and commentators, who argue that this remains the primary goal of the institution, and that it is therefore an agent of government, to be subjected to relentless critique.

3

Antiquity Fever

>∙⥋∙⊙∙⥋∙<

In the summer of 1799, French soldiers were rebuilding the defences of Fort Julien, in a small village in the Delta north-east of El Rashid (now Rosetta) which overlooks the final mile of the River Nile before it joins the Mediterranean Sea. In a wall, an engineering officer came across a block of grey rock, about 4 feet long and 2½ feet wide, which was quite different to the rubble around it. Carved onto the slab in separate sections were three scripts. On the bottom was ancient Greek, a language in which men of their time were well versed. In the middle was demotic, the common script of ancient Egypt, which a few of their day could read. On top was what appeared to be Egyptian hieroglyphs, a script that no one had been able to understand for millennia. This rock would become known as the Rosetta Stone.

Scholars accompanying the soldiers knew that the discovery was significant. Reading the Greek text, they could see that it was written in 196 BC and issued in Memphis, the ancient capital of Egypt, when the Ptolemaic pharaohs of Greek descent ruled. Greek was the language of Ptolemy, and the two forms of ancient Egyptian—demotic and hieroglyphics—were used for administration. Written on the stone is a decree by a congress of priests in the ninth year of Ptolemy V's reign, repealing taxes and issuing instructions in relation to the priests. Ptolemy V was a weak king, then only 13 years old, and the decree was issued to re-establish the rule of the kings after an internal revolt. The priests held great authority and the king needed their support. We can infer from the list of his good deeds on the stone how he secured their favour.

The find is of interest to specialists of the Ptolemaic period, but what made it so important was that it was pretty much the same text written in three different scripts. This had major implications for the understanding of the third, then incomprehensible, text. Hieroglyphs fell out of use at the end of the fourth century AD, and nobody had been able to read them for around 1,400 years. 'From time immemorial these obelisks and their inscriptions have been in Rome and so far no one has been able to decipher them,'[1] bemoaned the Jesuit scientist Athanasius Kircher in 1589, attempting to do so with little success, although he made breakthroughs in documenting the link between ancient Egyptian and the modern Coptic languages. Kircher had hoped that this link would show that his Christian religion was compatible with the ancient wisdom of the pagans.

One small block of what has turned out, on closer inspection, to be granodiorite rock would end this quest for understanding forever. After discovering the Rosetta Stone, with scholars comparing and analysing the three sections for decades, they cracked the code, deciphered the hiero-glyphs, and as a consequence could read countless other texts, inscriptions, writing on monuments—ultimately, ancient Egyptian culture. During their invasion of another country, the soldiers and engineers had made an accidental discovery that held major ramifications for our knowledge of the distant past.

In the eighteenth and nineteenth centuries, antiquarians, adventurers, and political leaders and their men rooted around Italy, Greece, and the Middle East. They sketched and sometimes took old sculptures and great monumental pieces, all with the permission of the rulers. They dug deep down into the ground, chopped blocks off monuments, and carted the treasures away. Many sites were excavated by what were, in effect, amateur archaeologists—it would take some time before professional standards were in place. And whilst warnings were voiced about removing antiquity from its original context, as this would separate artefacts from the contextual information essential to understanding what they were and what they were for, there were few restrictions on taking material away. Finds were quickly appropriated by Europe, especially Britain and France, where their study would lead to an expansion in the knowledge about other civilizations.

Some of the most famed artefacts in the world were discovered during this period. In addition to the Rosetta Stone, there is the colossal head of Rameses II, now in the British Museum (see Figure 4), and huge statues of great winged human-headed bulls from the North-West Palace of Ashurnasirpal II, carved in Assyria (now northern Iraq) in 883–859 BC.

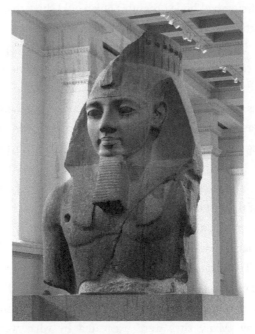

Figure 4. Colossal bust of Rameses II, the 'Younger Memnon'. The British Museum.

© The Trustees of the British Museum.

As well as in Iraq, these statues can now be found in the British Museum, the Metropolitan Museum in New York, and the Oriental Institute of the University of Chicago.

It was during this period that the Elgin Marbles were removed from the Acropolis in Athens and shipped to London. The fight over the Elgin Marbles that ensued as they landed was less over their ownership and circumstances of acquisition (although this was under question) than it was over their value and meaning. The sculptures arrived at a time when antiquity was being ordered into both a chronological and evaluative system, during a period that saw a shift in taste and order—a move away from neoclassicism to romanticism—and they became the focus of raging debates about aesthetics. Overall, the arrival of the Elgin Marbles changed the understanding of Greek classical style, crystallized an ideal of ancient Greece, and dethroned Graeco-Roman idols of a later period.

Driving some of the excavations was the intention that antiquity be used to legitimize political leaders, mostly associating the present-day regime with an authoritative antique past. In addition, the resulting display of artefacts expressed ideas about progress or great art that were often linked to certain stages in history, and certain peoples. However, despite these intentions, it was not possible to control how ancient artefacts were received. Upon their entry into European museums, these artefacts radically changed what people knew about previous human civilizations, provoking questions about how to categorize and place them and their creators in the chronology of history, and how cultural achievements should be assessed.

NAPOLEON IN EGYPT

When the soldiers found the Rosetta Stone, the French military—thirteen ships and 31,000 men—were advancing on El Rashid as part of Napoleon Bonaparte's campaign in Egypt. Egypt was a province of the Ottoman

Empire, which ruled the Middle East, the North African coast, and the Balkans. The French had the strategic motivation of interrupting Britain's communications with its growing interest in India, a source of much of its wealth; and the two empires were competing for dominance over the Middle East and Africa. If France controlled Egypt, it could control Jerusalem and the overland trade route to India. The *Expédition d'Égypte* was intended to halt the British Empire without a direct attack.

Napoleon was a young commander, aged just 28, with ambitions to rule continental Europe. By this stage, he had already defeated larger Austrian armies and conquered most of northern Italy. He had set his sights on the Mediterranean. 'The time is not far away', he wrote to the Directory on 16 August 1797,

> when we shall feel that, in order truly to destroy England, we must occupy Egypt. The steady death of the Ottoman empire obliges us to think in good time of taking steps to preserve our trade in the Levant.[2]

Napoleon modelled himself on classical conquerors. He dreamed of walking in the footsteps of Alexander the Great, the Macedonian king who united Greece and conquered the Persian Empire. 'I saw myself on the road to Asia,' Napoleon later reflected:

> riding on an elephant, a turban on my head and in my hand the new Koran that I would have composed to suit my needs. In my undertaking I would have combined the experience of the two worlds, exploiting for my own profit the theatre of all history.[3]

Egypt was the next step in his dream of conquest. 'Great reputations', he believed, 'are only made in the Orient; Europe is too small.'[4]

Newly formed following the Revolution, the French army claimed to arrive for liberation. They were there, they said, to free the fellahin (the peasants) from the Mamluks, who ran the area for the Ottomans, and to bring liberty and equality. The fellahin people, however, were more circumspect. They did not rise up and join the French army. And the

French support for Egyptian independence lost them the sympathy of the sultan. The Ottoman Empire was weakening, which made it more reliant on foreign support; this strengthened the British position and gained the sympathy of the sultan in relation to the excavation and exporting of antiquities—in particular, the Elgin Marbles.

Accompanying Napoleon on his Egypt campaign were the savants, the 167 members of the Commission des Sciences et Arts d'Égypte, a learned body of engineers, technicians, artists, and men of letters who carried the latest tools for surveying, drawing, recording, and digging. The savants had multiple purposes. They were there to assess the feasibility of building a canal through Suez, giving the French a direct nautical route to Asia. Egypt was also envisaged as a replacement for the sugar colony of Saint-Domingue. The Atlantic economy had collapsed and slavery was abolished during the Revolutionary Wars, and France needed Egypt, with its rich goods of cotton, sugar, and indigo, as a colonial alternative.

Alongside the military campaigns of the Napoleonic Wars ran a scientific and intellectual campaign. Napoleon established an Institut d'Égypte in a complex of palaces on the outskirts of Cairo. It had chemistry and physics laboratories, an Arabic press, conference halls, a library, and a museum: the first Egyptology museum. The 'principal objects' of the Institut were listed as follows:

> 1. The progress of knowledge and its propagation to Egypt; 2. Research, study and publication of the natural, industrial and historical facts about Egypt; 3. To give advice on the various questions upon which it may be consulted by the Government.[5]

The Institut was divided into four sections, devoted to mathematics, physics, political economy, and literature and the arts. All general officers of the French army were permitted to attend sessions held there on these areas. Whilst much of the attention was devoted to technical questions, such as the methods of purifying the Nile, or how to make beer without hops, they also investigated the ancient culture: the expedition would send two scientific commissions to study antiquities. One of the experts, Dominique Vivant Baron Denon, was an artist and diplomat, who sketched the antiquities along the way. Sometime later, in 1802, Denon was appointed by Napoleon to the position of director general of museums and head of the Musée Napoléon—the Denon Wing of the Louvre is named after him.

One scholar, Abd al-Rahman al-Jabarti, observed and chronicled the French expedition first hand in *Ajaib al-Athar* (*History of Egypt*), in which he documents an early period of the occupation. Describing the French as anti-religious materialists, he is dismayed by Napoleon's cynical attempts to win favour by proclaiming sympathy with Islam: 'these people are opposed to both Christians and Muslims, and do not hold fast to any religion'.[6] Lamenting that they 'soiled' and 'plundered' the Mosque of al-Azhar,[7] he depicts the French as immoral ('they have intercourse with any woman who pleases them and vice versa') and dirty: ('whenever a Frenchman has to perform an act of nature he does so wherever he happens to be, even in full view of people, and he goes away as he is, without washing his private parts after defecation').[8] If only they would leave: 'May God hurry misfortune and punishment upon them, may He strike their tongues and their dumbness, may He scatter their hosts, and disperse them, confound their intelligence, and cause their breath to cease.'[9]

Al-Jabarti visited the Institut's library and laboratory. Despite his severe judgement of the intervention, he recognized the European desire for learning, noting their interest in the ancient ruins and archaeology:

> By nature and desire they like to study curious objects and inquire into trivial details, especially ancient ruins and wonders of the land, paintings and statues found in caves and ancient temples in Upper Egypt and elsewhere. Some of these Englishmen rove all over the world for such purposes, spending great sums of money for their supplies and hired

attendants. They even went to the Southern border of Upper Egypt and brought back pieces of stone bearing carvings, writing, and pictures: they also found white marble sarcophagi containing corpses still in their shrouds[10]

Intrigued, he visited the house of Henry Salt, the British consul general in Cairo whose collections, acquired by the British Museum, included the great head of Rameses II (about 1250 BC), the third king of the Nineteenth Dynasty of Egypt and one of the greatest, most powerful pharaohs in history. Al-Jabarti was impressed with the ancient Egyptian artefacts: 'We admired their craftsmanship and uniformity and the sheen of their surfaces that have endured through centuries unnumbered save by the Knower of the invisible.'[11] He verges on praising the hard work and determination of the excavators in 'removing a great deal of dirt and dung' as well as 'bat excrement' in the digs.

Europe at this time was greatly interested in ancient Egypt, a fascination that goes back much earlier in time to the Greeks. Ancient Egypt had also intrigued the Romans, who removed great obelisks—tall, four-sided monuments, topped with a small pyramid—eight are now in Rome, and one stands right in front of the Vatican. Early knowledge of Egypt was based on the biblical tradition and Greek writers such as Herodotus. It had been heavily romanticized and was the focus of much speculation, evoking the Bible, the Romans, and the Quran. As Florence Nightingale would imagine whilst travelling in the mid-nineteenth century:

> Here Osiris and his worshippers lived; here Abraham and Moses walked; here Aristotle came; here, later, Mahomet learnt the best of his religion and studied Christianity; here, perhaps, our Saviour's Mother brought her little son to open his eyes to the light.[12]

Travel to Egypt became easier towards the end of eighteenth century, and visitors from western Europe started to publish accounts of the sights and the antiquities. With time, the debate about how to accommodate Egypt in a biblical account of the development of civilisations moved on to questions about the worth of Egyptian antiquities for their own sake.

Ancient Egypt was distant and mysterious for the Egyptians of the early nineteenth century, who lacked the Graeco-Roman accounts, and probably knew less than the Europeans. The French invasion of Egypt eliminated Mamluk rule and ushered in a new leader, Mehmet Ali, the Albanian-born Ottoman ruler of Egypt from 1805 to 1849. He readily gave permission in the form of firmans—the official permission of the Ottoman authority—for a great many artefacts to leave Egypt. Mehmet Ali was mostly interested in modernizing, and he needed to win favour with Europe in order to do so: he required technical and diplomatic support for his plans, and antiquities greased the way. Mehmet Ali was not particularly interested in the ancient past.

However, the historian Donald Reid places a caveat on the conventional account of this time, which suggests that only Europeans saw the Pyramids and ancient Egypt as symbols of Egypt. Reid argues that this is overstated, adding that Mehmet Ali, too, expressed 'intellectual curiosity' in the ancient culture.[13] Reid points to the dismay expressed by Ali at the exhumation of mummies, and the stamp of a pyramid on his official journal. Even so, it was a French scholar—Jean-François Champollion, who would go on to help decipher the Rosetta Stone—who pushed for Ali to protect the ancient sites and antiquities that were under threat. The threat came not only from European collectors, but also from development and modernization—the ancient temple complex of Dendera was being used as a quarry for a cloth factory. Champollion warned Ali that the great temples were disappearing, at risk of being destroyed forever, as were a many great monuments.

In 1835, Mehmet Ali issued a decree that established a governing body to control the traffic in antiquities. A ban was put in place on the unauthorized removal of artefacts. The decree designated a building in

Cairo to serve as a storehouse, and ordered the building of a museum. European museums were cited by Ali as the inspiration:

> the Europeans have buildings for keeping antiquities; stones covered with paintings and inscriptions, and other similar objects are carefully conserved there and shown to the inhabitants of the country as well to the travellers...such establishments bring great renown to the countries which have them.[14]

But the plans for the museum stumbled and failed, although a small collection was retained. And for some time the ban on removing antiquity was ignored, including by Jean-François Champollion, who took quite a few things for himself. Sites continued to be dynamited in the course of modernization.

Although Europeans would remove great quantities of Egyptian antiquity, they also played a part in founding research centres within Egypt. Between 1858 and 1908 they contributed to the founding of four museums: the Egyptian Museum, the Graeco-Roman Museum, the Coptic Museum, and what is now the Museum of Islamic Art, originally called the Museum of Arab Art. The Antiquities Service (then called the Service des Antiquités) was set up in 1858 by Said Pasha, the viceroy of Egypt, and run by French scholars for over a century. With time, the Egyptians used archaeology for their own ends, evoking it in nationalist challenges to the European control of Egypt.[15] In the 1950s, when the British colonial troops left Egypt, the Antiquities Service was organized and run by Egyptians.

The Rosetta Stone

In 1801, the British and the Ottomans defeated the French at Alexandria. The French occupation was brought to an end, and the dispute over the ownership of the Rosetta Stone began.

After its discovery, the Rosetta Stone was kept by General Jacques-François Menou. After the French defeat, he wanted to keep the stone as personal property, haggling over the terms of surrender, but General Hutchinson, Menou's British opposite number, refused this claim of ownership—he wanted it for himself. A witness, Edward Daniel Clarke, recalls their stormy argument:

> We remained near the outside of the tent; and soon heard the French General's voice elevated as usual, and in strong terms of indignation remonstrating against the injustice of the demands made upon him. The words *'Jamais on n'a pille le monde!'* [Never has the world been so pillaged] diverted us highly, as coming from a leader of plunder and devastation[16]

Menou failed to hold on to the Rosetta Stone. The diplomat William Hamilton, then secretary to Lord Elgin, landed in Egypt to help oversee the evacuation of the French, and helped to foil an attempt to smuggle it to France.

The Rosetta Stone was ceded to Britain under the Treaty of Alexandria in 1801, along with the fourth-century BC sarcophagus of the pharaoh Nectanebo II and other sculptures. The relevant part of the Treaty stated: 'the Arabian manuscripts, the statues, and the other collections which have been made for the French Republic, shall be considered as public property, and subject to the disposal of the generals of the combined army'.[17]

Upon arrival in Britain, the Rosetta Stone was received in nationalistic terms, as a symbol of triumph over the French. It was moved to the Society of Antiquities, in London, which was charged in its Royal Charter of 1751 to aid 'the encouragement, advancement and furtherance of the study and knowledge of the antiquities and history of this and other countries'.[18] Four plaster casts were created and sent to the universities of Cambridge, Oxford, Edinburgh, and Trinity College Dublin. Prints were also circulated among scholars in Europe, to stimulate study. The real thing was then sent to the British Museum. By this stage, stamped on the stone was a fourth language—English—as two additional sentences reinforced ownership: 'Captured in Egypt by the British Army in 1801' and 'Presented by King George III'. A series of engravings published in 1803 trumpet the stone and the objects obtained at the same time, as 'a GLORIOUS TROPHY OF BRITISH PROWESS, which the VAN-QUISHED THEMSELVES have been compelled to supply'.[19] The stamp on the stone has since been allowed to fade.

It was in London that early advances in understanding the stone were made. Thomas Young, an English physicist, made a major breakthrough when he worked out that the seven elongated ovals in the hieroglyphic section spelt, phonetically, the royal name of Ptolemy, and realized that this meant that the hieroglyphs had more than just symbolic meaning—they served as a spoken language. But it was difficult work. Writing in the 1816–24 edition of the *Encyclopædia Britannica*, Young voiced concerns that the lack of progress in deciphering the script meant that the object was largely valued as loot, rather than the door to knowledge that it could be. He worried that it had ceased to be a scholarly achievement and instead was 'useless, though a glorious trophy of British valour'.[20]

After years of studying the scripts, the French scholar Jean-François Champollion worked out what the seven demotic equivalents were. He then began tracing these demotic signs back to hieroglyphic signs, enlarging Young's list of phonetic hieroglyphs until, in 1822, Champollion established the foundations of the ancient language. Finally, it was possible to read history from the perspective of ancient Egypt. Received authority was displaced: with the knowledge unlocked by the Rosetta Stone, the Hebrew Old Testament could be challenged, scriptural tradition could be questioned, and the writing of the ancient people could be understood. It was such a breakthrough that the very name Rosetta Stone has come to be a powerful symbol of discovery, a term used in multiple instances and contexts to denote a key to knowledge.

Champollion became director of the Egyptian Museum at the Louvre in 1826, taking his first expedition to Egypt two years later. It was to be his last. He died of a stroke while researching a dictionary and grammar guide to Egyptian hieroglyphics. Thanks to his efforts, and those of Thomas Young, the Rosetta Stone is one of the most popular exhibits in the history of the British Museum, with thousands of visitors every single day jostling in front of it, trying to get a closer look.

The birth of Egyptology

The removal of the artefacts in Egypt took place under a failed and destabilizing attempt by the French to occupy Egypt and turn it into a colony. But it also stimulated European scholarly interest in Egypt and the founding of Egyptology.

Napoleon's expedition to Egypt had a major scientific result. Research on the excavated material led to the discovery of ancient Egypt and its documentation. Indeed, with the failure of Napoleon's military aims, the scientific investigation was amplified—the savants needed somehow to contribute to glorifying Napoleon in the absence of victory. (Despite this failure, he was crowned 'Emperor of the French' a few years later.) *The Description de l'Égypte* was the result of their efforts: an ambitious twenty-three-volume publication documenting archaeological sites, many of which were previously unknown. It was published in sections between the years 1809 and 1829, with 7,000 pages of text, 837 copper engravings, and over 3,000 illustrations. The *Description* was later described by the literary critic Edward Said as 'that great collective appropriation of one country by another'.[21]

The *Description*'s original cover is revealing. A large stone doorway frames a view of an ancient land with striking archaeological ruins.

Across the top of the frame, Napoleon is depicted as a conquering deity—perhaps Apollo or Alexander—riding a chariot beneath an imperial eagle, driving back the Mamluks against the Pyramids. Behind him are the nine Muses marching in procession. There are no modern buildings, or people. There are no Islamic references; it is as if they did not exist. The relics in the centre include Pompey's Column, Cleopatra's Needle, the Rosetta Stone, and the Dendera Zodiac. Of these relics, three of Cleopatra's Needles are no longer in Egypt, but in London, Paris, and New York; the Rosetta Stone is in the British Museum; and the Dendera Zodiac is in the Louvre. Pompey's Column, a Roman capital, remains in Egypt. But despite a certain amount of creative imagining, the drawings within the *Description* were carefully executed, with precise measurements of the monuments, sculptures, and buildings, as well as detailed recordings of manuscripts and wall paintings. It is the only record of some ancient monuments, which have since been destroyed.

The sometime head of the Musée Napoléon, Baron Denon, published *Travels in Lower and Upper Egypt During the Campaigns of General Bonaparte* (1802), a two-volume bestseller that was translated into German and English and reprinted in twenty editions. A fashion for Egypt spread across a European society already enchanted with the ancient civilization. The impact of the intervention by the French and their discoveries accelerated the birth of Egyptology—the scholarship of the history, language, and civilization of ancient Egypt. There was an Egyptian Revival in design. No world fair, like the Crystal Palace Exhibition in London of 1851, was complete without an Egyptian room, collection, or exhibit—the influence of the ancient culture of Egypt was everywhere. Napoleon ordered the making of a porcelain dinner set—the *Sèvres service égyptien*—with ancient Egyptian themes and motifs, and the Sèvres porcelain factory also made Egyptian inkwells. In Britain, Wedgwood created porcelain curios with pharaohs and hieroglyphs, and Antwerp zoo built an Egyptian temple to house its ostriches. Egyptomania spread into everyday life.

Belzoni: 'The greatest plunderer of them all'

After Napoleon was defeated by the British, the acquisition of collections from the ancient lands of Egypt continued for both the British and the French, with growing interest from Germany and Italy.

Although the British Museum, unlike the Louvre, was never intended as a museum of conquest, it was the first point of call after a British military victory, and for British diplomats with a collection to donate. As a consequence, in the first part of the nineteenth century the museum came to hold an important collection of ancient sculpture. Britain's position in the world was sustained by extensive and successful foreign diplomacy, together with the Mediterranean fleet. This aided the museum's collection, not least because the navy surveyed coastlands and transported many pieces. Nonetheless, what was acquired was often the result of informal arrangements and haphazard acts by individuals.

Henry Salt, British consul general in Alexandria from 1815 to 1827, was a key figure for the Egyptian collection of the British Museum. He was appointed to Alexandria with the help of Joseph Banks, who encouraged him to look for antiquities on behalf of the museum. But the precise arrangement was unclear and there was some disagreement. Salt had suggested to Banks that he procure the antiquities for a small annual sum: 'If I were allowed to draw upon the Trustees of the Museum for one or two hundred pounds per annum, I think I might be able to augment with great advantage their Egyptian Collection,'[22] Salt wrote to Banks, in the hope that the money from antiquities would bolster his income from the Foreign Office. But there was no confirmation of this in the museum minutes. In the end, the museum did not fund Salt but it did purchase, for £2,000, his first collection. The Louvre, on the other hand, paid five times that price for his second collection.

Working for Salt was Giovanni Battista Belzoni, who became his main agent and was then known as 'The Great Belzoni'. Nowadays he is assailed as a 'tomb robber' and derided as 'the greatest plunderer of them all'.[23] Born in Padua, Italy, Belzoni started out as a showman—a 6-feet-tall strongman in a circus, billed as 'the Patagonian Sampson'—but in reality he was a frustrated hydraulic engineer. Belzoni had left the circus and tried to start another career, attempting to sell a waterwheel in Cairo in 1815 to Muhammad Ali Pasha. Ali Pasha ruled Egypt for the Ottomans, increasingly independently, and was employing Western technicians to develop industry and agriculture, but Belonzi had little success. When his hydraulic schemes failed, he changed direction again and started to look for antiquities for Salt.

Belzoni is responsible for obtaining some of the most magnificent pieces now in museums in Europe. For the British Museum, he brought back the colossal sculpture of the head of Rameses II, a towering monument of the famous pharaoh that weighs 7¼ tons. The sheer size of the head stunned Belonzi when he discovered it in the Ramesseum, the mortuary temple of Rameses at Thebes. Belzoni anticipated its trip abroad: 'I found it near the remains of his body and chair with his face upwards and apparently smiling at me, at the thought of being taken to England.'[24]

It took fifteen days to move the bust to the Nile—the river was ¾ mile away. A team of around eighty men worked hard, using ropes, levers, and a wooden sledge to move it in hot, dusty conditions: Belzoni's engineering knowledge was finally put to use. He was pleased with the results of their strenuous efforts, and also with the triumph over the French, who had designs on the sculpture but had failed to transport it:

> It is almost two miles from the Palace known as the Memnonium to the Nile . . . and the already mentioned size of this Colossus was the reason why it was preserved, since it had fallen face down and remained in this position until the time of the French, who tried to cut it into two pieces by

placing a mine in its chest so they could transport it; but then, fearing that facial features would be ruined, they abandoned the undertaking.[25]

Once on the river, the bust travelled to Alexandria where it was shipped to London. It is said to have inspired the poet Shelley to write 'Ozymandias', which meditates on the fall of a great power:

> 'My name is Ozymandias, king of kings:
> Look on my works, ye Mighty, and despair!'
> Nothing beside remains. Round the decay
> Of that colossal wreck, boundless and bare,
> The lone and level sands stretch far away.

On another occasion, Belzoni stumbled upon a beautiful sarcophagus made from a single piece of translucent alabaster, covered with intricate, decorative details, the base of which was carved with a picture of the goddess Nut. The day, and the find, was 'one of the best, perhaps, of my life,' he wrote, for he felt, 'that extreme pleasure which wealth cannot purchase—the pleasure of discovering what has long been sought in vain'.[26] The sarcophagus was at the very bottom of a very large tomb in the valley of Beban el Malouk, near Gournon, buried in the Valley of the Kings. Belzoni noted that it was 328 feet long—later excavations have put it at 446 feet—with interconnecting chambers and tunnels.[27] He had found the tomb of Egyptian king Seti I, father of Rameses II. Henry Salt thought it 'exquisitely painted, with the colours as fresh as on the day it was completed; it throws everything else, as far as colour goes, completely into the background'.[28] Seti was no longer resting inside. The mummy was later discovered, having been hidden by priests in a cleft in a cliff to protect him from thieves and subsequently taken to the Cairo Museum for the Royal Mummy room. Belzoni was to become well known for finding 'mummy pits', where mummies were rooted out of what was supposed to be the final resting place of the dead, deep in the ground. Once discovered, if still in their cases, mummies were sent to museums or ground up into dust by the locals, used as a panacea for all sorts of ills.

Seti's sarcophagus is now in Lincoln's Inn Fields in London, snapped up for £2,000 by the architect and collector Sir John Soane for his home and museum after the British Museum decided they did not have the funds for it. When the sarcophagus arrived in London in 1825, Soane threw a party that lasted for three days and to which 800 people were invited. Members of the royal family, the prime minister Robert Jenkinson, and the Conservative politician Robert Peel all rubbed shoulders in front of Seti's sarcophagus, joined by the artist William Turner and the poet Samuel Taylor Coleridge. It was placed in the centre of the basement, lit up with over 100 candelabra and oil lamps. The sarcophagus was a sight it was to behold, wrote one partygoer:

> Seen by this medium, every surrounding object, however admirable in itself, becomes subservient to the sarcophagus—the ancient, the splendid, the wonderful sarcophagus is before us, and all else are but accessories to its dignity and grandeur; a mingled sense of awe, admiration, and delight pervades our faculties, and is even oppressive in its intensity, yet enduring in its association.[29]

Belzoni is now regarded in an unfavourable light by modern archaeologists. His excavation techniques were careless. He tore monuments out of the ground, on occasion using a battering ram to enter closed and complex tombs; he blew a hole in the pyramid of Khephren with dynamite, and the burial chamber still bears his signature on the wall. But while cavalier, careless, and forceful, this treatment was not particularly unusual for the time: and it did bring results. Belzoni died of dysentery in 1823, while trying to find the source of the Niger.

ANTIQUITY IN THE BRITISH MUSEUM

When the British Museum opened, there was no department dedicated to archaeological collections. There were no Elgin Marbles. That would change dramatically in the nineteenth century, when the British Museum changed from being something akin to a cabinet of curiosities and was reorganized as an institution with a clear focus on art history and archaeology. As it did so, the British Museum became, in the words of Jacob Rothenberg, author of a study of the acquisition of the Elgin Marbles, a 'universal shrine'[30] to the greatest antiquity of all: that from fifth-century BC Athens. Associated with the museum ever since they were acquired, Ian Jenkins, senior curator in the Department of Greek and Roman Antiquities at the British Museum, explains that the Elgin Marbles sculptures were revered in the nineteenth century 'with near religious awe'.[31] But they did not start out that way.

Collectors in Britain became interested in antiquity in the seventeenth century, a century later than the rest of the European continent. The British nobleman developed an enthusiasm in the eighteenth century. In 1732, the Society of Dilettanti held its first meeting in London. This was initially a dining club, and one of a number of flourishing clubs and societies in this period. Its members had to travel to Italy: indeed, many had met on the Grand Tour, the finishing school for gentlemen that took them to Rome, Venice, Florence, Vienna, and Paris. The Dilettanti earned a reputation for hedonistic exploits—it was described by Horace Walpole as 'a club, for which the nominal qualification is having been in Italy, and the real one being drunk'.[32] But as the Society of Dilettanti became more serious and prominent, it advanced the study of antiquity.

Collectors were in thrall to ancient Rome. It was commonly accepted that the greatest artistic creation was to be found in ancient Italy: in Rome; first and foremost, followed by Florence and Naples. Works,

especially the Graeco-Roman *Apollo Belvedere* and the *Venus de' Medici*—
with their smooth, polished, and poised limbs—were copied and vener-
ated. There was a thriving market in restoring broken and battered work
to improve the finish and elegance of the piece—arms, heads, and noses
were replaced, if needed. And there was little concern then that restoration
might spoil the authenticity of the piece: collectors wanted the perfect
model, often decoratively displayed in the English mansions in which there
was a building boom, and where many are still on show to this day.

Joshua Reynolds, a painter and founder of the Royal Academy set up
to advance an English school of art, was a proponent of neoclassicism, a
philosophical aesthetic movement influenced by Italian Renaissance theories.
Neoclassicism was fashionable, inspired by the order and rationality of the
Age of Reason. Reynolds wrote of the desired achievements of such work:

> Its essence is correctness: and when to correct and perfect form is added
> the ornament of grace, dignity of character, and appropriated expression,
> as in the Apollo, the Venus, the Laocoon, the Moses of Michael Angelo,
> and many others, this art may be said to have accomplished its purpose.[33]

In the early nineteenth century, the British Museum started to be filled
with classical remains. The first great archaeological collection, acquired
by the then Department of Natural and Artificial Productions, was that of
the antique Roman and Greek vases, bronzes, coins, and marbles assembled by William Hamilton during his ambassadorship to Naples and
arriving in the museum in 1772. Joseph Banks was involved in depositing
the marbles of the Society of Dilettanti in the museum. Additionally,
Horatio Nelson wrote to Banks with news of a cargo of Greek antiquities
seized from a French ship in 1803. He needed someone who could deal
with the British government regarding this haul, and Banks was only too
happy to help:

> I Shall undertake your Commission with Pleasure, and Execute it with Zeal
> I will take Care to offer the Sculpture you have Capturd to government in

a Proper manner to State the Value of it with Justice & Correctness, &, in Case of their Chusing to Purchase it for the advantage of the Arts in Britain, I will see that your brave and meritorious Tars are not deprivd of any part of their Rights.[34]

In 1803, the first curatorship in antiquities were appointed. On the recommendation of Charles Townley, Taylor Combe—a collector of classical sculpture—was appointed as an under-librarian in the Department of Natural History. Townley was a significant collector, assembling one of the foremost collections of classical sculpture: this was displayed in his Westminster home which had become a meeting place for connoisseurs and artists. Townley was also a trustee of the British Museum.

Plans were made to expand and to reassess the collections of the museum in general, with a number of reviews and discussions about restructuring. There was a discussion about charging for admission, a proposal that was rejected. The result was the commissioning of new buildings, and a significant change in the ordering of the collections: the division of antiquity from natural history. In 1807, forty-nine years after the museum opened, the Department of Antiquities and Coins was founded, with Taylor Combe as its first Keeper.

Joseph Banks, William Hamilton, and Charles Townley were on a committee that recommended and supervised the building of a new wing intended to house the Egyptian antiquities that had started to arrive after Napoleon's defeat. Opening in 1808, it included Charles Townley's collection of Graeco-Roman works, purchased for the nation when he died. One of his last acquisitions had been a Roman copy of the Discobolus—a naked male athlete throwing a discus, one of the most famous classical sculptures of all time. It is still in the museum, as are Townley's letters and documents.

In 1817, what became known as the Elgin Marbles arrived, after a stormy reception in London and a battle over their artistic value.

In 1751, the Society of Dilettanti sponsored James Stuart—an architect, archaeologist, and painter—and Nicholas Revett—also an architect and painter —to take an expedition to Athens, where they made drawings of the ruins of Greek antiquities and monuments. Their resulting publication—*The Antiquities of Athens*, an archaeological record, treatise, and reference work in Grecian taste—signalled a shift in the history of aesthetics. It followed on from the researches of the Frenchman Julien-David Le Roy and his *Les Ruines des plus beaux monuments de la Grèce*, published in 1758. The Dilettanti went on to sponsor work in Ionia in 1764, contributing to a developing archaeology of ancient Greece.

There followed a move away from a neoclassical ideal to a more Romantic one. The latter was concerned with the emotions and a

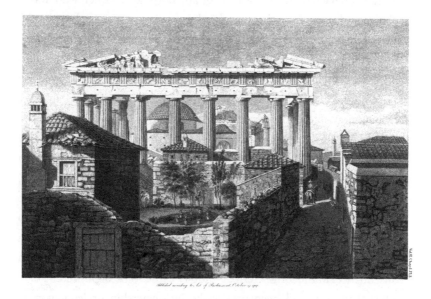

Figure 5. 'A view of the Eastern Portico of the Parthenon'.
James Stuart & Nicholas Revett. Antiquities of Athens (London, 1787), vol.2, chapter 2, plate I.
© RIBA Library Photographs Collection.

concept of the immediate, the instinctive, and the given in nature, defending the senses and experience. By contrast, the neoclassical approach was seen as passionless and over-idealized. However, it should be pointed out that, in England especially, there was never a fixed dividing line between the two, and thinkers would move between them, sometimes bridging them. Joshua Reynolds, for example, would argue, on occasion, that art should seize the imagination, drawing on Romantic ideals at times.

Whilst the neoclassicists had Joshua Reynolds advocating their cause, the Romantics were fuelled by Johann Joachim Winckelmann, one of the most important theorists of ancient archaeology, whose scholarship would change the way antiquity was understood. Winckelmann was a Prussian archaeologist and art historian, born to a father who was a cobbler and a mother who was the daughter of a weaver; but despite these modest beginnings, Winckelmann went on to achieve great heights. He started out studying theology, intended to become a physician, and ended up as an authority on Roman and Greek sculpture. In 1755, at the age of 40, he gained significant recognition when he published an essay on the imitation of Greek painting and sculpture.

Winckelmann didn't reject the concept of the absolute advocated by Reynolds, but advocated a more empirical approach—careful observation and comparison—and the delineation of stages in the progress of beauty. He was the first to publish a systematic chronological account of antique art, one that included the Etruscans and the Egyptians, and he tried to isolate the stylistic characteristics of different periods. Winckelmann praised the 'noble simplicity and sedate grandeur'[35] of Greek art. As a consequence, in the longer term, antiquity came to be organized by date rather than as it had been previously, by ownership or iconography. Remarkably, Winckelmann did this with very little first-hand knowledge of ancient sculpture: with the domination of the eastern Mediterranean by the Ottomans, from the fifteenth century, not much of this art had reached the West. There were Roman copies, which were different to the originals, and a few drawings, as well as literary sources such as Pliny the Elder and Pausanias—but little of the real thing.

It was his *History of Ancient Art*, published first in German in 1764, that became a significant European work. Winckelmann tried to systematize the different stages of Greek sculptures into four periods and he identified cultural factors in their creation. He was convinced that the Greeks were superior to the Romans. And he argued that the greatest Greek art had been brought about by specific geographical, political, and religious circumstances: 'Beauty... was not a general quality, even among the Greeks', but Athens was able to achieve it because, 'after the expulsion of tyrants, a democratic form of government was adopted, in which the entire people had a share'.[36] Political freedom was the essential precondition for the greatness of their art, he averred:

> The superiority which art acquired among the Greeks is to be ascribed partly to the influence of climate, partly to their constitution and government, and the habits of thinking which originated therefrom, and, in an equal degree also, to respect for the artist, and the use and application of art.[37]

According to this line of thinking, when the Greeks lost their freedom, they also lost their genius; and this genius would never be recreated, although attempts should be made to do so.

Winckelmann's career ended early, in tragedy. In 1768, at the age of 50, he was murdered in Trieste, seemingly for the theft of a few valuables he had on his person. He never saw the Greek art that he so championed. He never got to see the Elgin Marbles. But his work served as an intellectual backdrop for the reception that would interpret them as perfect works of art.

The Parthenon Marbles

The Parthenon Marbles are a large collection of marble sculptures and architectural features taken from the ruins of the Parthenon, which once stood on the Acropolis in Athens, constructed in the fifth century BC. About 65 per cent of the original sculptures survive and are held in museums across Europe. Whilst there are a few pieces scattered elsewhere, in Paris, Copenhagen, Vienna, Würzburg, and Munich, around half the remaining Parthenon Marbles are now in Athens and half are in London. They include panels from a sculpted frieze, which once ran continuously around the exterior wall; metopes (panels, originally displayed high up above its columns), and pediments (life-sized marble figures from its gable ends).

Local traditions, heroic conflicts, and myths are depicted on the sculptures. Gods, goddesses, heroes, and mortals are artfully carved, as are lions, galloping horses with nostrils slightly flared, and cattle being led for sacrifice. The sculpted frieze that once circled the entire building above the colonnade, is usually interpreted as representing Athenians in religious procession.[38] In the central scene of the east frieze, figures escort the sacred robe of Athena to be dedicated to the wood statue of Athena Polias. People look as if they are moving; the robes draping the bodies appear soft and to ripple. On the metopes are battle scenes: a struggle between Greeks and their opponents in oriental dress; the fall of Troy; centaurs—part man and part horse—and Lapiths—humans from northern Greece. A victorious centaur leans over a Lapith who is sitting down, defeated and dying.

They are thousands of years old. Yet astonishingly the figures and forms appear alive: they are *almost* realistic. They are more natural than the Roman works, but they also retain something of an abstract and imagined quality. And it is these qualities—the ideal and the realistic combined—that were much debated when they arrived in England.

Today, the Parthenon is often the first thing people think of when they think of Greece, a point underlined by Melina Mercouri when, as Greek minister for culture in the 1980s, she asked for the return of the Elgin Marbles: 'the very name of our country is immediately associated with the Parthenon'.[39] The Parthenon has become a symbol of democracy, the image of Greece, and an icon of the achievements of classical Greece. But it did not start out this way.

The building of the Parthenon began around twenty-five centuries ago, when the Athenian assembly voted to use the revenue it had raised through taxes imposed on other city states to rebuild a temple to Athena, the goddess of warfare. The temple that preceded it had been destroyed by the Persians when they occupied Athens in around 480 BC. Overseen by Iktinos the architect and Phidias the famous sculptor, the Parthenon was built at the behest of the politician Pericles, who was elected general by the Athenian people. This was a military post and Pericles was aggressive with it: he was later involved in triggering the war with the city of Sparta that Athens lost in 404 BC.

The Parthenon was a political monument as well as a temple, part of an ambitious building project conceived by Pericles to demonstrate the city's wealth and power, and one of a series of buildings on top of the hill that formed part of the Acropolis complex, which included a monumental gateway. Indeed, it is the monumental gateway, the grand Propylaia, which the Greek historian Thucydides highlights as the important building. As is often the case with such construction plans, Pericles' rivals criticized them as too expensive. What a waste of money, they said; an insult to their allies, whose defence budget was being squandered on the city of Athens.

Work on the new temple was completed in 432 BC. A large 40-feet statue of Athena made from gold and ivory was the centrepiece. Much of that which may have been the important focus for visitors, such as this statue, sacred objects and dedications, are all lost or destroyed. No one is certain what exactly the building was for, or even what it was called initially—few historical sources remain. In what is left of their accounts, Greek and Roman writers do not dwell on it; but it is thought that the 'Parthenon' may have been the name of one of the inner rooms, which came to be the common name for the whole building.

When you see parts of the Parthenon today, it is hard to believe that it is centuries old. When you hear what the building has been subjected to over time, including the ravages of nature and the fury of man, it comes as a surprise that anything is left in one piece.

The statue of Athena lost her gold plates in 296 BC, when they were stripped from her by the Athenian tyrant Lachares to raise funds to pay for his army. In the fifth century AD, the Parthenon was closed by the order of the imperial government in Constantinople; it is thought that around this time, the statue of Athena was taken to Constantinople where she was later lost. The Parthenon was then converted into a Christian church, dedicated to the Holy Wisdom, when the metopes on the north-west and east were defaced due to their pagan images. The Crusaders dedicated it to the Virgin Mary and renamed it the Metropolitan church of Athens. Having been a Christian church for centuries, in 1458 the Ottoman Empire turned it into a mosque, which was used by the garrison; the Christian bell tower—a Byzantine addition—was transformed into a minaret, and the mosaics and frescos were painted over. In 1687, a Venetian army took Athens in a fight with the Ottomans, as part of an alliance of European powers led by Venice that was trying to drive them out of Greece. The Ottomans stored their ammunition inside and the building was subject to attack: a mortar bomb damaged the roof, the damage from which was extensive and it was no longer fit for use. Adding to its woes, the Venetian Commander Francesco Morosini tried to remove the sculptures of horses on the west pediment so that he could take them back to Venice, but they were too heavy and were smashed in the process.

'As much as possible': Elgin takes his Marbles

In 1798, Thomas Bruce, the seventh Earl of Elgin, was British ambassador to the Ottoman government, known as 'Ambassador Extraordinary and Minister Plenipotentiary of His Britannic Majesty to the Sublime

Porte of Selim III, Sultan of Turkey'. Elgin's architect in Scotland, Thomas Harrison, made a suggestion that casts from Athenian monuments would contribute to the knowledge of ancient Greece that was starting to be advanced by James Stuart and Nicholas Revett (following their trip to Athens in the 1750s) and others. A young artist needed casts truly to understand these works, Harrison ventured.

Elgin agreed and was enthused. He approached painters, architects, and draughtsmen to draw the ancient monuments of Athens and make casts. These included William Turner, who was just beginning to be recognized as an artist. Turner was willing, but there was a disagreement about terms. He demanded a salary Elgin considered too high; Elgin demanded ownership of Turner's drawings and that the painter teach Lady Elgin to draw. So it was not to be. William Hamilton, the diplomat whom we met earlier in connection with the British Museum, was Elgin's private secretary; and the landscape painter Giovanni Battista Lusieri was appointed as an illustrator to assist him in drawing and making casts of the Acropolis, as did a few others. Philip Hunt, chaplain at the British Embassy in Constantinople, worked with them.

In northern Europe interest in the antique world was burgeoning, but it was not of great interest to the Ottomans or to the local people at that time. The Acropolis complex was being used by the Ottomans as a garrison, and the Parthenon was crumbling, treated as a quarry. The sculptures, as well as the plain building blocks, were being put to practical use—carted off where possible to be reused in housing.

In early 1801, Elgin's men received permission to access the site for the purpose of drawing, for which they were charged the considerable sum of a daily rate of 5 guineas. 'My whole plan', explained Elgin later to the Parliamentary Select Committee that would investigate whether the collection should be purchased, 'was to measure and draw every thing that could be traced of architecture.'[40] Philip Hunt became concerned that they were making minimal progress. Hunt had also become very keen on the monuments. He pushed for a firman that would allow them not only to cast the works, erect scaffolding, and dig (which was new), but also to 'take away any sculptures or inscriptions which do not interfere with the works or walls of the Citadel'.[41] This was first mention of such a scheme, and Elgin agreed with him.

In his later testimony to Parliament, Elgin explained that, although he had not begun with the intention of taking parts away, he changed his mind once it became clear that the building was in danger. '[T]he Turkish government attached no importance to them,' he said of the sculptures, but 'every traveller coming, added to the general defacement of the statuary in his reach: there are now in London pieces broken off within our day.' Even worse, 'the Turks have been continually defacing the heads and in some instances . . . they have pounded down the statues to convert them into mortar'.[42]

There was some toing and froing between Elgin and the Ottoman authorities. Elgin was initially given a firman thought to have authorized their entry into the Acropolis to make drawings, erect scaffolding, and to make moulds, but his request for permission to do more made little headway, at first. The team were then forbidden from entering the Acropolis for the purposes of drawing and moulds. Then, political developments dramatically altered these inhospitable circumstances: after the British won a victory against the French forces, all resistance came to an end. Elgin rejoiced:

> about the middle of the summer of 1801 all difficulties were removed; we then had access for general purposes. Yes; the whole system of Turkish feeling met with a revolution, in the first place, from the invasion of the French, and afterwards by our conquest.[43]

The Ottomans granted Elgin a second firman, of which only an Italian translation survives. They did not receive payment, but did receive gifts, which was the custom.

The academic William St Clair discovered the second firman in the archive of Philip Hunt's papers and has analysed it (there is no sign of the first firman). In his comprehensive and authoritative study of the acquisition of the Marbles, he notes that the firman gave Elgin's agents the right to enter the Acropolis freely, erect scaffolding, draw, make moulds, remove obstructions from the monuments, and 'to conduct excavations, taking away anything of interest which the excavations yielded'.[44] He notes also that it gave the first permission to dig. St Clair finds that it did not explicitly state they could remove sculptures from the actual building or damage it.[45]

Lady Elgin, the wealthy heiress Mary Bruce, wrote to her father of the news, describing Hunt as in 'raptures' and herself as in the 'greatest glee, for it would have been a great pity to have failed in the principle part, after having been at such an expense'. This firman, she details,

> allows all our artists to go into the Citadel, to copy and model everything in it, to erect scaffolds all round the Temples, to dig and discover all the ancient foundations, and to bring away any Marbles that may be deemed curious by their having inscriptions on them.[46]

Work progressed. A large group of Greek men were hired to help. Sculptures were picked off the ground where they had fallen. But the workmen then prised off a considerable quantity from the building. The key moment appears to have been when Philip Hunt pushed for authority from the voivode (the local Ottoman administrator) to remove pieces from the building. The voivode was either encouraged to believe the firman already granted permission to remove sculptures from the buildings or else he believed it was in his power to approve. He therefore agreed to the request. Some time later, Elgin received letters from the Ottoman government approving what the voivode had done.

The metopes and corner blocks were removed. Philip Hunt wrote to Elgin enthusiastically of the excavations that were taking place, of the statues that were being detached and lowered down from the Temple. 'If I said all I could, I should not say anything in comparison with their merit. I am sure there is nothing so perfect of this kind in all the universe.'[47] He ended his letter with the triumphant news: 'The most beautiful of statues is now in the Consul's yard. We have been forced to get a gun carriage and a train of thirty men to bring it down.'[48] Bits of marble were chiselled off and broken into pieces to make them portable, with the excess material discarded.

Elgin, who was in Constantinople, wrote to Lusieri asking for original pieces for Broomhall, his home in Scotland:

> I should wish to have, of the Acropolis, examples in the actual object, of each thing, and architectural ornament—of each cornice, each frieze, each capital—of the decorated ceilings, of the fluted columns—specimens of the different architectural orders, and of the variant forms of the orders—of metopes and the like, as much as possible. Finally, everything in the way of sculpture, medals, and curious marbles that can be discovered by means of assiduous and indefatigable excavation. This excavation ought to be pushed on as much as possible, be its success what it may.[49]

He explained he wanted pieces to enhance the art of the nation—an escalation in intent from merely adorning his home:

> The scale I am upon is the result of much enquiry from scientific and practical artists . . . and has been carried through with great trouble and expense . . . I am flattered with hopes the whole will constitute a very great national acquisition.[50]

As parts were taken, the building was damaged. Lusieri described these actions himself, in a letter written to Elgin:

> I have, my Lord, the pleasure of announcing to you the possession of the eighth metope, that one where there is the centaur carrying off the woman. This piece has caused much trouble in all respects and I have been obliged to be a little barbarous.[51]

Elgin justified his actions as a heroic preservation of historic treasures in the service of the fine arts and as a great national acquisition.

Others considered it a vile desecration. Criticism came first from British travellers in Athens, who saw Elgin's agents at work. Edward D. Clarke complained that the workmen damaged the architecture of the building while removing the metopes and the horse-head from the east pediment:

> We saw this fine piece of sculpture raised from its station between the triglyphs, but the workmen endeavouring to give it a position adapted to the projected line of descent, a part of the adjoining masonry was loosened by the machinery and down came the fine masses of Pentelican marble, scattering their white fragments with thundering noise among the ruins.[52]

As an aside, it is worth noting that few of those men making accusations about Elgin could themselves be considered pure. Clarke was a keen collector who a few years earlier had stolen a statue from Eleusis, thought to be by Phidias. This statue, now in the Fitzwilliam Museum in Cambridge, is now known to be a Roman caryatid.

Robert Smirke, a proponent of the Greek Revival architecture, who later designed the main block and facade of the new British Museum building, was also in Athens and witnessed the work. He noted ambivalent feelings towards the excavation:

> Though I was at first pleased with the Idea of our Country coming in possession of such valuable remains . . . I could not but feel a strong regret when I considered their being taken as a sort of signal for the annihilation of such interesting monuments . . . Each stone as it fell shook the ground with its ponderous weight with a deep hollow noise; it seemed like a convulsive groan of the injured spirit of the Temple.[53]

At this stage, and for some time, it was assumed that the sculptures would be restored. They were incomplete, parts had been broken, and restoration was common practice. Even Winckelmann was not opposed to the restoration of antiquity in principle, so long as it was clear what was and was not original. It is quite possible then that the Elgin Marbles could have looked very different today. But William Hamilton was unsure about such plans, from early on:

> Lusieri speaks to me frequently of his Expectation that you intend to send the mutilated originals which are carried away from Athens, to Rome to be restored...I cannot think it will ever be worth while to risque such valuable monuments in a place where all that is precious is every moment in danger of falling into other hands.[54]

Hamilton appears to have been worried that were the sculptures to go to Rome for the work—common practice with antiquity at that time—they might be seized by the French. Hamilton also ventures that restoration might be inappropriate for these particular sculptures, that they should be left as they are, for aesthetic reasons: 'it may be said that few would be found who would set a higher value on a work of Phidias or one of his Scholars, with a modern head and modern arms, than they would in their present state'.[55] He was wrong at the time—when they appeared in London, their ruined and disfigured state was derided by many—but in the end Hamilton was right. In 1803, the sculptor Canova refused the suggestion that they be restored by him, saying, 'it would be sacrilege in him or any man to touch them with a chisel'.[56] Elgin also asked the sculptor John Flaxman to perform such an act, and Flaxman also refused. They were not restored; and today it is unimaginable that they might have been.

Elgin neither looted nor stole the sculptures. They were removed under changing circumstances under the command of an enthusiastic individual and an equally keen team, with permission from the Ottomans who had, by that stage, run Greece for 350 years. Travellers and anti-quarians from northern Europe were taking various pieces that they could realistically carry. Elgin's workmen took considerably more than these travellers (200 tons of sculpture were shipped) with greater zeal, but he also took them with the knowledge and consent of the rulers. Elgin's agents, who carried out the excavation, probably took more from the actual building than they were supposed to, and were brutal in doing so. The terms of the agreement were also vague.

No court of law would find in favour of Greek complainants who would make an argument that the Marbles were illegally taken. According to the legal scholar John Merryman, whilst Elgin arguably 'exceeded the authority granted in the firman', nonetheless, 'the argument that they were taken illegally or immorally does not survive careful examination', and 'the law favours the British case'. Merryman continues:

> Although the original firman provides only slender authority for the removals, subsequent ratification of Elgin's actions by the Sultan and the passage of time since Greek independence both support the proposition that the British own the marbles. If Greece were to sue the Trustees of the British Museum today for their return, the remedy would be denied unless a quite different version of the facts were found.[57]

Besides, who knows what would have happened to those statues and friezes had they not been taken away by Elgin's men? The Parthenon was already falling down; it had been abandoned and was in pieces. Travellers and locals were grabbing what they could carry away for multiple purposes. If Lord Elgin had not taken them it is likely that the French or Germans would have. Years later, the Acropolis would be battered again in the Greek War of Independence, when it was besieged twice. Elgin may, or may not, have rescued the sculptures. We will never know.

The Parthenon in Athens

Over two decades later, with the Greek War of Independence, the Ottomans were defeated. In 1832 Greece was recognized as an independent nation with an appointed Bavarian king—Prince Otto, son of King Ludwig of Bavaria. In a matter of years the Greek Archaeological Service was founded, and a law passed for the control and regulation of antiquities.

Plans were made to build on the Acropolis. Friedrich Schinkel, the leading Prussian architect of his day and builder of Berlin's Altes Museums and Concert Hall, designed an elaborate royal palace on top of the hill that he intended would sit next to the decorative ruins of the Parthenon. Otto rejected the plans in the end, but it could have gone the other way—a new palace might have been the lasting image we came to have of Greece. As it turned out, Otto had very different designs on the Acropolis. He aimed to build a new nation state imbued with images of the Greek Golden Age. It was with Otto that ancient Greece was revived in Greece: only then did the Parthenon became the emblem of a new modern country.

Ancient Greece as we know it and see its remnants today is a reasonably recent construction, the product of a time when the political elite identified its history as integral in the creation of the new nation of Greece. The classicist Mary Beard explains that 'it was the Bavarian monarchy, looking for legitimation and bringing its own traditions of investment in ancient Greek culture, that made the connection between classical antiquities and Greek nationhood absolutely inextricable'.[58] The interests of the Bavarian monarchy chimed with Greek intellectuals, who were echoing the idealism about the glories of ancient Greece.

The visual linkage of ancient Athens with the new Greek state was expressed in a great pageant on the Acropolis in August 1834. The elaborate spectacle suggested that the new leaders were rightful inheritors of this great and ancient past, rather than recent and imposed incomers presiding over a new country. The new king watched the ceremony in his finery, having ridden to the Acropolis on horseback. Franz Karl Leopold von Klenze, master of ceremonies and the German architect involved in the reconstruction, made an opening statement:

Your majesty stepped today, after so many centuries of barbarism, for the first time on this celebrated Acropolis, proceeding on the road of civilisation and glory, on the road passed by the likes of Themistocles, Aristides, Cimon, and Pericles, and this is and should be in the eyes of your people the symbol of your glorious reign . . . All the remains of barbarity will be removed, here as in all of Greece, and the remains of the glorious past will be brought in a new light, as the solid foundations of a glorious present and future.[59]

The new king, the pageant suggested, had his rightful place within this list of magnificent leaders. The recent past, one of barbarism and invasion, could be put aside.

From 1835, there was a systematic attempt to the restore the Acropolis so that it looked more in keeping with plans to build the future of the new state on a long distant past. Old buildings and Turkish villages were removed, along with a tower, once believed to be Florentine, now thought to have been Byzantine, and a Renaissance palace that had been built into the Propylaia. There were complaints about this destruction— the pulling down of the tower in 1875, in particular, was regretted—but they were ignored. In the process of purifying the site of later building projects, those excavating came across sculptures from the sixth century BC, and other artefacts that would contribute to a better idea of what the appearance and layout of the Acropolis once was. Ancient monuments were reconstructed. The finds were put on display in a new purpose-built museum that opened in the 1860s, next to the east of the Parthenon. Subsequently, there have been numerous arguments about what to build near and around the building, so as to not obscure the view of ancient Greece.

In 1835 the British Museum offered casts of the Elgin Marbles in exchange for casts of the Parthenon sculptures in Athens, but in response the Greek government asked instead for the return of the Marbles. In 1890, the Greek minister in London, Ioannes Gennadios, asked that the architectural fragments be sent back to Greece, but this was refused.

Nearly 100 years later, in 1983, Melina Mercouri asked officially, as the Greek minister of culture, that the Marbles be returned—a request that the British government denied a year later.

'A mass of ruins': The Elgin Marbles arrive in London

Shipments of the material were arranged from March 1802 to transport the material from Athens to England. The arrival of the 'cases of curiosities' was first reported in the London press in August.[60] Crates would continue to arrive for the next decade. Elgin took a little longer: he was captured on his return and held prisoner by the French, and only released in 1806.

As the cases of sculptures arrived in London, they remained unopened for some time, passed around various houses—including the London abode of the Duchess of Portland—until they ended up in Elgin's new townhouse at Park Lane near Piccadilly. It was there, in 1807, that the Marbles first went on show, bunched together. They attracted considerable attention. John Flaxman, the sculptor who had been a pupil of Canova, was an early visitor. He declared them 'very far superior' to all the treasures of Italy.[61] This was an important concession for he was trained to hold in the highest esteem copies of lost Greek originals, such as the *Apollo Belvedere*. Others, however, were not so positive.

A degree of hostility built up towards Elgin and the Marbles. The Society of Dilettanti were a little cool on him, or at best silent. Over dinner one evening, one of their members—Richard Payne Knight, who was something of a neoclassicist and an authority on taste—shouted at Elgin, 'You have lost your labour, my Lord Elgin, your marbles are overrated; they are not Greek'—they were in fact 'Roman, of the time of Hadrian'.[62] He hadn't even seen them by that stage. Payne Knight helped to turn much of the Dilettanti against the Marbles. A few years later in his work *Specimens of Antient Sculpture*, Payne Knight argued that the friezes and metopes were probably executed 'by workmen scarcely ranked among artists'.[63]

Other visitors included the Royal Academician Humphrey Ozias, who remarked that they had 'something great and of a high style', but described the lot as 'a mass of ruins'.[64] The strongest and most well-known fury directed towards Elgin and the Marbles would come later from Lord Byron, fuelled by a certain amount of personal animosity. The sculptures, he said, were 'mishapen monuments', and 'mutilated blocks of art' on which Elgin had wasted thousands.[65] Byron deplored that Elgin had 'ruined Athens', that, 'I know no motive which can excuse, no name which can designate, the perpetrators of this dastardly devastation'. He continued: 'the wanton and useless defacement of the whole range of the basso-reliefs, in one compartment of the temple, will never permit that name to be pronounced by an observer without execration'. Byron raged that 'the honour of England' was not 'advanced by plunder, whether of India or Attica'; and these Marbles would bring a curse on those who acquired them:

> Curst be the hour when from their isle they rov'd
> And once again thy hapless bosom gor'd
> And snatched thy shrinking Gods to northern climes abhorr'd![66]

While criticism mounted of their retrieval and questions were raised about their quality, there was also an enthusiastic response: 'their fame is spreading every Day and the Value set upon them by public Voice will . . . be increased fourfold from what it was six Months ago: the Townley Collection is unanimous in your favour,' William Hamilton, by then Under-Secretary of State for Foreign Affairs, wrote to Elgin who was away in Scotland.[67]

The young painter Benjamin Robert Haydon took on the cause of the Marbles—writing and talking about, drawing, and praising them. He was of a more Romantic persuasion. After seeing them, 'I dozed and dreamed of the marbles. I rose at five in a fever of excitement, tried to sketch the Theseus from memory, did so and found that I comprehended it.' He went back to Park Lane, and found 'the impression was more vivid than before'.[68] He spent hours drawing the Marbles. In venerating them, Haydon went against the tradition of Joshua Reynolds and the academy, who valued the ideal above the actual form. The Elgin Marbles were praised and critiqued along the lines of the shifting ideals in taste. One reason why they became caught up in this battle, perhaps, is that that there is something to their aesthetic that appealed to both sides. The pieces are more natural than their later copies and the Roman sculptures, but they also retain something of the classical ideal. This meant that the various protagonists involved in the tussle over 'ideal' taste could each find something in them not only to adore but also to criticize.

Whilst on display, the Marbles became a backdrop for comparisons between the sculptures and the real thing: live human bodies. The anatomist Charles Bell describes attending such an occasion: 'On Saturday, when I came home I found that Lord Elgin has called, and written a note requesting me to come and see an exhibition of the principle sparrers, naked in his museum.' Two leading boxers, admired for their physique and strength, were exhibited, with nothing on, in various poses, alongside the figures, examined by the watchful academicians. Bell was 'much pleased. The intention was that we might compare the well-formed men with the remains of antiquity.'[69]

As the Marbles became the subject of lively argument about ideal art and aesthetic evaluation, Elgin was down on his luck and in poor health. He was suffering from syphilis, to which he had lost his nose, a misfortune in which Lord Byron publicly took pleasure. Elgin was also broke. He had spent a considerable amount of money in removing the sculptures and was on the verge of bankruptcy. Nor was this the end of his troubles. He had lost his very wealthy wife to her lover, and he had lost his seat in the House of Lords. Lord Elgin hoped to sell the Marbles, which would at least improve the health of his finances.

Elgin petitioned the House of Commons to appoint a Select Committee to investigate the circumstances of acquisition and to recommend on what terms, if any, they should be sold to the government. Elgin wanted £73,600, which he felt would be his 'just expectation'.[70] This sum, he argued, was far from their worth, but would cover his expenses. He noted that private individuals had paid considerably larger sums for other collections of art.

With the serious and pressing problem of the Battle of Waterloo in the background, the debate over the sale was put on hold. It may have helped Elgin's cause, for during the delay the well-known sculptor Canova travelled to London to see the Marbles, and was taken around by Hamilton and Haydon. Canova swooned in their favour: 'Oh! That I were a young man, and had to begin again, I should work on totally different principles from what I have done, and form, I hope, an entirely new school.'[71] The fan club for the Marbles gathered momentum.

Parliament reopened in 1816 and Elgin resubmitted his petition. A debate, held in February, heard testimony from eleven speakers. Some spoke about the great value of the collection. Others, however, raised questions about the right of Elgin to acquire it—though, in all the debates of 1816, nobody suggested it be sent back immediately. The petition was agreed to and an inquiry by a House of Commons Select Committee was launched to investigate 'whether it be expedient that the Collection mentioned in the Earl of Elgin's petition...should be purchased on behalf of the public, and, if so, what Price may be reasonable to allow for the same'.[72] It was to consider four questions in reaching this decision: on what authority the collection from the Parthenon was acquired; the circumstances under which the authority was granted; the merit of the sculptures and whether making them public property would add to the purpose of promoting the study of the fine arts in Britain; and finally, the value as objects of sale.

Artists were among those called to assess the worth and the value of the sculptures. The central question concerned the claims made for their exceptional quality: were these marbles as good as others, especially in relation to the *Apollo Belvedere*, the *Venus de' Medici*, the *Torso Belvedere*, and other Graeco-Roman works? A detailed discussion and debate about the different periods of sculpture, the varying artistic achievements, and specific qualities of the Marbles, ensued. The sculptor Joseph Nollekens declared them 'very fine; the finest things that ever came to this country', so good that he compared them to the finest marbles from Italy, but he did not make a valuation.[73] Nor did the sculptor John Flaxman, who nonetheless considered them 'the finest works of art I have seen . . . With respect to their excellence, they are the most excellent of their kind that I have seen'. Flaxman also found it hard to say definitively that the Marbles were better than the *Apollo*.[74] Richard Payne Knight's testimony to the Committee was mixed. He said that the mutilated parts lessened their value, and that it was more difficult to assess their artistic merit. Certain parts were 'second rank', not first class, but some metopes were some of the 'best works of high relief'. Parts were even worthless as furniture. He also doubted the Phidian origin.[75]

'Do you think it of great consequence to the progress of art in Britain, that this Collection should become the property of the Public?', the Committee asked. Flaxman's answer was emphatic: 'Of the greatest importance, I think; and I always have thought so as an individual.'[76] Richard Westmacott of the Royal Academy valued the Elgin Marbles above the Townley Collection on artistic grounds, but rejected the suggestion that they be broken up and sent around to different parts of the country in the service of instruction, responding: 'I think it would be a pity to break such a connected chain of art.' The chain of art was the idea of progress in art that followed the taxonomic approach to the natural world. The idea was that ancient art and ancient civilizations would be documented, and the best, and its influences, be identified.

It was a complex discussion. The ideas of neoclassical taste and the antique models of perfection were openly and officially questioned. New ideas were emerging for standards of excellence, but they were not entirely accepted. The argument over the Marbles was part of that transition. Reynolds's idea that perfection was only achieved in the grand manner of abstraction from form was in abeyance, although it was not put aside completely.

Reporting on 25 March 1816, the Committee recommended the Marbles be purchased for their aesthetic merit, and kept as an 'entire School of Art, and a Study for the formation of Artists'.[77] The Committee concluded that the cultivation of fine arts contributed to the 'reputation, character, and dignity of every Government by which they have been encouraged', and that no country could be better suited than Britain to honouring the greatness of ancient Greece. Here, it was hoped, artists would learn to 'imitate, and ultimately to rival them'.[78] Their acquisition was compared favourably to the methods of French conquest; the Committee cleared Elgin from the charge of illegality and misuse of ambassadorial powers, though it was made clear that Elgin had not been encouraged to remove the Marbles; and the Committee was tactically mute on the question of which antiquity was the greatest. It advised that £35,000 would be a sufficient price.

In June, it was the turn of MPs to assess if they were worth the money and if the acquisition should be recommended. Questions were raised about spending considerable sums on bits of old marble when the country was recovering from the costly Napoleonic Wars. Lord Broughton argued that money should instead be spent on the men discharged from the navy. Members wondered whether Elgin had been right to use his role as ambassador to acquire them. Sir John Newport MP asked some pointed questions about Elgin's actions:

The Honourable Lord has taken advantage of the most unjustified means and has committed the most flagrant pillages. It was, it seems, fatal that a representative of our country looted these objects that the Turks and other barbarians had considered sacred.[79]

Unease was expressed about possible comparisons to the extensive looting under Napoleon in France, where artefacts were currently being returned to their original owners following Napoleon's defeat at Waterloo. Mr Banks defended Elgin, asserting that his actions 'bore no resemblance to those undue and tyrannical means by which the French had obtained possession of so many treasures of art, which he rejoiced to see in the possession of their rightful owners'.[80] Taking a different point of view, Hugh Hammersley MP demanded an amendment to the resolution, because of the way the Marbles were obtained, and asked

> that Great Britain holds these marbles only in trust till they are demanded by the present, or any future, possessors of the city of Athens; and upon such demand, engages, without question or negotiation, to restore them, as far as can be effected, to the places from whence they were taken.[81]

Hammersley's amendment was not passed. The questions of how the Marbles would justify the economic expense, and why they belonged in Britain, were answered by John Wilson Crocker MP, Secretary to the Admiralty. The same questions raged in the past about the sculptures, he said, but then—as now—the answer is that

> it was money spent for the use of the people, for the encouragement of arts, the increase of manufactures . . . not merely to please the eye of the man of taste, but to create, to stimulate, to guide the exertions of the artist, the mechanic, and even the labourer, and to spread through all the branches of society a spirit of improvement, and the means of a sober and industrious affluence.

With these sculptures, the cultural and moral achievements of ancient Greece, intertwined as they were, could be born again in England:

> Your Committee cannot dismiss this interesting subject, without submitting to the attentive reflection of the House, how highly the cultivation of

the Fine Arts has contributed to the reputation, character, and dignity of every Government by which they have been encouraged, and how intimately they are connected with the advancement of everything valuable in science, literature, and philosophy.

He continued, evoking the free spirit of ancient Athens:

In contemplating the importance and splendour to which so small a republic as Athens rose, by the genius and energy of her citizens, exerted in the path of such studies, it is impossible to overlook how transient the memory and fame of extended empires, and of mighty conquerors are, in comparison of those who have rendered inconsiderable states eminent, and immortalised their own names by these pursuits.

Crocker concluded:

if it be true, as we learn from history and experience, that free governments afford a soil most suitable to the production of native talent, to the maturing powers of the human mind, and to the growth of every species of excellence, by opening to merit the prospect of reward and distinction, no country can be better adapted than our own to afford an honourable asylum to these monuments of the school of Phidias, and the administration of Pericles: where secure from further injury and degradation, they may receive that admiration and homage to which they are entitled, and serve in return as models and examples to those, who by knowing how to revere and appreciate them, may learn first to imitate, and ultimately to rival them.[82]

English artists, even the morality of the country, could well be inspired by these works and ultimately by ancient Athens. This was a narrative that became important. Ian Jenkins, senior curator of Greek collections in the British Museum, explains: 'Waterloo became England's Battle of Marathon, and acquisition of the Elgin Marbles by the British Museum was hailed as confirmation of the ancient claim that liberty and the arts rise and fall together.'[83]

Parliament voted 82 for, 30 against. An Act of Parliament was passed that secured the purchase of the Marbles for 'Thirty five thousand

Pounds', a condition of which was that the whole collection should be kept together in the British Museum, that it should be 'open to Inspection, and called by the name of 'The Elgin Marbles', and that every person who should attain the rank of Earl of Elgin should be added to the Trustees of the British Museum.

The Elgin Marbles were officially transferred to the British Museum on 8 August 1816. It was a victory of sorts for Elgin. Although he remained ruined financially, he was added to the Trustees of the British Museum.[84] In 1817, the *Gentleman's Magazine* announced that the public would very shortly have access to the 'spacious rooms' built to contain the Marbles, adding: 'They are a proud trophy, because their display in the British Metropolis is the result of public taste, and also a pleasing one, because they are not the price of blood shed in wanton or ambitious wars.' Thus the actions of the British were again compared to those of the French.[85]

The Marbles went on show at the British Museum in 1817. The artist Benjamin Haydon recorded in his diary their popular reception:

> On Monday last there were one thousand and two people visited the Elgin Marbles! A greater number than ever visited the British Museum since it was established. It is quite interesting to listen to the remarks of the people...We overheard two common looking decent men say to each other, 'How broken they are, a'ant they? 'Yes,' said the other, 'but how life like.'[86]

John Keats is thought to have been inspired to write the mournful 'Ode on a Grecian Urn':

> Who are these coming to the sacrifice?
> To what green altar, O mysterious priest,
> Lead'st thou that heifer lowing at the skies...?

The Elgin Marbles were awarded their own gallery in 1831. They were displayed with the intention that artists would draw them and be inspired. Sculptures were placed on turning posts, so that those sketching

could twirl them around and get a better look.[87] There was one suggestion, made in 1850, that the Marbles and other sculptures in the British
Museum be moved to the National Gallery, to be presented next to the
paintings as art. In the 1930s the Marbles were cleaned, destructively
scrubbed with wire by Lord Duveen, in the aim of making them whiter. It
was then thought that they were white in ancient Greece: in fact originally, they were brightly painted, probably placed against a blue background, a fact that caused considerable upset when suggested by Stuart
and Revett in *The Antiquities of Athens* in 1762.

The Marbles did not stimulate great art in England, but they did
transform our understanding of ancient Greek art.[88] By 1830, they were
the leading model in academic training, and the *Apollo Belvedere* was
relegated. Their fame spread across Europe and the world. They were the
influence for a classical building style in Europe and the US. Soon after the
acquisition, casts were made and supplied on demand to museums all over
the country and country houses. Gift sets were cast and given to the courts
of Rome, Naples, and Prussia. Russia, Bavaria, and Württemberg paid for
a set. Most major cities in Europe and America came to have casts of some
if not all the Elgin Marbles by the middle of the century. Interestingly, for
a short while, they appear to have been valued by some in a similar light as
the original work: in 1819, the Louvre offered an original metope in
exchange for a set of casts of the Elgin Marbles.

PALACES WITHOUT RIVAL

From the ninth to the seventh century BC, Assyria went from being a
small nation state to becoming the largest empire ever known, encompassing what is now Iraq, Syria, Jordan, Israel, Egypt, Turkey, and Iran. It
was ruled by a series of kings.

King Ashurnasirpal II, whose name means 'the god Ashur is the
protector of the heir', came to the throne in 883 BC. He launched

aggressive military campaigns, expanding his territory and consolidating the conquests of his father, Tukulti-Ninurta II, leading to the establishment of the New Assyrian Empire. King Ashurnasirpal II conducted a massive building programme at Nineveh and Assur, as well as at the new capital of Kalhu—now Nimrud, north of Baghdad—and spent the great wealth that had flowed into the kingdom from the local rulers. Kalhu was transformed from a small provincial city into the new capital, benefiting from nine new temples, palaces, offices, and administrative buildings, with a strong protective mud wall stretching 5 miles around it.

Upon its completion, the king held a festival for the people to celebrate. One inscription speaks of 'the happy people of all the lands together with the people of Kalhu—for ten days I feasted, wined, bathed, and honoured them and sent them back to their home in peace and joy'. It is claimed that 69,574 people went to the party.[89] The traces and evidence left suggest that the new capital was both imposing and magnificent, built to overwhelm and impress everyone with the wealth and power of the great man. Inscriptions written on the walls and on the carvings of narrative scenes on what are now ruins of the palace at Nimrud celebrate Ashurnasirpal II's achievements: 'I built thereon [a palace with] halls of cedar, cypress, juniper, boxwood, teak, terebinth, and tamarisk as my royal dwelling and for the enduring leisure life of my lordship.'[90] They boast of great stone animals that looked down on the visitor: 'Beasts of the mountains and the seas, which I had fashioned out of white limestone and alabaster, I had set up in its gates.'[91]

Ashurnasirpal II's successors built their own palaces. King Sargon II (721–705 BC) commanded the construction of a whole new city called Dur-Sharrukin, known now as Khorsabad. Upon his death, the new king Sennacherib (704–681 BC) moved the capital to Nineveh and made it the largest city in the known world, constructing a 'palace without rival'. It was splendid and well decorated. Around seventy great rooms were lined by limestone slabs with carvings detailing the great deeds of Sennacherib.

Alabaster wall reliefs recount violent battles, grand building projects, processions, hunts, gods, and royal pageants. These warriors glorified their victorious lives and exploits in stone.

But the Assyrians were not successful forever. The empire started to disintegrate, and the army and court were finally defeated in 609 BC, when they were conquered by the Babylonian Empire. The three capitals were sacked and burned, the people deported, and the cities fell into ruin. The palaces without rival, the great reliefs, beasts of the mountain and the seas, and the battles came to be distant memories, then forgotten. Over time, they were covered in sand, dust, and dirt. The traces of the Assyrians were almost lost, living on only in biblical records and in the writing of classical historians.

Having been mostly schooled in Mesopotamia, through the classical authors and the Hebrew Bible, most people in Europe knew it to be the site of the Holy Land, home to some of the oldest civilizations in the world. But the Victorians knew very little about the great palaces or their culture. As the excavator Austen Henry Layard commented, after he helped to rediscover them:

> Although the names of Nineveh and Assyria have been familiar to us from childhood, and are connected with our earliest impressions derived from the Inspired Writings, it is only when we ask ourselves what we really know concerning them, that we discover our ignorance of all that relates to their history, and even to their geographical position.[92]

The ignorance that Layard describes was gradually dispelled. After a slow start, the impressionistic speculation about the ancient Assyrians was challenged, replaced by knowledge based on archaeological evidence.

In the early nineteenth century, the only Mesopotamian object conserved in Europe was the Michaux Stone, a stone marker (or 'kudurru') brought back in 1786 by the French botanist whose name it was given, and bought by the Bibliothèque Nationale in Paris. After which time,

British diplomats and officers retraced the stops of Herodotus to the site of Babylon, which they explored perfunctorily. In 1826 the British government, acting on behalf of the British Museum, bought for 1,000 livres a small Mesopotamian collection brought back from the Orient by the Baghdad Resident Claudius James Rich.

In 1842, the Frenchman Paul-Émile Botta started excavating for traces of the ancient Assyrian civilizations. He was sent as the French consular agent to Mosul, and began digging at his own expense on the site of Nineveh. Botta discovered Sargon's palace at Khorsabad.

The mud-brick walls of the palace had been lined with slabs of alabaster delicately carved in relief, depicting the king's triumphs. In addition, some of the palace gateways were guarded by massive stone colossi, the 'beasts of the mountains and the seas'. These are human-headed bulls and lions that once adorned the throne rooms. They have great wings but despite their beast-like body they have human heads on the top of which are crowns, with stylized geometric carvings on their muscled body. From the front they appear to be standing. From the side, with the clever addition of a fifth leg, they appear to be walking. The finds were sent by sea to Paris arriving in February 1847; the following May the two-room Assyrian Museum opened in the Louvre.

After that, there was no holding the excavators back. French success inspired an explorer from the British side. In 1845, Austen Henry Layard started an excavation at Nimrud. Layard had set out for Ceylon in search of work as a solicitor, but on the way he secured an advance of £200 from the publisher John Murray to write a travel book. He changed his course, taking an overland route through Syria, Palestine, and Persia.

Layard worked, unofficially, with Colonel Robert Taylor (the British Resident in Baghdad) and then with Ambassador Stratford Canning, gathering information on troubled spots in the Ottoman Empire. The literary and cultural theorist Shawn Malley argues that Canning would help fund Layard for two reasons. Firstly, he had antiquarian interests. Secondly, archaeology was a subtle extension of Canning's larger political goals in the region. It acted as a display of European civilization to the Turks, and was part of manoeuvrings between different European nations staking claims in ancient Assyria. Writing to Layard in December 1845, Canning explained: 'I think we might manage to transmit some sculpture to Europe as soon if not sooner than the French. This would be very important for our reputation.'[93]

In 1846, Canning had secured permission from the grand vizier of the Ottoman sultan, which gave Layard free reign:

> The British Ambassador has asked that there shall be no obstacles put in the way of the above-mentioned gentleman taking the stones which may be useful to him...The sincere friendship which firmly exists between the two governments makes it desirable that such demands are accepted. Therefore no obstacle should be put in the way of his taking the stones which...are present in desert places, and are not being utilised; or of his undertaking excavations in uninhabited places.[94]

British and French agents vied to discover ancient Mesopotamia. The Assyrian agent to the English, Hormuzd Rassam, dug clandestinely at night at the site of Kuyunjik (Nineveh), in order to remove some of the most interesting pieces as the Frenchman, Victor Place, slept.

Nineveh and Its Remains was Layard's published book on his travels, a colourful account, embellished with made-up observations of devil worship, biblical history, evacuation, and adventure (see Figure 6). The book sold 8,000 copies in the first year and was published in six editions, making it the first archaeological bestseller in England. Within, Layard describes unearthing gigantic sculptures with the body of a lion, the wings of a bird, and the head of a man:

> What more sublime images could have been borrowed from nature, by men who sought, unaided by the light of revealed religion, to embody the wisdom, power, and ubiquity of a Supreme Being? They could find no better

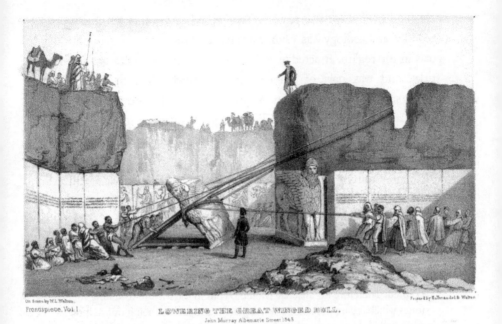

On Scene by W.L. Walton.
Frontispiece. Vol. I

LOWERING THE GREAT WINGED BULL.
John Murray Albemarle Street 1843

Figure 6. Layard supervises the lowering of the Great Winged Bull, removed from the Palace of Sennacherib at Tell Kuyunjik, the site of the citadel of Nineveh.

Frontispiece to Austen Henry Layard, *Nineveh and its Remains: with an Account of a Visit to the Chaldaean Christians of Kurdistan, and the Yezidis, or Devil-Worshippers; and an Inquiry into the Manners and Arts of the Ancient Assyrians* (1853).
© Mary Evans Picture Library.

type of intellect and knowledge than the head of a man; of strength, than the body of the lion; of rapidity of motion, than the wings of the bird.[95]

How different things were centuries after their creation, he reflects. 'But how changed was the scene around them! The luxury and civilisation of a mighty nation had given place to the wretchedness and ignorance of a few half-barbarous tribes.'[96] Layard seems to view the Arabs as ignorant but himself as a civilized man, one mark of which is his respect for Assyrian antiquity. The conceptual linkage between 'being civilized' and a respect for heritage was thus clearly underlined.

The massive stone colossi can now be seen all over the world, where these tremendous animals now tower above many human beings in different contexts. Go to the Louvre, the British Museum, the Metropolitan Museum, the Pergamon Museum in Berlin, the Chicago Institute of Art, or the National Museum of Iraq and you can see them today, because they were rediscovered by the French and the British in the mid-nineteenth century.

Will the public taste deteriorate?

At the end of June 1847, the first shipment of material arrived in London. Assyrian sculptures, including eleven wall reliefs and a massive head, were put on temporary display alongside other antiquities in the entrance hallway of the British Museum. But their reception was uncertain. For a start, there was not much space and curators were unsure where to put them. This was a problem that went beyond physical constraints—it was unclear just how to assess the Assyrian artefacts. Were they art? How did they compare to the rest of the antiquities? And what impact would they have upon the understanding of other civilizations? Such comparisons can be disruptive and unpredictable.

Layard was in no doubt that the Assyrian artefacts were art, praising them and comparing them favourably to Egyptian antiquity:

> [The Assyrian sculptures] are immeasurably superior to the stiff and ill-proportioned figures of the monuments of the Pharaohs. They discover a knowledge of the anatomy of the human frame, a remarkable perception of character, and wonderful spirit in the outlines and general execution. In fact, the great gulf that separates barbarism from civilised art has been passed.[97]

Others disagreed. Henry C. Rawlinson, the British consul in Baghdad and a supporter of Layard, was unconvinced: 'I still think the Nineveh marbles are not valuable as works of art.'[98] He saw them as an aid to understanding history, but no more:

> Can a mere admirer of the beautiful view them with pleasure? Certainly not, and in this respect they are in the same category with the paintings and sculptures of Egypt and India . . . I admit a certain degree of excellence in the conception and execution of some of the sculptures, but when we come to value, *a certain degree* won't do. We have specimens of the very highest art—and anything short of that, as a work of art . . . [is] valueless for it can neither instruct nor enrapture us. I hope you understand the distinction and when I criticise design and execution, will understand I do so merely because your winged God is not the *Apollo Belvedere*.[99]

Seven years later, the question of their value as art was the object of scrutiny of a Parliamentary Committee. The political class were concerned that the inclusion of such material in the British Museum might mean that the public's appreciation of the Elgin Marbles would be threatened. One questioner asked:

> Do you think there is no fear that by introducing freely into the institution objects of more occasional and peculiar interest, such as for instance as the sculptures from Nineveh, may deteriorate the public taste, and less incline them than they otherwise would be to study works of great antiquity and great art?[100]

The response from Sir Richard Westmacott, professor of sculpture at the Royal Academy and sculpture adviser to the British Museum, was in the negative. The Elgin Marbles were art; the Nineveh sculptures were not, they were merely interesting objects from history. 'The Nineveh marbles are very curious, and it is very desirable to possess them,' he said, but

> I look upon it that the value of the Nineveh Marbles will be the history that their inscriptions, if they are ever translated, will produce; because if we had one-tenth part of what we have of Nineveh art, it will be quite enough as specimens of the arts of the Chaldeans, for it is very bad art.[101]

Worried that the public taste might be 'corrupted' by the Nineveh Marbles, the questioner pursued this line of concern: what would happen if the Elgin Marbles were 'side by side' with the Nineveh sculptures? Westmacott responded:

> persons would look at the Nineveh Marbles and be thinking of their Bible at the time they were looking at them; they would consider them as very curious monuments of an age they feel highly interested in; but the interest in the Elgin Marbles arises from a distinct cause; from their excellence as works of art.[102]

Bringing together great work from different ancient peoples—ancient Athens, ancient Egypt, and the Assyrians—allowed comparisons, but these comparisons threatened to be destabilizing. After all, Greek art of a particular period—fifth-century Athens—was thought to be the supreme moment of perfection. With new excavations, that claim would be scrutinized, and with an understanding of ancient Assyria, the domination of Hellenism would gradually loosen.

The majority of Layard's finds were sent to the British Museum. Several of the reliefs and colossi found their way to other institutions. Some were acquired by American missionaries working in Iraq, who saw the carved slabs as evidence for biblical history. Other sculptures entered private collections, such as that of the financier J. P. Morgan. Layard had a cousin at Canford Manor in Dorset, England, to whom he sent a number of reliefs, where they installed the Nineveh Porch. Thus, in this very English manor house, you could find great doors flanked by human-headed bull colossi and stained-glass windows composed of patterns drawn from wall paintings found at Nimrud. In 1919, eighteen of the sculptures were sold and they eventually moved to the collection of John D. Rockefeller Jr; he donated them to the Metropolitan Museum in 1932 where they have been ever since.

Cracking cuneiform

Between 1845 and 1847, while at Nineveh, Layard discovered a large section of what was perhaps the greatest Assyrian palace built by Sennacherib. Here, Layard found over 2 miles of clay slabs with a strange script on them. It was the great library of Sennacherib's grandson, Ashurbanipal. Somehow it had survived the centuries, protected under the sand. Layard had discovered one of the earliest known forms of writing: cuneiform.

Layard's find would mean that ideas and records from 5,000 years ago could be read, but no one could understand them at first—the squiggles on the clay were incomprehensible. Like the Rosetta Stone, the language needed to be studied and deciphered. In the early 1840s, nobody could read Assyrian cuneiform. By the late 1850s they could, with help from scholars at the British Museum, thanks to another remarkable breakthrough in the study of another ancient culture.

Ashurbanipal was a learned and proud man. 'I am Ashurbanipal', proclaim inscriptions on some of the early tablets. Much of the rest of the writing relates to money and taxes. On the tablets are letters about administrative matters: financial and legal documents, lists of people, animals, and goods. In some respects they are a little dull, a far cry from the profundity of poetry and literature, but appearances can be deceptive—this is evidence about the beginnings of a state, informing us how human beings ran an early society thousands of years ago.

The British Museum became the focus for Assyrian studies, making numerous breakthroughs. In 1872, George Smith, a regular visitor to the museum, became obsessed with the tablets and made an important discovery. Smith had spent a considerable time working away on the tablets, often during his lunch hour; it paid off when he deciphered a neo-Assyrian seventh-century BC tablet from Nineveh, revealing a story of how Utnapishtim was warned by the gods that there would be a great flood that would destroy the world, and in response built a boat and loaded it with everything he could find. Utnapishtim survived the flood, although mankind was destroyed. Smith was astounded to read the tale. It turned out to be the most famous of the Gilgamesh stories—the story of the Deluge. Smith's immediate thought was, 'I am the first man to read that after two thousand years of oblivion.' Then, 'he jumped up and rushed about the room in a great state of excitement, and, to the astonishment of those present, began to undress himself!'[103] Smith was overcome with excitement. Under his very eyes, what was understood as a Hebrew biblical story was written on a Mesopotamian tablet, chiselled into the clay 400 years before the oldest version of the story in the Bible. Reading this proved that the biblical story of Noah was not unique.

The value of museums

The scientific character of these interventions and scholarly activities in the nineteenth century had a huge impact upon the understanding of antiquity. The invading or wandering Europeans stimulated an appreciation of ancient pasts both within and outside the countries in which they intervened. Museums were filled with these artefacts in Europe as a consequence. In Egypt, they were built after the arrival of the invaders, at times with their support.

Seen through the eyes of the present, there is no question that the military interventions were questionable, if not plain wrong, and that many of the archaeologists' actions during this time were cavalier. Many presumed that the artefacts were 'theirs' to take to Europe or America, where antiquity was often used to endorse political projects and legitimize leaders. These acts appear dubious to us today, to say the least. How should we think of them? What judgement should we place upon them?

Things were different in the past. Actions and deeds were permitted and approved of then that would not be now. Looking back is a privileged and elevated position from which to view the past, and it is one that is often distorted by current preoccupations. We should guard against the simplistic and easily acquired feelings of superiority that we can have by surveying the past through contemporary mores, centuries later. It is far better—and harder—to try to understand than to condemn. We should judge the past on the terms of the past, rather than by what we feel is right today.

Further, the result of the excavations described above helped to open our understanding of history to perspectives beyond the ancient accounts. The Rosetta Stone and the Assyrian cuneiform tablets, especially, revealed the ancient language so that the culture of these civilizations could be read and understood. No longer could words be put so easily into their mouths by later writers; no longer would we have to rely on classical accounts. Deciphering these ancient scripts meant that received authority—scriptural authority—could be challenged, and it changed the way people thought about the past and the people who lived there.

We know about these ancient cultures today because of the acts of the excavators and invaders. It was only by digging down and taking monuments and sculptures out of the ground and making them available for scholars to study and decipher that breakthroughs could happen. And it is for this reason that it is, on balance, right that these great monuments and sculptures were taken from their original context and are now on display for all to see their wonders.

When sculptors in Assyria carved the winged beasts for their king, they had no idea that their creations would end up on show all over the world. They were not made for museums. The most valued artefacts to us today were made to be used elsewhere by someone else: in a palace, a home, or a religious space, sometimes to glorify powerful and mighty princes, politicians, and kings. Soon after any object is made, it passes out of the hands of the creator into the hands of others: patrons, family, friends, thieves, and new owners, crossing continents and centuries. There is no one 'home' for any object. Every object is, by definition, decontextualized. Ancient objects sometimes belong in museums, often far away from their creation and discovery, where they can be cared for, studied, and shown to the world.

The Rosetta Stone, the cuneiform tablets, and the Parthenon Marbles, as well as the many different artefacts in museums, all originally adorned different spaces—none of these were intended for our eyes. They were not made to be placed on a pedestal inside any museum, but this is where they bring the past to life. Collecting necessitates taking artefacts or parts of an object from one part of the world, from a particular time and place, and preserving it in a separate sphere. The fact that objects are in a museum in the first place by definition entails a disjuncture from one context and the creation of a new one. This act of separation removes objects from their original use, but then generally situates them in a wider, richer framework of relationships. An icon or a religious painting that was once an object of devotion in a church, becomes in a gallery an object of inspiration or beauty, or a social text to be read. Next to other artefacts they provoke questions, illustrate relationships, and take on an elevated meaning. That is the value of museums.

4

Cases of Loot

⊱─┼─◆➤─○─◆┼─⊰

'For three long years he so thoroughly despoiled and pillaged the province that its restoration to its previous state is out of the question,'[1] Roman orator Marcus Tullius Cicero declared in his opening statement to one of the most well-known legal cases in history. Cicero was the prosecutor in the trial of Verres, a powerful Roman governor on trial for extortion. Adding to a litany of abuses, Cicero highlighted Verres' voracious appetite for taking art, statues, and public monuments, none of which belonged to him:

> ancient monuments given by wealthy monarchs to adorn the cities of Sicily . . . were ravaged and stripped, one and all, by this same governor. Nor was it only statues and public monuments that he treated in this manner. Among the most sacred and revered Sicilian sanctuaries, there was not a single one which he failed to plunder.[2]

Cicero linked these crimes to the moral decline of the Senate. Verres fled into exile at the start of the trial which was never completed, but Cicero published his speeches and his prepared case in the *Verrine Orations*, which have set the terms of discussion about the illicit removal of art and antiquity ever since.

The trial against Verres shows not only that people have taken objects in dubious circumstances for centuries, but also that questions about these acts and artefacts have been debated for just as long: When is their removal legitimate? What should the consequences be for those who take treasures in this way? Why are these artefacts significant to us?

One reason for the constant and passionate interest in the rights and wrongs of the removal of art and antiquity, suggests the historian and archaeologist Margaret Miles, is that their fate came to be tied to major events in people's lives. In Roman times, the taking of enemies' treasures established this practice as associated with glory. The Romans were acquisitive as they expanded their empire; as they moved into southern Italy, Sicily, and then into Greece, highly esteemed antiquity was ripped out of buildings and wrenched from the hands of the defeated. Looting came to be conducted systematically as part of warfare. The booty was carefully divided up: some objects were put aside for the gods, and others used for exacting reparations, funding the army, or luring mercenaries.

Bringing these artefacts to Rome played a significant role in political triumphalism. Treasures were displayed in the Roman Forum, in the heart of the ancient city. The Forum was the centre of public life—a meeting point of political, cultural, and civic activities, with temples, law courts, government offices, and senate house. It was here that the Roman military triumphs were held, on the return of commanders who had achieved a military victory, to thank them and to pay public tribute. Art and artefacts were carried back and shown off, to stimulate admiration for the generals and support for their imperial enterprise. Processions heralding their return became more elaborate. Paintings of battles and placards accompanied these captured trophies, together with descriptions of where the original works came from and why they were special.[3] Rome verged on being a museum itself: the centre of the city held the great works of Greece, Egypt, and Asia Minor. It was a fantastic spectacle of conquest. 'Its fate', Miles says of the art and artefacts, 'reflected the effects of war on people.'[4] They soon associated its acquisition with triumph or with loss.

When power shifts, treasures of the past follow. The movement of art and artefacts is now conducted mostly via the marketplace, where they sell for thousands, if not millions, of euros, dollars, or pounds. China has recently entered the fray, spending billions of yuan on art and artefacts; they are a hot commodity in Saudi Arabia, upon which millions of Saudi riyal are spent. But in previous times, thousands of objects and pieces of art were commonly taken during war.

We have seen that with the birth of archaeology as a discipline and the concurrent growth in cultural competitiveness between nations, spectacular monuments and sculptures were carted back to (mainly) European museums. Most were taken with permission, though that permission was occasionally partial; there are plenty of other cases where artefacts were taken by force, but even then many of these acts were legal. We now turn to a few of those thorny cases, when collections in museums were taken as spoils of war by soldiers. First, we look at post-revolutionary France and Napoleon; second, we examine two cases from the Age of Imperialism—the plundering by the British army of the Benin Bronzes and the sacking of the Chinese Summer Palace in Peking by the British and French armies.

History shows that looting has taken place for centuries, but much has changed. In the final sections of this chapter, we examine the present state of play. There have been a number of shifts in both practice and law: seizure is no longer an accepted part of warfare, but problems remain. Material is often removed from archaeological sites to sell, but this is illegal, and it is done by individuals and organized networks rather than the emperor and the soldiers of a nation.

NAPOLEON

Two figures have been popularly compared to Verres. One is Thomas Elgin; the other is Napoleon (see Figure 7). Of the two, it is Napoleon who deserves the reputation for being the greatest looter of them all; he

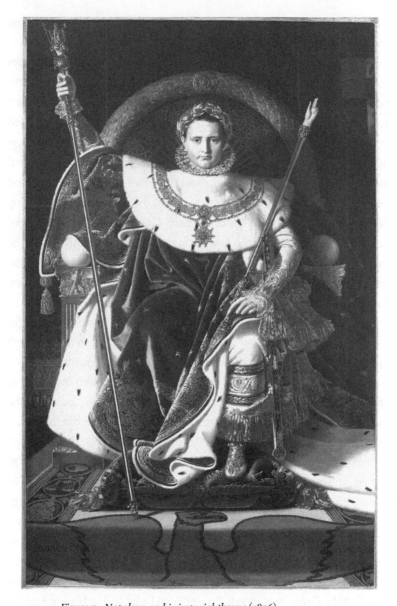

Figure 7. *Napoleon on his imperial throne* (1806).
Jean-Auguste-Dominique Ingres (1780–1867).

© Paris–Musée de l'Armée, Dist. RMN-Grand Palais / Emilie Cambier.

continued a programme of the appropriation of art and antiquity that was in place before he was in power, taking it to another level.

In 1794, one year after the Louvre opened as a museum, French forces won a victory in Belgium, leading to occupation and the French government's authorization of the appropriation of artworks. The seizure of art from the clergy and royalty that had happened within France was applied to the defeated in wars abroad, in what was an escalation in practice: although there had been looting, earlier campaigns in the Netherlands had not been followed by official confiscation. It is often said that this extension was fuelled by, or that it at least relied upon, the ideas developed during the French Revolution. Art historian Cecil Gould argues that the social context of the opening of the Louvre and its symbolic status led to the more formalized approach in taking material from defeated powers. Had the museum not opened as a symbol of the Revolution, Gould argues, then the scale of the ensuing seizures might never have taken place.[5]

The Temporary Commission of the Arts appointed a subcommittee of its members, which included Lebrun, a specialist on Dutch and Flemish painting; Abbé Grégoire; and Varon, a member of the Louvre Conservatoire, to accompany and advise the French army in Belgium in respect of what to confiscate. Others would join them in their quest, including the painters Luc Barbier and Jean-Baptiste Wicar, and an archaeologist, a biologist, an antiquary, and an architect.

In 1794, paintings and sculpture taken from Belgium were shipped to France in seven convoys. The first included works by Rubens—*The Descent from the Cross* and *Erection of the Cross* (both from Antwerp Cathedral), and the crucifixion scene *Le Coup de Lance*—as well as a sculpture by Michelangelo of the Madonna. Le Brun had singled out these works for great praise in his book *Galerie des peintres flamands*, which had been published two years earlier. As the material was transported, Abbé Grégoire boasted: 'Crayer, Van Dyke and Rubens are on the way to Paris; the Flemish school rises in a body to adorn our museums.'[6]

Confiscation by the French began under the National Convention. It continued through the Directory, the Consulate, and the Empire. Broadly, over this time three rationales were provided. First, there was the argument that masterpieces should reside in the seat of liberty. 'The fruits of genius are the patrimony of liberty,' as Luc Barbier proclaimed in a speech to the National Convention which celebrated and justified the confiscations. 'For too long', Barbier continued, 'these masterpieces have been soiled by the gaze of solitude.'[7] The second argument was that France should be the capital of art and culture, and should rightly be compared to the ancient civilizations of Greece and Rome. Thirdly, ancient precedent was cited, referring to the normal practice of nations where plunder was the reward for victory. For instance, when, in 1794, Grégoire celebrated the arrival of the confiscated Flemish artwork, hoping that the troops would be victorious in Italy, he announced a desire to acquire the *Apollo*: 'Certainly, if our victorious armies penetrate into Italy, the removal of the *Apollo Belvedere* and of the *Farnese Hercules* would be the most brilliant conquest.'[8]

This was not looting, it was legal seizure. It did not violate international law, as the legality of taking works depended on the right of conquest; thus, it was already a standard part of military conquest and part of the common law of warfare. Also, importantly, by the time they got to Italy Napoleon was in charge—and he made sure to further secure the work with the use of contracts. Napoleon signed treaties with the defeated, specifying the cession of works of art. Sometimes this list documented every single painting, sculpture, and artefact.

After the French army defeated the Duke of Modena in northern Italy, the armistice promised: 'The Duke of Modena undertakes to hand over twenty pictures. They will be selected by commissioners sent for that purpose from among the pictures in his gallery and realm.'[9] Art was formally tied as payment and reparations for the war, the first of many such contractual arrangements with the vanquished. It was to be taken back to France, occasionally marked out specifically for the Louvre. Writing to the Directory, Napoleon mentioned in passing:

> You will find attached the conditions of armistice that I have accorded to the Duke of Parma. As soon as possible I will send you the most beautiful pictures of Correggio, among others a *Saint-Jerome* that is said to be a masterpiece; I hope you will give him the place of honour in the Museum. I repeat my request for a few known artists to take charge of the choice and transport of the fine things we shall think fit to send to Paris. All arrangements are made for the 10,000 men from the Army of the Alps. There will be no difficulty over their passage.[10]

Such arrangements would even include the Papal States. In 1797, Pope Pius VI signed the Treaty of Tolentino. Article 8 pledged to give the following:

> A hundred pictures, busts, vases, or statues to be selected by the commissioners and sent to Rome, including in particular the bronze bust of Junius Brutus and the marble bust of Marcus Brutus, both on the Capitol, also five-hundred manuscripts at the choice of the said commissioners.[11]

The French wanted eighty-three sculptures, including the celebrated *Apollo Belvedere* that was taken from the Vatican, although it took some time for the works to be boxed up and sent to them.

The Commission of the Arts thought that the army and the art needed a grand entry into France; after all, their appropriation was of symbolic importance. A parade with a fanfare would also boost patriotism in difficult and turbulent times—the economy was limp, and measures were required to enlist public support for the wars, as well as for the Directory at home. A festival was organized in 1798 to mark the arrival of a third covey of objects and paintings, intended to emulate the great Roman Triumphal processions (see Figure 8).

The press reported each step of the journey taken by the convoy of crates to France, and the ensuing pageant. Bonaparte's Grand Army and

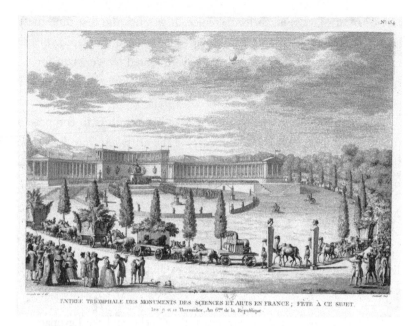

ENTRÉE TRIOMPHALE DES MONUMENTS DES SCIENCES ET ARTS EN FRANCE ; FÊTE À CE SUJET.
les 9 et 10 Thermidor, An 6me de la République.

Figure 8. Triumphal entry of monuments of science and art into France, 9–10 Thermidor,
An VI (27–8 July 1798)
Pierre-Gabriel Berthault. Paris (1802).
© Bibliothèque nationale de France.

the commissioners played leading roles (nobody saw the actual artwork,
as it remained stored in the crates). A military band led the march,
together with the cavalry. Singing choirs, marching museum administra-
tors, and art students led the 'Third Division of Fine Arts' section, joining
two divisions that made up the rest of parade: Books and Manuscripts,
and Natural History, which included seeds, tropical plants, scientific and
agricultural instruments, as well as exotic animals including lions, ele-
phants, and camels. There was even a bear. One banner in the 'Third
Division of Fine Arts' section read: 'Monuments of Antique Sculpture.
Greece gave them up; / Rome lost them; / Their fate has twice changed; /
It will not change again.'[12] The procession included the four bronze

Horses of St Mark's, taken from Venice. It was not the first time these horses had been carted off by soldiers—they were only placed on the facade of St Mark's Basilica after they were looted by Venetian forces, from the Hippodrome of Constantinople, during the sack of the city in 1204.

The French minister of the interior asked songwriters to compose a tune that would celebrate the conquests of the art taken from Italy, one that the ordinary public could sing during the ceremony. They duly came up with a ditty:

> Rome n'est plus dans Rome
> Elle est toute à Paris[13]

Rome is no longer in Rome. It is all in Paris. Official speeches, such as this one, constructed a story of justifiable conquest akin to the Romans:

> The Romans plundered the Etruscans, the Greeks, and the Egyptians, accumulated the booty in Rome and other Italian cities; the fate of these products of genius is to belong to the people who shine successively on earth by arms and by wisdom, and to follow always the wagons of the victors.[14]

Despite the great fanfare, many of these crates were left unopened for eighteen months, until Napoleon came across them towards the end of 1799, and protested at the way his plunder had been treated. New galleries were then arranged in the Louvre, inaugurated a year later.

But although they were legal, some of the seizures were condemned. As the spoliation of Rome was planned, the historian and theorist Quatremère de Quincy spoke out against it, winning some support. He was aghast that the modern world could revive the 'absurd and monstrous right of conquest of the ancient Romans, which made men and chattels the property of the strongest'.[15] Arguing that these works should remain in Rome, de Quincy emphasized that context and customs were vital to appreciate them:

> The museum of which I am speaking, is, it is true, composed of statues, of colossi, of temples, of obelisks, of triumphal columns, of baths, of circuses, of amphitheatres, of triumphal arches, of tombs, of stucco decoration, of frescos...but it is also composed fully as much of places, of sites, of mountains, of quarries, of ancient roads, of the placing of ruined towns, of geographical relationships, of the inner connections of all these objects to each other, of memories, of local traditions, of still prevailing customs, of parallels and comparisons which can only be made in the country itself.[16]

In a letter to the *Courrier universel*, Quatremère employed multiple arguments against Napoleon's actions. The plan for despoiling conquered countries, he warned, would result in 'the total destruction of the arts'.[17] It would deprive the vanquished of their models and traditions, and nobody would then pay artists to create new work. Art belonged in its original context, and that included the environment in which it was created: art, he reasoned, derived its meaning not just from its aesthetic qualities, but from its geography and the local customs. Quatremère questioned whether museums were the best place for artefacts, arguing that they should be a location almost of last resort, to be used only when the original home was no longer viable. Nor would France benefit, he argued, from this seizure. The imported work would depress the appetite for new work, at a time when artists were already suffering due to the demise of Church patronage.

A petition was sent to the Directory to protest against the seizure of antiquities in Italy. It gathered fifty-one signatures, including those of Quatremère de Quincy, the architects Pierre Fontaine and Charles Percier, and the painters Pierre-Henri de Valenciennes and Jacques-Louis David. It may seem surprising to us now, but even Vivant Denon signed—this was before he was go to Germany and Egypt with Napoleon, to play a role in the removal of antiquities there. Indeed, a number of these signatories either supervised or at least supported later expropriations.

Charles-Joseph Trouvé, a politician who had served as general secretary to the Directory, launched a counter-attack. He refuted the petition. Where would it end, if objects were sent back to Italy and Germany? It would lead to the destruction of France. Everything else would go, as well as the art:

> Before long, opponents of the confiscations will form a jury that will declare that there was a French plot against Germany and Italy and that as a result not only artistic monuments but also weapons, pecuniary contributions, and towns [whose seizure] rewarded French valour must be returned—and that, most importantly, the republican government must be destroyed.[18]

Trouvé argued that keeping the booty and displaying this great art would benefit France and art generally. Paris was a great public centre where the art was on show for everyone, whereas in Italy, he chastised, it was hidden in private collections, only available to the people at the owner's whim. The former was unquestionably better than the latter, which was politically backward as it was only for an elite group of privileged people.

French museums expanded between 1804 and 1814 with military conquest. The invasion of the Netherlands led not only to the cultural treasures going to France, but to the building of cultural institutions. Napoleon's brother, Louis, appointed as the first monarch of the Kingdom of Holland, tried to build such palaces of culture to emulate those in France. This led to the first National Museum (Rijksmuseum) in Amsterdam, as well the Royal Academy of Arts and Sciences.

RESTITUTION, TO A NEW HOME

Only when Napoleon was finally defeated at Waterloo was an end brought to his dreams of empire and further art seizures. With defeat, in various stages, arguments were mounted in favour of the restitution of the artworks taken by France (although the preliminary 1814 Convention and Treaty of Paris did not provide specific guidelines for the return of stolen art). These arguments were furiously resisted by Denon and his countrymen.

The pope complained in 1814 that he could not work without the return of his archive. Soon afterwards the Duke of Wellington, the British soldier and statesman who, with Blücher, had defeated Napoleon, argued that the 'day of retribution must come', and that while the people of France would be angry about restitution, these were feelings of 'national vanity only'. The motives for retention were suspect: 'It must be a desire to retain these specimens of the arts, not because Paris is the fittest depository for them . . . but because they were obtained by military concessions, of which they are the trophies.' The Duke continued:

> The same feelings which induce the people of France to wish to retain the pictures and statues of other nations would naturally induce other nations to wish, now that success is on their side, that the property should be returned to their rightful owners, and the Allied Sovereigns must feel a desire to gratify them.

He ended with this final sentence, recommending that France be taught a 'lesson':

> Not only, then, would it, in my opinion, be unjust in the Sovereigns to gratify the people of France on this matter, at the expense of their own people, but the sacrifice they would make would be impolitic, as it would deprive them of the opportunity of giving the people of France a great moral lesson.[19]

As we have seen, William Hamilton was involved in securing material from foreign lands for the British Museum. On this occasion, in his capacity of Under-Secretary of State for Foreign Affairs, he assisted in the removal of artworks from the French—Hamilton attended the

Foreign Secretary's mission to Paris, which was designed to work out the arrangements. Hamilton worked with the pope's agents to return Italian works, including the *Apollo*, which went back to the Vatican. Hamilton's hand in the process enraged Vivant Denon:

> What is most certain is that Mon. Hamilton has behaved in this matter like a maniac, that he has set on the entire destruction of the Museum and that he has got the support of Lord Wellington in the execution of his project.[20]

Denon accused Hamilton of wanting to destroy the then-named Musée Napoléon, so that the British Museum would be the best collection in Europe.

Correspondence suggests that the British briefly considered some of the artefacts for themselves. Lord Liverpool conveyed that the Prince Regent, the future George IV, expressed an interest in the statues and pictures 'for a museum or gallery here',[21] going on to claim: 'The reasonable part of the world are for general restoration to the original possessors; but they say, with truth, that we have a better title to them than the French, if legitimate war gives a title to such objects.' Lord Liverpool asked: 'Might there not be some compromise upon this question?'[22]

It appears, however, that the statesmen were wise to how this would look, and judged that it would not go down well with the public. After all, none of these works had been taken from the British, and they could be accused of hypocrisy by the French. Hamilton explained as much in a letter to the earl of Bathurst, in which he responded to the Prince Regent's desire to acquire some of the works from Rome, in return for helping Rome secure the return of the rest. Hamilton shunned the suggestion:

> It would throw an odium upon our exertions to receive stolen goods... If accompanied with any proposal to our own benefit the whole will fall to

the ground, and the French will remain undisturbed proprietors of what they are now afraid they are to lose; and they will have the additional gratification of owing it to our own mismanagement.[23]

The allies began to take apart the Musée Napoléon and to make arrangements for the restitution of its artworks. Art and antiquity once again was tied to the fate of a country. Forcing France to hand over these treasures was a way of reinforcing the defeat. French ladies are said to have cried at the loss of the *Apollo*.

Despite these efforts, it is estimated that only about 55 per cent of the art and artefacts that were taken was returned.[24] Historian Marie-Louise Blumer documents that out of 506 paintings removed from Italy, 249 were returned: 248 remained therefore in France, although nine disappeared.[25] Some of the treasure was too difficult to move, such as antique marble columns from Aachen Cathedral, Germany, which had been built into the fabric of the museum. Some was not even in the museum— Empress Josephine, the former wife of Napoleon, had taken work for herself; the rest had been sent to provincial museums, who tried—with some success—to ignore the demands for return.

The rest, however, was returned home. Or rather, it was sent to a new home. It is important to understand that the treasures sent back did not, usually, 'return' to the 'original' location. On the whole, artworks and antiquity that is 'returned' usually goes somewhere new.

One such example is the prized papal treasures. In 1815, the sculptor Canova was appointed by Pope Pius VII to retrieve them from the Louvre. It was not a straightforward process: after all, contracts had been signed, and turning over treaties such as these could set a dangerous precedent. But Canova's selection for the task was inspired—he could argue for their return from the position of art, as a sculptor, distancing himself from the politicians. And he was moderately successful, mounting many arguments for restitution, among which was the idea that the art could only be appreciated in Rome, the original location. Canova achieved the return of about half the artworks taken from the Papal States, and the British Prince Regent helped pay for their transport. But they were not returned to the original context of a religious space. Instead, Pope Pius VII appropriated them for his new museum: the Vatican Pinacoteca, which opened in 1817. The pope wanted his own museum, his own treasures on display.

More frequently than not, the treasures were sent to new museums, to Berlin, Brussels, The Hague, Madrid, Vienna, Rome, Milan, and Parma. Bavaria received books that had been taken from Salzburg. Elsewhere, King Willem I, the sovereign of the new Dutch nation, sent the professor and rector of the University of Leiden, Sebald Justinus Brugmans, to the Muséum d'Histoire Naturelle in Paris, tasked with retrieving Holland's natural history collection. He returned to the Netherlands with about 10,000 objects. But many specimens from the original collection did not return with him, while at the same time he took a great proportion of naturalia that was not part of the original collection. These objects all went to the University of Leiden and, five years later, were added to the Rijksmuseum of Natural History in Leiden during the period of national institution building.

IMPERIAL PLUNDER–THE BENIN BRONZES

In February 1897, regalia that included ivories and wood and brass sculptures were seized from the palace of Benin (now Nigeria), during an imperial rampage by the British in West Africa.

The city of Benin had been the head of a medieval African kingdom, founded in the tenth century. It was one of the earliest and longest-lasting participants in the European slave trade, and flourished with money from that—Portugal, the Netherlands, and Great Britain all purchased large slave cargos here (Portugal being the first, arriving in 1472). In the sixteenth century, the Oba—the king of Benin—commissioned the Bronze

Casters Guild (Igun Eronmwon) to make casts of significant events in the kingdom. These became the Benin Bronzes. Despite their names, they are made from brass, copper, and ivory. They skilfully depict life in the kingdom, aspects of life the king wanted to glorify: hunting, relations between people, animals, the army, battles, and court life—as well as himself.

The rise of Britain as an imperial power caused the downfall of Benin. After the abolition of the slave trade at the beginning of the nineteenth century, British attention on the West African coast turned to supplying trade goods in return for raw materials. A land-grab of Africa followed, with the carve-up of the country into spheres of influence by the European powers. At the end of the nineteenth century the British Empire spanned a quarter of the world, including an established presence along the coast of present-day Nigeria, with certain areas administered directly from Whitehall and others under trading company control. As the British Empire grew, trading conditions set by Benin became less acceptable and a power tussle ensued. Benin refused the conditions of trade and taxation set by the British, who retaliated by demanding that Benin be taken by force and the treasures of the kingdom sold to pay for the expenses accrued. The king was obstructive, causing trouble. He had to go, as Lieutenant James Robert Phillips, acting consul, reasoned:

> I am certain that there is only one remedy. That is to depose the King of Benin... I am convinced that pacific measures are now quite useless, and that the time has now come to remove the obstruction... I do not anticipate any serious resistance from the people of the country—there is every reason to believe that they would be glad to get rid of their King— but in order to obviate any danger, I wish to take up sufficient armed force... I would add that I have reason to hope that sufficient ivory may be found in the King's house to pay the expenses incurred.[26]

The British mission met resistance; they were ambushed. But the attack gave them an excuse for war and they raised a punitive expedition to sack the city. Within six weeks the city of Benin fell, largely destroyed after much of it had been set alight and burnt to the ground. The Oba was exiled and the Benin Kingdom was incorporated into the British Protectorate of Southern Nigeria.

Felix Roth was a medical officer with the expedition. He described the dramatic sight of the sculptures as they entered the king's compound:

> on a raised platform or altar, running the whole breadth of each, beautiful idols were found. All of them were caked over with human blood, and by giving them a slight tap, crusts of blood would, as it were, fly off. Lying about were big bronze heads, dozens in a row, with holes at the top, in which immense ivory tusks were fixed. One can form no idea of the impression it made on us. The whole place reeked of blood.[27]

Outside, 'all about the houses and streets are dead natives, some crucified and sacrificed on streets'. It was a gruesome scene. Roth reflected: 'I suppose there is not another place on the face of the globe so near civilisation where such butcheries are carried on with impunity.'[28]

The *Illustrated London News* recorded the destruction: 'Benin is indeed a city of blood, each compound having its pit full of dead and dying; human sacrifices were strewn about on every hand, hardly a thing was without a red stain.'[29] *The Times* newspaper reported the battle as concluding positively: 'No-one was injured,'[30] the paper stated, referring, of course, to the British army. The king was later captured, put on trial, and sent into exile.

Anthropologist and museum curator Henry Roth, brother to Felix, agreed with the general assessment that the war was justified. In *Great Benin: Its Customs, Art and Horrors*, published shortly afterwards in 1903, he wrote:

> while we cannot avoid feelings of regret that an interesting old town and its old-world institutions should have been destroyed, the horrors which met the Punitive Expedition, when it entered the sacred precincts, showed that the little war we waged was justification beyond all expectation.[31]

The collection of sculptures and plaques were gathered up by the British troops and given to the Foreign Office. As Phillips had suggested, they were auctioned by the Admiralty to help bear the expenses of the expedition.

The bronzes and plaques were sold off in London salerooms and, later, in America. The Ethnological Museum in Berlin bought a great many, today holding what is considered to be the most comprehensive and finest collection of Benin art in the world. Pitt Rivers Museum in Oxford holds about 100 artefacts from Benin—about a third taken by the chief of staff of the British Expedition, Captain George Le Clerc Egerton, before his family loaned them to the museum via the Dumas Egerton Trust. Sculptures and plaques also went to the Glasgow Art Gallery and Museum, the Horniman Museum in London, the Stuttgart Museum in Germany, the Metropolitan Museum of Art in New York, and the British Museum. The Seattle Art Museum also bought bronzes, and you can also see examples in the Chicago Art Institute and the National Museum of Scotland. There is a superb collection in the Boston Museum of Fine Arts, donated by the collector Robert Owen Lehman. Only a handful remain in Nigeria. Two artefacts were returned to the Oba Erediauwa, the head of the traditional state of Benin, Nigeria, in 2014, by Mark Walker, the great-grandson of Captain Herbert Walker—a principal figure in the British expedition in Benin.

When the sculptures first arrived in Europe, with time, they transformed the way people saw Africa. Europeans were surprised that Africans—a people whom they assumed to be backward—could make such refined artwork, as indicated by Charles Hercules Read, a curator from the British Museum, who secured the collection for the museum:

> It need scarcely be said that at the first sight of these remarkable works of art we were at once astounded at such an unexpected find, and puzzled to account for so highly developed an art among a race so entirely barbarous.[32]

It was a revelation to the Europeans that craftsmanship of this quality had been achieved in sixteenth-century Africa. In turn, European artists including Picasso emulated images found in Benin art. When artefacts move to new locations, they have an influence beyond, and sometimes contrary to, that which is intended or expected.

IMPERIAL PLUNDER: YUANMINGYUAN PALACE (THE CHINESE SUMMER PALACE)

Two robbers breaking into a museum, devastating, looting and burning, leaving laughing hand-in-hand with their bags full of treasures; one of the robbers is called France and the other Britain.[33]

So raged Victor Hugo, the French novelist, at the sack of the Chinese Summer Palace during the Second Opium War in 1860. James Bruce, eighth Earl of Elgin and Kincardine—the son of the Lord Elgin who acquired the Elgin Marbles—plundered the treasures of the palace in 1860, together with the French army. Rapacious and acquisitive, they even lifted the empress's Pekinese dog, christened him Looty, and presented him to Queen Victoria.

The Chinese government estimated that around 1.5 million items were taken, when, 150 years later, they launched a search to find the treasures, looking through museums and private homes around the world. As yet, there have been no official demands for repatriation, although many think it is only a matter of time, for it is slowly becoming a more prominent issue. Jackie Chan's popular film *Chinese Zodiac* tells the fictional story of a heroic attempt to reunite the bronze animals' heads, which were originally situated on the water-clock fountain in the grounds. Some in China would like to see this imagined happy ending come true.

For now, the Chinese government merely wants to investigate what is where—and that is not easy. The first problem is the scale. While the figure of 1.5 million missing items is speculative, even Elgin, who ordered the razing of the palace, emphasized in his diaries the size of the palace complex and described extensive pillaging, as well as the quality of what was taken, or destroyed:

> It is really a fine thing, like an English park—numberless buildings with handsome rooms, and filled with Chinese curios, and handsome clocks, bronzes, etc. But, alas! Such a scene of desolation... There was not a room I saw in which half the things had not been taken away or broken in pieces.[34]

The Summer Palace (Yuanmingyuan, in Chinese) was built during the eighteenth and early nineteenth century. It was where the emperors of the Qing Dynasty lived and handled government affairs, a grand complex of buildings and gardens. Located on the outskirts of Beijing (or Peking, as it was then commonly known in the West), parts of the palace were notable for their emulation of buildings inspired by the Rococo period, after Emperor Qianlong, who reigned from 1736 to 1795, ordered the building of certain palaces to have a European inspiration. It was described by Victor Hugo as a 'masterpiece'; built of jade, marble, and porcelain, and constructed by architects 'who are poets', it was a 'dazzling cavern of human fantasy with the face of a temple and palace'.[35]

The root of the ransacking of the palace was a trade dispute with the British Empire over drugs. The First Opium War (1839–42) between China and Britain began when China resisted the opium trade, which the British were pursuing with poppy seeds from fields in India controlled by the British Raj. War broke out when China tried to stop the importing of opium. Britain won and the Treaty of Nanjing provided for the cession of five ports for British trade and residence. Despite these concessions, the British continued to be unsatisfied. They wanted to extend further their trading rights in China.

The catalyst to the renewal of hostilities in the Second Opium War (1856–60) came when Chinese officials boarded the British ship *Arrow*, allegedly lowered the British ensign, and tried to charge the crew with smuggling. The British Parliament gained French support to send an expeditionary force to China. Admiral Sir Michael Seymour led the joint British–French naval force; Lord Elgin led the British army. In 1860, British and French forces marched inland from the coast and reached Peking. As they did so, British and Indian troops, including two British envoys and a journalist for *The Times* newspaper, were taken prisoner, tortured, and twenty of them killed. This was the trigger for the destruction of the palace.

The troops tore in, grabbing and smashing the delicate porcelain and jade works of art, ripping down the elaborate textiles, looking for gold and silver and anything else they could get their hands on. '[T]hey seemed to have been seized with a temporary insanity,' observed Deputy-Assistant Quartermaster General Garnet Wolseley, describing how, 'in body and soul they were absorbed in one pursuit, which was plunder, plunder'.[36]

Elgin instructed the soldiers to set the buildings on fire. Troops burned the libraries and rare books, then all of the palaces: the temples, halls, pavilions, the Jade Fountain Park, and the grand Main Audience Hall with its marble floor. Elgin appears to have experienced feelings of regret about the acts he sanctioned: 'Plundering and devastating a place like this is bad enough but what is worst is the waste and breakage.'[37]

It is said to have taken three days and over 4,000 men to leave the palace a blackened shell, covering the city in a smoky haze. Robert Swinhoe, a British interpreter, writes of how he subsequently came across French soldiers selling 'a string of splendid pearls', 'pencil-cases set with diamonds', and 'watches and vases set with pearls'.[38] As well as looting by French and English soldiers, the local Chinese people made off with numerous goods, which they then sold on to travellers.

A candid letter home by Major General Charles George Gordon, known as 'Chinese Gordon' because of his campaigns there, reveals how wretched he felt:

> You can scarcely imagine the beauty and magnificence of the places we burnt. It made one's heart sore to burn them; in fact, these palaces were so large, and we were so pressed for time, that we could not plunder them carefully. Quantities of gold ornaments were burnt, considered as brass. It was wretchedly demoralising work for an army. Everybody was wild for plunder.[39]

But despite reservations, Elgin remained resolute about the action. Plundering and burning the palace was unquestionably the best option available: 'I came to the conclusion that the destruction of the Yuen-Ming-Yuen was the least objectionable of the several courses open to me.'[40] It was expedient—they wanted to leave Peking before winter, and needed to deliver quick and efficient punishment to the emperor and his court; one which would not harm the Chinese people. Elgin elaborated:

> It was the Emperor's favourite residence, and its destruction could not fail to be a blow to his pride as well as his feelings ... The punishment was one which would fall, not on the people, who may be comparatively innocent, but exclusively on the Emperor, whose direct personal responsibility for the crime committed is established.[41]

The usual practice was to auction the booty through official channels when back in Britain, but in this instance Major General Gordon departed from the norm, and held the sale immediately. The items were sold on the spot and the money realized (£26,000) was distributed between the men according to rank. First-class officers received £60, sergeants £7, and the Indian soldiers, who made up a third of the army, got nothing—they were, however, allowed to keep the objects they had taken. This hierarchy of distribution reinforced notions of order and place, which served to legitimize the whole project. And it needed to be legitimized.

In a letter to Sidney Herbert, the Secretary of State for War, General Grant explained his decision to hold the auction immediately. The frenzy that seized the army had to be calmed; it had to leave them with 'no reason to complain'.[42] Grant worried that not sanctioning the plunder would endorse ill-discipline within the ranks in the future. He was concerned about the consequential threat to order and obedience, believing that the lower ranks would see the widespread looting as permissible behaviour and as an endorsement of reckless acts more generally, which in turn could threaten his authority. The troops needed to know their place and that they must control their passions. By selling off the objects quickly, General Grant reasoned, their lust would be satisfied: and crucially, the auction would lend a semblance of order to what had happened. The auction was held there and then to wrest back control over the troops, and to authorize their actions.

In Britain, the arrival of the treasures served as material proof of British dominance and the humiliation of the Chinese. Many of the objects were sent to Queen Victoria, where they took their place alongside other spoils from the victories of the British army. A large collection was sent to France, whose soldiers had also taken part in the pillaging. Pekinese dogs were taken from the palace and brought to Europe, including Looty, seized by a captain J. Hart Dunne and later presented to Queen Victoria; it lived at Windsor Castle for a further eleven years. A number of portraits of this little dog were made, including a drawing by Edwin Henry Landseer and a painting by Friedrich Wilhelm Keyl, which was displayed at the Royal Academy in 1862. The painting is now part of the Royal Collection (see Figure 9).

Summer Palace loot first appeared in auction houses in London in 1861. The first public display was in the Tuileries in Paris in April that same year, and included items given by the French army to Napoleon III. One reporter commended the transfer of objects from one ruler to another, lamenting that other artefacts had fallen into the hands of

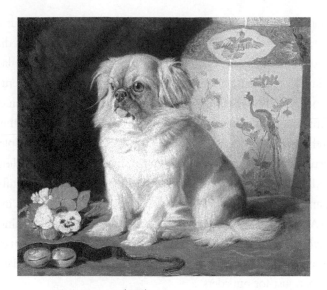

Figure 9. *Looty* (1861).
Friedrich Wilhelm Keyl (1823–71).
Royal Collection Trust / © HM Queen Elizabeth II 2012.

people of lower orders who he described as 'unappreciating amateurs'.[43] Guillaume Pauthier, a French scholar of China, concurred, writing in the art history journal *Gazette des Beaux-Arts* of his 'regret' that certain objects had fallen into the hands of soldiers, and bemoaning the fact 'that only a small sample has arrived in France, which, in itself, is far from sufficient in giving a full idea of Chinese art'.[44] He wanted to see more.

By the 1870s, the treasures began to enter museums. Displaying the objects as war loot demonstrated the power of the British army over the Chinese emperor, so they were often promoted as loot rather than art, in a narrative that emphasized British victory and domination. Artefacts were proudly labelled 'From the Summer Palace of the Emperor of China'. Indeed, the kudos was such that it is likely that more items were labelled loot than actually were. Many artefacts in the Victoria & Albert Museum in London were described as such until as recently as the late 1980s, when looting was no longer seen as something about which to boast; and this mislabelling is another reason why today it is difficult to pinpoint exactly what is and what is not from the Summer Palace.

We know that the Royal Engineers Museum at Chatham in Kent has a collection of chinoiserie brought back by General Gordon, including a large imperial couch with dragon carvings. The V&A has one of the most comprehensive collections of Chinese art in the West. On display are spectacular treasures from Yuanmingyuan, including a pair of cloisonné fishbowls, a filigree headdress with blue feathers and pearls, beautiful jade vases, and elaborately embroidered silk robes. Opening as it did in 1852, the V&A was able to take advantage of the growing fashion in Chinese art that developed after the 'Summer Palace' sales in the 1860s, when excited collectors realized they were seeing art created for the imperial court rather than just for outsiders.

The sacking of the Summer Palace was a turning point in the consumption of Chinese art and artefacts in Britain. Prior to this point, most objects of Chinese origin were those made for the export trade, for a mixture of Chinese and European taste. These objects from the Summer Palace, however, were made specifically for the Chinese emperor. The interest of collectors was stimulated by this because they wanted objects that had been owned by the grandees. The taking of private objects from the Chinese grandees further encouraged a blossoming desire for chinoiserie. Captain Lawrence-Archer's essay on Chinese porcelain gives a first-hand account:

> Fortunately the writer arrived in China immediately after the sacking of the Yuen-men-Yuen, when so many splendid or beautiful specimens, hoarded jealously for centuries in the imperial depositories, at length became known to the outer, and at that period scarcely appreciative, world; and when, for the first time, the matchless bowls and jars of the 15th and 16th centuries—when the art of ornamentation, in the most vivid as well as purest colours, had attained to what may be called perfection— proved that Imperial taste delighted not in the grotesque . . . but in true beauty of form and chaste embellishment.[45]

The problem of relations with China did not dampen a developing market. It added to the thrill of acquisition.

Since the late 1990s, the destruction of the Summer Palace has become a sensitive issue, seen as part of a 'century of humiliation' when China was not only defeated in the Opium Wars, but lost Taiwan and suffered from Japanese invasions. Efforts have been made to retrieve the objects and art ransacked during this period, especially those from the Summer Palace, where there is now a viewing area where visitors can watch the restoration of objects that the Chinese are starting to bring back, primarily through purchase at auction.

China is concentrating on buying items as they come up at sales, but these are extraordinarily expensive. So as well as collectors paying large sums for the artefacts, there is a programme of researching the institutions and collectors where they may have ended up: perhaps with the hope of one day applying diplomatic pressure. At the end of 2009, a team of Chinese experts on cultural relics visited the United States. Eight major organizations, including the Metropolitan in New York, permitted them to look through their stores. The team discovered relics that were unknown to the experts, including a painting dating back to the Song Dynasty (AD 960 to 1279) on display in the Boston Museum. They found and are scrutinizing historical records written by visiting Westerners about what they saw at the Summer Palace, as well as photographs that are documentary proof of what it was like.

France and Britain are on their list of institutions to investigate. This approach has already paid off in respect of the actions of private collectors. In 2013, a wealthy French businessman agreed to return two bronze animal heads to China. More may follow. Victor Hugo's wish, that the 'booty' is returned to 'despoiled China', may one day be granted; although it will be too late for poor Looty.

KNOWLEDGE THROUGH COLLABORATION

The cases discussed thus far are instances of the removal of artistic treasures in circumstances that are now frowned upon. It is important to remember, however, that there are thousands of artefacts in museums today that were not acquired through any bloodshed, duplicity, or arm-twisting. Millions of objects are on display today because of straightforward collaboration, born out of sharing knowledge and material across countries. One such example is given by exchanges between Swedish and Chinese scholars.

In the early twentieth century it was common for Western scholars to argue for the Western origins of Eastern civilizations. This reflected the world as they saw it, due to the dominance of world powers based in the West and an absence of any evidence that the rest of the world had a prehistory. It was a view transformed with the research findings of the Swedish geologist Johan Gunnar Andersson, who was crucial to the discovery of prehistoric China. The story shows how scholars in different countries have worked together and produced major breakthroughs in understanding.

Johan Gunnar Andersson was director of Sweden's National Geological Survey. In 1914 he was invited by the Chinese government to be a mining adviser, training China's first geologists and locating valuable resources, in a team organized and led by Chinese geologist Ding Wenjiang. A few years later Andersson visited a small village south of Beijing: Zhoukoudian, named Chicken Bone Hill by the locals as it was well known for its abundance of small fossils. A return trip in 1921 and subsequent excavations led to the finding of two human teeth, which were identified as the first remnants of what is now known as Peking Man: one of the first specimens of *Homo erectus*.

In collaboration with Chinese scholars such as Yuan Fuli, excavations further revealed prehistoric Neolithic remains in Henan and unique artefacts, from a period that begun around 10,000 BC and concluded about 8,000 years later. What we now know about China's past began with this groundbreaking discovery. There had not been any finds of ancient human fossils in Asia up until this moment, and the prehistory of China was completely unknown. Andersson's discovery would trigger the study of the prehistory of China, having identified man in Asia without the Western origins that had been previously assumed.

Their research and excavations led to the creation of the Museum of Far Eastern Antiquities in Stockholm in 1926. By permission of the Chinese government, many of the cultural artefacts discovered were sent to Sweden, where they formed the basis of the museum. Andersson served as its director for ten years. Today, the museum holds some of the most valued antiquities from China. It is the most important collection outside China, with stoneware and porcelain from the Song, Ming, and Qing dynasties.

CONVENTIONS IN PLACE

For centuries the removal of private property from the enemy was common practice in warfare, but no longer is this the case. In *Prohibiting Plunder*, the American political scientist Wayne Sandholtz traces the emergence of norms and laws against wartime looting and how they have developed over the past 200 years.[46] Sandholtz delineates the ideas that were important in bringing about significant changes in practice and regulation. In the eighteenth century, the veneration of art would come to imply that it held a special status and deserved protection. In addition, Enlightenment thinking gave rise to the idea of a 'rationalist' war, one that only justified applications of force necessary to achieve military objects, rather than further punitive action. The concept of a national heritage, which was brought about with the rise of the nation state and indeed national museums, also contributed. But although during the second half of the eighteenth century, the idea that cultural treasures should be immune from war became respectable, it was not the norm. French plundering would trigger considerable debate and lead to some changes. And it was only with the Hague Conventions of 1899 and 1907 that the first formal statements were made, together with attempts to protect cultural property from all nations and prohibit the removal or seizure of enemy property, unless specifically demanded by the imperative of war. These statements signalled a significant shift in attitudes.

But the Conventions had little practical effect, especially during the Second World War. Although the German Reich and the Russian Empire signed the Hague Conventions, they (or, more precisely, the regimes which succeeded them) disregarded them only a matter of decades later. Both Nazi Germany and Soviet Russia robbed museums in occupied territories, after which further regulations in the form of the 1949 Hague Convention were put in place. The 1954 Hague Convention imposed procedures on the intervening party, outlining that they should protect cultural heritage, refrain from directing any hostility against it, and prevent the export of cultural property from the occupied territory. It expressed the idea that heritage was a collective good that should be protected for everybody. The preamble begins:

> [We are] convinced that damage to cultural property belonging to any people whatsoever means cultural damage to the heritage of mankind, since each people makes its contribution to the culture of the world.

As of 2014 it had been ratified by 126 states, including in 2009 the United States, but not Andorra, Ireland, Philippines, or the United Kingdom. In 2015, the new culture secretary, John Whittingdale, committed the British Conservative government to ratifying the Hague Convention on cultural property, as a response to the devastating destruction of antiquities in Syria and Iraq.

In 1970, the United Nations Educational, Scientific and Cultural Organization (UNESCO) Convention on the Means of Prohibiting and Preventing the Illicit Import, Export and Transfer of Ownership of Cultural Property was adopted by a large number of signatories including the United States of America, but not the UK, Japan, or Switzerland. It had the aim of discouraging the international trade in stolen antiquities, and targeted individuals and institutions—rather than nations and political leaders, which had ceased to be a problem. Compared to the 1954 Treaty, the 1970 Convention emphasized heritage less as a collective good for mankind and more as the property of the nation state.

CONDITIONS TODAY

In 2003, during the American invasion of Iraq, thousands of priceless antiquities from the ancient civilizations of Babylon, Ur, and Nineveh were systematically looted from the National Museum in Baghdad. The museum was stripped of its collection of precious antiquity that reached back to the birth of civilization. Over 15,000 objects were taken including irreplaceable cuneiform tablets, around 5,000 valuable cylinder seals, pottery, pendants, and the sacred vase of Warka: a 5,000-year-old carved alabaster stone vessel.

The museum had opened initially as a small room in a government building, devoted to housing artefacts found at Assyrian, Babylonian, and Sumerian sites. Gertrude Bell, the British explorer and amateur archaeologist, who played a role in the foundation of the Iraqi state, helped to set up the museum—then the Baghdad Antiquities Museum—and was its director until her death in 1926. It is due to her efforts that many artefacts stayed in Iraq after they were found. Bell left £50,000 to the museum to ensure its survival; in 1966 a new building was built specifically for it, and it was named the Iraq National Museum.

Museums were also a target for looters during the First Gulf War of 1991, but that was nothing compared to the organization and the scale of the looting in 2003. Nor was the museum the only target. Important archaeological sites were scavenged beyond recognition. Commentators were angry that the American military had not done more to stop the looting, which was predictable and preventable. Historic artefacts that include cylinder seals and cuneiform tables were subsequently swept into the black market. An international effort to find them was launched, through universities, websites (which listed catalogues and showed pictures), and international customs agencies. With such a concerted effort, the search campaign has achieved the return of around 4,000 objects. But despite these strenuous attempts, it is estimated that only about 50 per cent of that which was taken has been recovered.[47] Objects turn up in auction houses, with uncertain provenance, mostly likely through dealers operating a questionable practice, and are whisked off into private collections.

Look at any war-torn country with an antique past and you will find an illegal trade in their treasures. Iraq is a particularly bad case. Egypt, Syria, and Afghanistan have all suffered. There are many archaeological sites that are difficult to protect. The problem with such looting is not only that the artefacts are lost: removing them in this way takes them out of their original context, which it is important to record in order to understand what that object is and how it was used.[48]

These recent cases are worrying examples of the ongoing attempts to steal and remove valuable artefacts for personal gain. But, they are markedly different to the other cases discussed earlier. What we have here is the work of individuals and well-run gangs motivated by profit. It is a serious problem, and one that is difficult to address: these countries are torn apart by war, the antiquities fetch a good price, and although it is illegal it is understandable that people in difficult circumstances sell and buy such material—there is a market for it. Even so, looting by individuals and gangs is illegal, condemned, and resisted: a state of affairs that is very different to the days of Napoleon and the British Empire—or the era of the Second World War. Similar, extensive acts are no longer possible due to major changes in attitudes and law.

Museums are more careful about where their artefacts come from. Some professionals try to exert influence on the prevention of looting and the understanding of cultural heritage. The director of the V&A, Martin Roth, travelled to Syria to brief relief organizations and NGOs on the importance of Syria's cultural heritage and its history, because he was concerned at reports that ISIS was looting and trafficking antiquities to fund its activities. In other instances, museum professionals have gone out of their way to help to return objects. In 2012, 843 artefacts were returned to the National Museum of Afghanistan in Kabul, with the assistance of the British Museum. The Art and Antiques Unit of the Metropolitan Police found the artefacts when there was an attempt to smuggle them into Britain. In addition, a private collector spotted some of the artefacts on the black market and bought them back in order to return them to the Kabul museum, including a sculpture of Buddha and the Begram Ivories—fragile Indian carvings that were once set into furniture and which date back to the first century AD. The British Museum stored the objects and conserved them, as well as helping to identify them and trace their route—in some cases, they had come from the National Museum of Afghanistan, which had suffered substantial thefts in the Civil War of 1992–4. The British Museum signed a three-year agreement with the National Museum of Afghanistan to work together to identity and return artefacts that had been stolen and illegally exported out of the country. They have had a small degree of success building on earlier attempts: records show the total number returned thus far is around 2,330.[49] In June 2015, the director Neil MacGregor told *The Times* newspaper that the British Museum was guarding an artefact that was looted from Syria, in the hope of returning it when the country is stable.[50]

In the past, some curators dealt with antiquities sellers who had acquired objects in questionable circumstances. Today, museum directors take care to demonstrate that this behaviour is no longer acceptable. Buyers of undocumented antiquities have started to recognize the uncertain status of objects without known provenance acquired after 1970. This came about in part due to growing concerns from within archaeology, in the 1960s and 1970s, about the loss of cultural context that attends looting, as well as later campaigns, spearheaded by Professor Colin Renfrew in the 1990s, calling for greater museum accountability in relation to the antiquities market. The operation of the art market relies, to some extent, on looted artefacts and there have been attempts to limit that. But it is difficult to stem and regulate the black market.[51] Curators and collectors have subsequently been placed under increased scrutiny within the museological establishments and have engaged in self-regulation, although many suggest this has not gone far enough. There is greater accountability, but this remains a fraught area, and there has been something of a breakdown of partnerships within the professional and academic circles around museums.

Countries of origin have pressured prominent museums and collectors to give up antiquities that are thought to have been taken illicitly since the 1970s. And a good number have been repatriated over the past decade as a consequence. Several North American museums have been shaken by claims from countries, especially Italy, that objects in their collections were acquired illicitly. In 2007, the Getty returned forty ancient works to Italy, and other major institutions followed suit, including the Metropolitan Museum of Art and Boston's Museum of Fine Arts. In 1972, the Metropolitan Museum of Art paid US $1 million for the 2,500-year-old Euphronios Krater—an ancient Greek terracotta bowl, used for mixing wine with water, created around the year 515 BC. It was not looted or stolen by armies or any nation, but had been purchased from Robert Hecht, who was subsequently put on trial in Italy on charges of conspiring to deal in looted antiquities. The statute of limitations expired on the case before it was brought to trial, but it had a major impact nonetheless. It became clear that a number of individuals had been selling questionably obtained items to museums, or that the museum had accepted them as generous donations, when it should not have done so. The Euphronious Krater was returned to Italy in 2008, in exchange for the right to display comparable artefacts on loan.

In 2010 Marion True, a former curator to the J. Paul Getty Museum, who had been on trial for five years on charges related to artefact trafficking, was released when an Italian court ruled that the statute of limitations had expired. It brought to an end a long legal battle over whether or not True had knowingly acquired ancient objects of illegal provenance for the museum. She was the first American museum official to be criminally charged by a foreign government. It should be pointed out that during her tenure as curator, True returned several pieces of questionable provenance to Italy and triggered a move to enforce more stringent standards for checking attribution. Although her case was finally dismissed, it has acted as a game changer in the debate. The case has put pressure on museums to account better for where and how they acquired their artefacts. The prominence of this prosecution has increased pressure on museums in the US to refuse to acquire artefacts, or to give them back, if they cannot be confident of their provenance.

The journalists Jason Felch and Ralph Frammolino document that between 2005 and 2010, American museums returned 102 objects to Italy and Greece.[52] This number excludes later announcements, including, in 2013, the news that the J. Paul Getty Museum agreed to return a fourth-century BC terracotta head to Italy. Although the Getty had bought the bust in 1985, they came to realize that it had been stolen in the 1970s. Indeed, in the wake of the scandals at the Getty over looted antiquities, the museum has put substantial efforts into trying to verify the ownership histories of 4,500 antiquities in its collection, and intends to publish them online.

Things are different to how they used to be. Yet despite these positive developments, it is common to assume looting is endemic and that museums continue to acquire stolen property. The prevailing wisdom, it would seem, is that a museum is simply a display case of plunder, that there is little difference between current practice and past practice. And this outlook can distort our understanding of how things are and what is happening.

In January 2011, as the Arab Spring took hold of the Middle East, the Cairo Museum in Tahir Square—home to some of the most important ancient Egyptian art in the world—suffered a break-in. Display cases were smashed and a number of objects looted. The news of the break-in spread like wildfire: reports, email circulars, Twitter feeds, and Facebook updated readers constantly about looting at the museum. Rumours proliferated. A number reported that looters had beheaded two priceless mummies, and were accompanied by photographs of the human heads— one against a background of bones. *Discovery News* said that 'the mummies of King Tutankhamen's great grandparents might have had their heads ripped off as a result of the recent turmoil in Egypt'.[53] Other experts eagerly piled in with their theories, with one suggesting that the head belonged to the mummified body of a teenage girl.

After considerable conjecture and rampant speculation, it turned out that the long-dead pharaohs were wrapped up, unharmed, with their heads firmly attached to their bodies, in the museum. What seems to have happened is that the robbers picked up two skulls that are usually kept in a storeroom to test a CT scanner and then left them behind. It appears that they were on the lookout for items to sell, targeting the gift shop in particular. During the break-in, some exhibits were damaged, but the mummies were unharmed. Depending on which report you read, between twenty and seventy objects are now in need of some repair and restoration. This is by no means a good thing, but it could have been much worse. More serious was the reaction, which revealed a tendency to see greater damage and looting than was actually taking place, reflecting the assumption that organized looting on the scale of Iraq was just waiting to happen. Seeing all activity though loot-tinted glasses can mean that the reality of a situation is misunderstood.

Today, strong criticisms of museums and their collecting practices are expressed in academic literature, books aimed at a general market, and journalism on the question of looting. Serious accusations are levelled at museums. For example, in *Chasing Aphrodite: The Hunt for Looted Antiquities at the World's Richest Museum*, journalists Jason Felch and Ralph Frammolino tell the story of how the prestigious Getty acquired illicitly looted objects. 'The museum world's dirty little secret came to light amid revelations about paedophile priests in the catholic church,'[54] their opening pages begin, as if collecting illicitly acquired objects was somehow comparable to systematic child abuse. They continue: 'Museums have fuelled the destruction of far more knowledge than they have preserved.'[55]

I am intrigued as to why museums stimulate such hostility, not only in relation to *historical* collecting practices but also with regard to their role today. I believe that past practices are often conflated with current ones, without an adequate appreciation of the significant changes that have taken place. I very much doubt that museums have fuelled the destruction of more knowledge than they have preserved. On the contrary, they have added to a great expansion of knowledge—but no longer is this commonly recognized. And I am concerned that contemporary critics are failing to take into account the work museums do, across nations, to stem looting: for example, the assistance given by the British Museum's curators to scholars in Iraq in the aftermath of the Gulf Wars, when people worked together to track down looted antiquity and to try and monitor the state of excavations.

This chapter began with the prosecution of Verres. It is interesting to note that Cicero's legal case was not, in fact, about looted artefacts. Cicero flagged up Verres's flagrant taking of art as a way of gaining sympathy for the case that he was actually prosecuting: maladministration in a foreign province, which was important but less emotive. His discussion of looting was a way of attracting attention to his case, a way 'of making his case urgent to a Roman audience that might otherwise be indifferent', explains the historian and archaeologist Margaret Miles. It is worth remembering that accusations of loot are often used to reinforce other battles: in this instance, one of political corruption and mismanagement.[56] And in that vein, it is time to explore why we hear so many critical statements about looting and museums today. What is being said? Why? By whom? What are the underlying dynamics to the demands for repatriation today? Addressing these questions is the focus of the following chapters.

PART II

5

Museum Wars

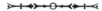

Towards the end of 2010, officials at the Natural History Museum in London, in collaboration with the Natural History Museum in Asunción in Paraguay, were finalizing plans to investigate parts of a distant forest in South America. They intended to send sixty botanists and zoologists to the remote Dry Chaco region of Paraguay, to better understand the little-known biodiversity of the area. The team included experts on insects, plants, lichens, cyanobacteria, moss, microorganisms, worms, molluscs, mammals, and fossils.

The organizers hoped the expedition would yield new information about fragile habitats. 'The information and specimens collected on this trip will help scientists to understand the richness and diversity of the animals and plants in this remote region,' explained Professor Richard Lane, head of science at the Natural History Museum, London. The investigation was urgent, he stressed, because 'we are losing the Earth's biodiversity at a shocking rate and we need to gather appropriate evidence of the nature of this change as well as what's in danger of being lost'.[1] They planned to make the information available to the Paraguayan government and policymakers, conservation groups, and local people, so it could be used better to manage and protect these kinds of habitats. The trip had taken several years to arrange and was an ambitious undertaking.

Others took a very different view of the project. Concerns were expressed about the indigenous people who live in the forest and have no contact with the outside world. Iniciativa Amotocodie, an indigenous people's protection group, wrote an open letter to the Natural History Museum in London, asking for the expedition to be immediately cancelled. 'The expedition you plan', cautioned the director, Benno Glauser, 'constitutes beyond any doubt an extremely high risk for the integrity, safety and legal rights of life and self-determination of the isolated Ayoreo, as well as for the integrity and stability of their territories.' Glauser warned of the harmful impact it could have both on indigenous peoples in the area and on the scientists: 'There exists a considerable menace and risk also for the safety of the scientists taking part in the expedition, as well as the rest of the expedition's participants.'[2]

The organizers tried to reassure the opponents. Steps had been taken to ensure there would be no contact with the indigenous communities in the area, Professor Lane explained, and they had worked with local people to assist them in their travels: 'our collaborators have enlisted an Ayoreo elder, who has volunteered to guide our team in the forest'. But their attempts to placate the critics did not ease concerns. Jonathan Mazower, advocacy director for Survival International, which campaigns for the rights of tribal people, was not persuaded. Indigenous people were mobile, he countered, always on the run, and therefore not easily avoided. Any unexpected contact could turn violent. The project was suspended to allow for further consultation. After consultation, it was cancelled. Preparations and plans were aborted.

This cautious approach is very different to that which underpinned the expeditions undertaken 250 years ago by Captain Cook. Cook set sail without knowing where he was going, or who he would meet, and continued regardless. In this more recent instance, investigating the natural world was seen as risky and potential contact with people dangerous—so much so that the expedition did not go ahead.

Understanding the natural world was felt to be of lesser importance than the negative impact the expedition might have on the flora, animals, and the local population, despite the potential for addressing the threat of climate change.

In Chapter 2, we saw how the idea of the museum was formed over the centuries. In the Renaissance period there was an attempt to get to grips with the works of ancient thinkers. Cabinets of curiosities were formed that were, in part, an attempt to understand, and even manipulate, a tumultuous world. They were a demonstration of power and status. Later, a more modern outlook reordered the museum as an attempt to understand the world through things. Collections came to be ordered taxonomically, at first concentrating on natural history—an approach that was later extended to include art. These two approaches—the Renaissance and the modern—differed from one another in many ways, but both were at bottom confident about the possibility of understanding the world. In recent decades a different way of thinking about knowledge has become influential. It is an approach that recognizes that the pursuit of knowledge is difficult because a full and complete understanding is inevitably partial. It is an outlook that is concerned that the quest to know has had negative consequences, that it operates in the interest of the powerful and can harm the vulnerable. This chapter explores this approach, and its impact upon how museums are understood to operate.

TROUBLE IN ENLIGHTENMENT

Towards the end of the eighteenth century, an influential movement developed in opposition to Enlightenment thinking. This movement questioned rationalism and the autonomy of the individual, and came to be known as the Romantic movement. The relationship between Enlightenment and Romantic thinking dominated the nineteenth century, with thinkers moving between and within these poles of thought.

Whereas Enlightenment thinkers were generally united on the need to challenge what they regarded as irrational prejudices, superstition, and the possibility of progress with rationality, the Romantics were unconvinced: this is exactly what they feared. The danger was, they argued, that emotion, sentiment, and feeling would be drained away from our understanding of human beings. Nature was an arena for spiritual contemplation, they felt, rather than a site that was to be ordered and categorized.

Whilst Enlightenment philosophes saw a civilization of mankind, suggesting there was something held in common between people, Romantic thinkers focused on the differences. That is, they understood humankind as being from distinct and different cultures that needed protection. For example, according to the German thinker Johann Gottfried Herder, reality was not understandable in a universal sense, or subject to objective rational investigation: rather, each historical period and human culture was different, partial, and possessed its own unique culture. This culture was central to national identity, the *Volksgeist* ('soul of the people'). As Herder said: 'Let us follow our own path...let men speak well or ill of our nation, our literature, our language: they are ours, they are ourselves and let that be enough.'[3] Herder was one of the first to express and develop ideas about Romantic nationalism and the particularities of nations. His fledgling nationalism was never political—he did not assert the superiority of particular nations or his own culture, but argued that cultures are neither comparable nor commensurable: 'No man can convey the character of his feeling, or transform my being into his.' People and cultures are different, such that 'The Negro is as much entitled to think the white man degenerate...as the white man is to think of the Negro as a black beast...The civilisation of man is not that of the European; it manifests itself, according to time and place, in every people.'[4]

This is a different view of human society to that of the Enlightenment thinkers, who argued that human beings held common characteristics and that the natural world and society were subject to universal laws which could be understood by rational inquiry. As the philosopher David Hume put it, expressing the classic universalist Enlightenment position: 'Mankind are so much the same at all times and in all places that history informs us of nothing new or strange.'[5] Mankind was, wrote Voltaire, 'generally speaking, always what he is now'.[6]

The Romantic approach, on the other hand, saw progress as dangerously eclipsing other more spiritual forms of knowing and culture. But it was only in the twentieth century, especially after the Second World War, that Enlightenment thinking came to be significantly challenged in a way that is pertinent to this study. Thereafter the role of rationality was profoundly problematized. Rationalism was perceived as having played a key part in the events that led to the creation of concentration camps, not least because Germany had specific intellectual roots in the Enlightenment project. In the *Dialectic of Enlightenment*, the Frankfurt School philosophers Theodor Horkheimer and Max Adorno identified forces within secularization—the drive to know and to rationalize—as having led to the domination and destruction that reached its horrific conclusion in the Holocaust. The objectification central to the Enlightenment was understood as having turned on human beings.[7] In *Modernity and the Holocaust*, the sociologist Zygmunt Bauman advanced the theory that the Holocaust was not a malfunction, an aberration, nor a unique event, but connected to—and a product of—modernity and its rationalizing tendency. More starkly and forcibly, the contemporary philosopher John Gray argues: 'Progress and mass murder run in tandem.'[8]

On the whole, it was thinkers on the political Right who initially advanced a critique of modernity, suggesting that it was dehumanizing and potentially destructive. But this began to change in the 1950s and 1960s, when the New Left began to lose faith in the progressive potential of the class struggle. This group of thinkers and activists had become disillusioned with the grand narratives and ideologies of the early twentieth century, and began to look more to Third World liberation movements, feminism, and the role of culture to bring about social change. And they scrutinized the old ways of thinking: the reliance on rationality, truth, and progress. This laid the foundations for the intellectual trends of postmodernism, postcolonialism, and cultural studies.

Postmodernism is an approach and a method of understanding that is sceptical about the very possibility of knowledge, and explicitly questions whether any truth is possible. The literary theorist Terry Eagleton describes the outlook of postmodern thinking as follows:

> the contemporary movement of thought which rejects totalities, universal values, grand historical narratives, solid foundations to human existence and the possibility of objective knowledge. Postmodernism is sceptical of truth, unity and progress, opposes what it sees as elitism in culture, tends towards cultural relativism, and celebrates pluralism, discontinuity and heterogeneity.[9]

Zygmunt Bauman makes a helpful distinction between the eras of modernism and postmodernism, helping to differentiate them. Bauman explains that while it is debatable whether philosophers of the modern era ever established the foundations of objective knowledge, the point is that they pursued it with 'conviction'.[10] They believed that in striving for knowledge, glimmers of the truth would be in reach. With postmodernism, Bauman argues, the search for truth was understood to be impossible and discarded.

In this context, thinkers began to be sympathetic towards ideas about the particularity of cultures. Theories of cultural difference could help explain differences in how the world was organized. As a consequence, particularism—a perspective that sees irreconcilable differences instead of commonalities—began to have some sway. Theorists started to argue that Western thought disguises those differences, thus acting as an instrument of domination. And by the 1980s, Western rationality was derided as one of many potential social constructs, seen as an oppressive and colonizing enterprise that dominated everyone and forced the 'Other' into positions of inferiority. As thinkers across the political spectrum began to embrace these ideas, they shaped the dominant strands of intellectual inquiry in the academies of the West.

CRITIQUING THE MUSEUM

Museums were somewhat isolated at first from these ideas. Museum scholar Eilean Hooper-Greenhill notes that these struggles took longer to significantly impact on the museum sector than others, such as education and the media, which were subjected to such debates earlier in the 1980s.[11] Up until the late 1980s, much of the literature on museums was technical, discussing how best to display and conserve artefacts, reporting on exhibitions, or describing the history of various institutions. This changed when a body of work called the 'new museology' emerged, which intended to introduce a new philosophy around the function of museums, and which advocated a different kind of relationship between the institution and communities.[12] This was not a completely new approach, as we shall see, but this is when it came to be influential and increasingly dominant in museum studies.[13]

Museums subsequently became the focus of ideological struggles. A broadly questioning and critical outlook is now the prevailing analysis in the academic and professional literature, an attitude described by the historian Ralph Starn as having resulted in a 'tidal wave of museum studies'.[14] This outlook can be broken down into three arguments. First, museums function in the interests of the powerful; secondly, the narrative or intellectual framework of the institution presents itself as the truth, but it is neither *a* truth or *the* truth—rather, it is subjective opinion, and inherently biased; thirdly, museums and their narratives can be harmful to people.

I want to start by illustrating the voices arguing for the first position: that museums serve the interests of the elite. An early manifestation of this thesis was advanced by French sociologist Pierre Bourdieu who, drawing on research conducted in the 1960s, examined the structures of society, taste, and cultural practices. Bourdieu researched the public visiting French art galleries, and argued that attending galleries and museums was a marker of 'distinction'—primarily, an act of social positioning, which showed that one was 'civilized'. 'Museum visiting increases very strongly with levels of education, and it is almost exclusively the domain of the cultivated classes,' argued Bourdieu and his colleague, Alain Darbel.[15] The consumption of culture was not only a consequence of class, but also a direct reflection of class, which sustains and reproduces it: 'taste classifies and it classifies the classifier'.[16] The objective of art museums, then, is not to achieve the love of great works in everyone—what Bourdieu describes as 'upliftment'. Rather, it is to reinforce and underwrite existing cultural distinctions, naturalizing a stratified culture.[17]

In his groundbreaking book *Ways of Seeing*,[18] published in 1972, the art historian John Berger highlighted the hidden ideologies in art work and in galleries. It was a retort to the TV documentary series *Civilisation*, presented by Kenneth Clark, who had been director of the National Gallery in London, and held other prominent posts. Berger sought to counter Lord Clark's characterization of much of Western art as a monument to civilization. It was no such thing, argued Berger: Western art disguised privilege, oppression, and injustice. Art appears to be neutral and magnificent, but in fact it gives a spiritual credibility to the political elite, which contributes to the reproduction of existing power relations.

Bourdieu and Berger tackled important questions that encouraged reflection on the relationship between cultural institutions, art, and the social structures of society: about the disparity between the democratic promise of the institution and the failure to realize it. Both explored how habits in consuming art and visiting the art gallery were socially bound up in class and power: far from being for everyone, museums and art galleries were predominantly popular with, and frequented by, more elite sections of society, which in turn reinforced the social position of museums. The discourse of museums and galleries was one of truth, beauty, and art for art's sake; but this, these scholars insisted, hides and even reinforces their true social role. Feminist scholars, including Griselda Pollock and Linda Nochlin, towards the end of the 1970s and into the 1980s, would look in particular at the complicity of the arts in the subjugation of women.

Some of these issues had been raised before. In the Victorian period, writers and critics that included John Ruskin, William Morris, and Matthew Arnold explored the value of culture to society. In the recent scholarship in museum studies, which critiques the impact of culture and advocates using culture for particular social ends, there is a resemblance to the Victorian moralism that regarded culture as a tool to improve peoples' lives. But there are differences in the concepts of cultural value and ideas about subjectivity in the two periods. With the Victorian thinkers there was a belief in cultural authority, expertise, truth, and perfection, even if they were seen to be under threat. Thinkers influenced by Bourdieu and Berger strongly questioned these concepts. Further, as Munira Mirza, the cultural policy specialist, ventures, there are profound changes in the way the audience, indeed the human subject, is conceptualized in the two periods. As she explains, the liberal-humanist cultural discourse of the Victorian moralists was related to the expectation that the individual was able to transcend their everyday, 'particular' culture, in order to appreciate a 'universal' culture. Today, critiques of this notion of transcendence and universality dominate and have purchase. Cultural value is no longer regarded unequivocally as durable and transcendent, but relative to each society or community that produces it.[19]

The approach promulgated by Bourdieu and Berger was rapidly applied to the analysis of museums in an inflexible fashion. It became conventional wisdom in academic circles and in museum studies to argue that museums were established to reinforce the social position of the powerful, and that they continue to do so. Indeed, in the discipline of sociology, art is still mainly perceived as a means of distinction, with little attention paid to the possibility of aesthetic judgement. Scholars examine the dynamics of art production, and the common sociological understanding of the gallery or museum is that they are understood to function for the cohesion and reproduction of capitalist society. Museums are taken to contribute to civic ritual, ideals of nationhood, and the promotion of structural inequalities.[20]

This analysis of museums understood the purpose of the institution as reinforcing the power of the elites. The collections and their interpretation were seen not as representing truths about history or human culture, but as reinforcing the intellectual view and social position of the powerful. 'In Europe, the tradition of museums as institutions both reflecting and serving a cultural elite has been long established and, in many, is still maintained,'[21] argues the museum scholar and activist Moira Simpson. In a similar vein, according to the theorist Carol Duncan, the art museum is 'one of those sites in which politically organised and socially institutionalised power most avidly seeks to realise its desire to appear as beautiful, natural and legitimate'.[22] In an article in the *Museums Journal*, the professional journal for the sector in Britain, the curator Gilane Tawadros writes: 'originally a bastion of western military and imperial sovereignty, the Louvre in its contemporary role as museum, functions as a bastion of western cultural and intellectual sovereignty'.[23]

The role of the museum and galleries in sustaining power relations is, it is said, disguised by their claims that knowledge is objective. Mark O'Neill, director of policy and research at Glasgow Life, who has worked with Glasgow's museums for over twenty-five years, critiques this claim to objectivity by arguing that knowledge is culturally specific; it is related to social position and education, rather than something pure or disinterested. According to O'Neill, museums pursue a controlling agenda to secure the power of the elite. Museums, he elaborates, 'reinforce the existing power structure, not in some way peripheral to some other more central function, but because that is what they are for'.[24] For thinkers like O'Neill, the museums' mandate—to collect, preserve, interpret, and educate—is inherently an imposition of power. That is their primary objective.

The very order that the museum imposes on ideas and history pretends to be impartial, but, posits Sonya Atalay, a professor of anthropology, it is in fact an act of Western domination: 'Museums, collecting, anthropology, and archaeology were developed within, and are deeply entrenched in, a Western epistemological framework and have histories that are strongly colonial in nature.'[25] Moira Simpson is more forceful: 'To many Indigenous peoples, western-style museums are laden with associations of colonialism, cultural repression, loss of heritage, and death.'[26] Indeed, the association with colonization in general, Simpson suggests, is a good reason for repatriation, not just if the object was taken illicitly: 'The fact that material of origin was acquired legally is often used as a defence against possible repatriation. However, the debate cannot ignore the colonial ancestry of the collections or the insensitivity of the methods with which many items were acquired.'[27] In a similar vein, Catherine Bell, a law professor, contends that a refusal to return material taken during colonial times is a continuation of colonial oppression.[28]

Museums are 'colonising spaces', according to scholar Janet Marstine.[29] They 'naturalise the category of "primitive," in which non-western cultures are in arrested development and frozen in time—metaphorically dead'.[30] Marstine argues further that, 'In forming collections by appropriating—making one's own—objects from non-western cultures, museums reveal more about the value system of the coloniser than about the colonised.'[31] Museums, she writes, 'impose evolutionary hierarchies of race, ethnicity, and gender, they encode an agenda that effectively unifies white (male) citizens of imperial powers (the self) against conquered people (the other)'.[32]

These thinkers advanced a critical analysis of culture as only reinforcing the powerful and the status quo. Something should be done to change and counteract this domination, they claim. Having decided that the museum was simply a tool of control, theorists advised, in response, that they change how this tool is used.

The eminent cultural theorist Stuart Hall argued that the history of modernity in the Western canon needed to be continually reconsidered because 'museums are still deeply enmeshed in systems of power and privilege'.[33] This would be a never-ending project. The museum, suggested Hall, should constantly question its role, and continually rethink it. The museum

> has to be aware that it is a narrative, a selection, whose purpose is not just to disturb the viewer but to itself be disturbed by what it cannot be, by its necessary exclusions. It must make its own disturbance evident so that the viewer is not trapped into the universalised logic of thinking whereby because something has been there for a long period of time and is well funded, it must be 'true' and of value in some aesthetic sense. Its purpose is to destabilise its own stabilities.[34]

Here, Hall is advocating that members of the cultural profession, in continually questioning their roles, should not stop to think that they might be right about the research they conduct, or that they might understand their subject of specialism. He maintains there is little that can be considered genuinely 'true', or of 'aesthetic value': so much so that he has to put the terms between quotations marks. Rather, he suggests, museum staff should display uncertainty, and constantly question their intentions, perspective, and practice.

Museum theorist Tony Bennett argues that museums should refrain from trying to establish a singular truth, or establish any kind of narrative, because this is impossible. Nor, he states, should museums posit what they assume (incorrectly) to be universal standards of the best: these attempts would be fruitless and futile. Instead, he argues, curators and managers should show up truth claims as partial, and give different individuals and ethnic or social groups the opportunity to present their own versions of the past that they think is worth valuing.[35] Eilean Hooper-Greenhill holds a similar position, suggesting that the modernist museum of nineteenth-century construction should be 'reborn' as what she calls 'the postmuseum'. This is achieved by removing the curatorial voice and replacing it with many other voices, so one is not imposed: she wants 'the incorporation into the museum of many voices and many perspectives'.[36] With Tony Bennett, Hooper-Greenhill, and other critics, the museum as an institution that orders and narrates the past by interpreting artefacts is rendered invalid here. The old narratives and perspectives, it is argued, need to be jettisoned.

Such critics advocate changing the museum, on the grounds that the traditional institution dominates and harms people. For James Clifford,[37] museums should decentre the collection; this means removing or displacing it, and including more diverse arts, cultures, and traditions. Of course, museums have always displayed diverse arts and cultures. What Clifford appears to mean is that the curators should stop curating the collections; that they should rather leave this task to the particular cultures that are considered to have rightful ownership—ownership in an intellectual and moral sense—of the objects. Indeed, Clifford is ambivalent about collections altogether, proposing instead that museums should operate as a 'contact zone' and be orientated towards cultivating and sustaining relationships with communities and becoming 'places for dialogue'. Clifford argues that this shifts the location of authority away from the traditional sources, and in so doing, changes the museum for the better. It certainly *does* shift the institution away from being based on collections, or attempting to pursue the truth of different human cultures, replacing this role with a more nebulous social orientation.

DEFENDING THE MUSEUM AGAINST THE CRITICS

Whilst these critiques of museums may seem extreme, they are not simply based on a paranoid fantasy of the role of museums past. Let us recall that the Renaissance cabinets of curiosities, discussed in Chapter 2, *were* used in attempts to influence the world, securing reputations and as displays of power. As we saw in Chapter 3, antiquity *was* used to authorize leaders, including Napoleon and Otto, the Bavarian king of the new Greece, by associating present-day regimes and peoples with great ancient cultures. And there *were* attempts to use antiquity to resurrect the spirit of ancient Greece in England. So there should be no doubt at all that antiquity most certainly was used in the service of the powerful.

And as we will know from our own experiences, exhibitions and displays are constructions that reflect concerns and sometimes prejudices of the present day, even if they do so unintentionally. And despite recent attempts to expand the social demographic of visitors to galleries and museums, they remain predominantly visited by the upper and middle classes.

But while there is something salient in the observations and arguments about the role of the museum in sustaining the social hierarchy, the theorists cited above deny everything that is positive to the museum. They present a one-sided account that such institutions are merely handmaidens of privilege or institutions for the powerful. And yet there was always more to museums than vain displays of status and empty vehicles for the interests of the elite. Even when the cabinets of curiosities belonged only to private individuals, at the heart of them lay a tremendous spirit of enquiry that had a positive public impact in the long run. When monuments were brought back from Europe and used to endorse those in authority, the objects on display lasted longer than those men who took them for this purpose. They are still in museums, where we can look upon them in a different time and context. And despite the use of such objects in the service of authority, research on them contributed to the questioning of authority, leading to breakthroughs in understanding and the development of knowledge. The knowledge from this research disrupted the dominant ideas of the day.

It is equally important to note that aspirations to use museums as a tool for social control have not always been realized. When museum leaders in Britain in the nineteenth century hoped to calm social unrest by opening museums and galleries to the masses, these institutions manifestly failed to quell political agitation, unrest, and revolution. The public are not as easily manipulated as some managers and some theorists would have us believe.

This is a point made well by James Cuno, president of the J. Paul Getty Trust, in *Museum Matters*,[38] a book that aims to restate the purpose of museums in the face of these theoretical challenges. Cuno responds specifically to the museum theorist Tony Bennett, who, following the French theorist Michel Foucault, characterizes the museum as like a prison. Bennett asserts that the museum 'aimed to inveigle the general populace into complicity with power by placing them on this side of a power which it represented to it as its own'.[39] To which Cuno replies: 'At this point, one has to ask the obvious: Is this your experience of museums?' If you walk through your local gallery, Cuno asks: 'Do you feel manipulated by a high power—in Bennett's terms, an "archactor" and "metanarrator," the ruling elites of your city, or perhaps the state itself?'[40] Cuno makes the point that whatever the museum leaders' conscious or unconscious ambitions, visitors have minds of their own; they interrogate and interpret exhibits and displays for themselves. As he pointedly and rhetorically asks, referring to a well-known critical paper by the academics Carol Duncan and Alan Wallach:

> Do you think that the nearly ten million people who visit the Louvre every year experience it as 'the site of a symbolic transaction between the visitor and the state,' where 'in exchange for the state's spiritual wealth, the individual intensifies his attachment to the state,' as Duncan and Wallach would have us believe?[41]

Cuno concludes:

> I suspect, if your experience is anything like mine, your thoughts are on those ancient and distant places, on the people who made those things and looking on them in wonder as you are doing.[42]

Unquestionably, when the public museum was originally conceived, the elite's promotion of culture was self-interested and partial. But only to a point. There was much that was valuable when it was established, then and now, which led to the building of great museum collections and contributed to the world's understanding of people's lives and beliefs in centuries past. Such collections have also led to the appreciation and understanding of the technical ability and intention of craftsmanship that continue to inspire artists, designers, and laypeople. Furthermore, whatever their motives, the directors and managers of these old museums also believed in and displayed the power of art, the beauty and brilliance of craftsmanship, and the importance of understanding complex cultures and their material artefacts. Museum leaders nurtured specialist knowledge about some of the most interesting and innovative peoples of the past, who had previously been largely forgotten, or had their lives distorted by Scripture, or were simply the object of uninformed or idle speculation. They had a clear sense of the value of their collections: that they were key to scholarship about the past, and their display would enhance understanding and appreciation of humanity's achievements. About this, they were right.

Think back to the contribution made by researchers working to decipher the Rosetta Stone, or those examining the Assyrian reliefs, and the specimens brought back by the Cook voyages. Is the knowledge gleaned from them really just one of many perspectives? Does this information simply contribute to the domination of Western interests or those of the elites? Was the purpose of the research and their display *solely* to bolster the political class, a technique of surveillance to put the workers in their place? No. It may have been fuelled by particular interests, but what it generated and created as a consequence goes well beyond those interests.

What is more, objects hold our attention and distort and redirect the narratives in which they are placed, often despite the plans held for them. They are open to reinterpretation and, no doubt, misinterpretation—what we know is never finite, finished, or final. There is always more to know and ask these treasures about the history of which they have been a part. Our questions often change. And objects can only tell us so much: they still have to be interpreted in relation to other sources, and our thoughts and questions. That is why museums will continue to be relevant for generations to come.

We need to get the right balance on the relationship between culture and power. That Britain was an imperial state enabled it to collect many of its most important antiquities, but this was a consequence of imperialism. The British Museum did not drive imperialism; it benefited from it. The British Museum was not an explicitly political project, but it reflected the times in which it operated. Even with the Louvre, which was more consciously used in the service of Revolution and Empire, the museum did not make either of these events happen.

There is a significant limitation to this body of work that critiques the museum. It obscures the social forces and dynamics underpinning imperialism and colonization and it ignores the powerful forces of economics and national interests. It is also noteworthy that concerns about the role of museums in such social practices emerged as the social practices themselves were ending (with, for example, decolonization) and being supplanted. In sum, such a one-sided account can de-historicize the museum, by seeing it as only one thing—an agent of the elite—when it was never only that.

This critical body of work has, however, been highly influential, both in terms of ideas about the role of the museum and the practice that has developed inside it. The philosopher Hilde Hinde suggests that the museum is in transition, due to the embrace of pluralism in particular. This development, she ventures, has led the institution to become more responsive to public needs, as well as moving away from the presentation of the real thing—the object—and replacing it with of the production of experience. But this is a process that has left museums unmoored: 'Like most contemporary institutions, museums have descended from the heaven of authoritative certainty to inhabit the flatlands of doubt.'[43]

Andreas Huyssen suggests that museums are more commercial spaces now, like department stores.[44] Patty Gerstenblith's analysis holds that visiting a museum is now more like entering a warehouse with catering.[45] And the sociologist Nick Prior notes that museums have changed since the 1960s, having reacted to the critique that they are institutions of a dominant ideology. According to Prior, however, the new changes are not a serious disjuncture; rather, they are a continuation of the contradictions and fashions that have always influenced and been influenced by cultural institutions. Prior qualifies that these contradictions in purpose may be more pronounced in the contemporary period, and notes that the museum is a 'radically syncretic institution'[46] influenced, like all modern institutions, by the feature of institutional self-consciousness.

In my view, the shift has been more profound than this. As a consequence of the historical events and intellectual theories that informed the development of the museum—the pursuit of knowledge, culture, and science—the work of museums has today come to be viewed, not as universal or objective, but as a damaging reflection of the prejudices of European cultures. At the very least, the ascendancy of this approach has impacted on the museum, which is consequently less sure of its purpose. This threatens the maintenance and the future development and dissemination of knowledge. While much analysis of repatriation focuses on the claims made from community groups, I believe that in order to understand the rise of, and the reason for, such claims, we also have to look at the status of the museum today—how it is broadly viewed.

Museums are no longer considered the enlightened keepers of artefacts; indeed it is assumed that they use artefacts to reinforce their own social position, to force their biased interpretation onto others, and to harm different cultures. They are enveloped by the prejudice that they just want to hang on to stuff that does not belong to them, and for no good reason. The central argument of this book is that the negative cloud surrounding museum institutions is as damaging to their work as are the specific claims for the return of ancient treasures. The negativity around museums today invites repatriation claims, and undermines the good reasons for museums to hold artefacts.

POLITICIZING CULTURE

As theorists questioned the possibility of a disinterested pursuit of knowledge, and argued that, instead, cultural sites were a place of domination working in the interests of elites, museums and other cultural sites came to be identified as a site of political activism. Scholars and practitioners argued that museums could never be free from the agenda of state power; therefore they should be deliberately employed towards social good. This was a body of work that examined all culture, including literature and the arts, and advocated that it be used consciously to tackle contemporary political problems. Reformation rather than revolution was seen as the solution. Culture could be a site of liberation, if used strategically.

The work of Tony Bennett illustrates this development. For Bennett, there is, and can be, no such thing as a 'disinterested' museum; it is by definition a tool of citizenship and behaviour management. Bennett follows this train of thought to argue that the museum—and culture in general—could be more explicitly and deliberately employed.[47] In a similar vein, Janet Marstine posits that the 'post-museum'—by which she means the museum that has divested its authority—'seeks to share power with the communities it serves, including source communities'. Marstine continues: 'Most importantly, the post-museum is a site from which to redress social inequalities.'[48]

Museums have become a place for political activism, a site to deal with problems within society. This approach, which focused attention on the cultural sphere, is reinforced by ideas about the 'politics of recognition', which gained considerable ground in Europe and North America in the 1980s and 1990s. According to these theories, cultural and state institutions recognize particular identities, and the recognition of identity is as important as wealth distribution. For instance, the political theorist Nancy Fraser argues that institutions need positively to affirm people's identity by 'upwardly revaluing disrespected identities and the cultural products of maligned groups'.[49]

Mainstream society, it is said, excludes marginalized groups by not telling their stories or presenting negative images of who they are and what they are capable of. Instead of working against these groups, museums could play an active role in recognizing and affirming their identity, making them feel better about their lives. The political philosopher Iris Marion Young argued that 'groups cannot be socially equal unless their specific experience, culture and social contributions are publicly affirmed and recognized'.[50] Cultural institutions, it came to be thought, could engage and reinforce people's identity by showing ethnic groups' work and cultural habits in a good light. Museums and similar organizations came to be seen as central to telling people who they are.

It is a way of thinking that has been taken on board in some museums.[51] At a conference held by the Smithsonian Museum in April 2012, Clement Price, a professor at Rutgers University, argued that natural history museums have the potential to inform social change, because such museums could counter the 'master narrative' and provide a space for 'remembering' the experiences of forgotten or marginalized peoples.[52] A policy document on the future of museums, published by the UK Museums Association, titled *Museums Change Lives*, outlines how 'they contribute to strong and resilient communities' and 'create a fair and just society';[53] museums even 'improve mental and physical health', help 'marginalised sections of the community gain a sense of citizenship', and 'increase employability'.[54]

But there are limitations with an approach that identifies museums as a solution to social problems. Even Nancy Fraser, an advocate of the politics of recognition, draws attention to the way that 'cultural domination supplants exploitation as the fundamental injustice. And cultural recognition displaces socioeconomic redistribution as the remedy for injustice and the goal of political struggle.'[55] To put it another way: the concern for addressing inequality and identity through a 'soft' approach with the use of culture, and with cultural institutions, could be a convenient, if not a deliberate, strategy to divert attention from the structural causes of today's social problems and the solutions that are needed to solve them. As the philosopher Kwame Anthony Appiah comments, in a thoughtful piece about identity, culture, and what artefacts would be appropriate for the people of Mali: 'The problem for Mali is not that it doesn't have enough Malian art. The problem is that it doesn't have enough money.'[56]

Lois Silverman, author of *The Social Work of Museums*, argues that 'artefacts possess an undeniable power to elicit responses from people'. This sounds reasonable enough. But what sort of responses does she mean? Silverman continues: 'Objects serve as symbols of ourselves, our relationships, and our lives.' Thus, they can be used 'as therapeutic tools, and pathways to self-exploration and growth'.[57]

There is no question that many people gain solace and respite from museums, that they experience all sorts of feelings when looking at objects. After all, as visitors to a museum we bring ourselves to an encounter with an artefact; and it is therefore likely that what we see will provoke reflection about our immediate lives. Depending on our mood, we have a difference experience. But it is not all about us. Objects are not only there as tools and pathways to personal growth. More often than not, encounters with artefacts take us *away* from the everyday, helping us to forget, if only for a short while, about the things we have to do and the places we need to be, prodding us to think about other times and places far beyond our own lives. Sometimes these encounters can make us feel better; sometimes they can make us feel worse. The impact of an artefact is not predictable or measurable; and this means that it is difficult to use artefacts in the service of policy and politics, even if we wanted to.

The identification of the political role of culture coincided with, and reflected, growing disillusionment with the conventional framework of the politics of Left and Right. Intellectual debate came to concern itself less with a global politics of clashing empires than with a more personal politics and the politics of identity. And this is why it was so readily embraced: the interest in cultural politics replaced declining and failed traditional political concerns. Even Stuart Hall, the pioneer of cultural studies, admitted that 'The Centre for Cultural Studies was the locus to which we *retreated* when that conversation in the open world could no longer be continued: it was politics by other means.'[58]

It is for this reason that literary theorist Terry Eagleton argues that the turn to culture is utopian. The attempt to use culture to resolve fundamental structural contradictions will inevitably fail.[59] Taking a similar stance, the historian Steven Conn warns:

museum studies critics demand political penance from museums for the sins of colonialism and capitalism and redress for the complaints that arise out of identity politics. Too left-wing for some, not nearly left-wing enough for others, but at the end of the day, the real facts of politics remain unaltered.[60]

Using culture for political ends tends to get problems and solutions the wrong way round. Yes, culture can be political; it expresses ideas in which it is situated, but usually this is as a consequence of the outcome of a wider climate. Culture is mostly subordinate to politics. And while culture may be a product of particular circumstances, occasionally dubious ones, it can become detached from it. Great art may have been created to glorify authoritarian leaders, but it remains great art. The opposite is also true: work may have been designed for good, but it often ends up as agitprop. Political art of this sort rarely lasts.

The central problem with the way culture has been put to work in the service of politics is that it has come at a time that eschews even the consideration of genuine social and material change. Books and exhibitions are critiqued, while structural inequalities remain entrenched and unchallenged. By focusing on culture as an arena that requires change and struggle, activists have vanished into a dead end, where battles are fought primarily about language, image, and representation. This burdens cultural institutions with responsibilities to improve lives when they have little power to do so in the way that is required.

The ideas of arts practitioners and academics such as Stuart Hall and Tony Bennett, which called for greater attention to culture as a factor in political life—both as a source of oppression and of liberation—have helped to transform the museum. As a consequence, the academic Stephen Weil has described the museum as having moved 'from being about something to being for somebody'.[61] The social onus on museums is sometimes counterposed to its role in caring for collections. In this vein, Professor Richard Sandell, head of museum studies at Leicester

University, writes disapprovingly: 'Many museums continue to view the processes of collection, preservation and display, not as functions through which the organisation creates social value, but as outcomes in their own right.'[62] The centrality of the collection, preservation, and display is seen as a problem by Sandell, who believes that 'Museums and galleries of all kinds have both the potential to contribute towards the combating of social inequality and a responsibility to do so.'[63] At the Museum Association conference in 2013, Mark Taylor, the director of the Museums Association in the UK, rehearsed what is heard often in the sector—'Museums of the future will be spaces for debate and catalysts for social change'—and added that the way to do this was to get them to give up their voice: 'The key thing is getting museums to give up power, to say, "It's not my view that counts—what's your view?"'[64]

These changing ideas with regard to the role of the museum—what and who it is for—are one of the reasons why the institution is on less firm ground today. Effectively, its historical, conceptual foundation has been destabilized, and this is an important factor in why museums have become such sites of controversy and why the claims for repatriation have both escalated and resonated. In this context, claims for repatriation have purchase, and are amplified, even encouraged, within the museum itself.

MUSEUM WARS

These broader changes and their impact are evident in contemporary museum practice. They were first firmly evident in the 'Museum Wars' of the late 1990s, which took place in North America. Fifty years after the end of the Second World War, in 1994, the Smithsonian National Air and Space Museum in Washington DC planned an exhibition that would tell the story of the *Enola Gay* in the surrender of the Japanese. The *Enola Gay* is a compact aircraft with a wingspan of 141 feet and just enough

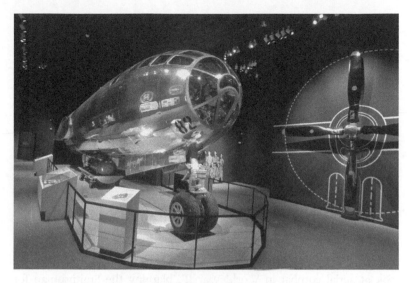

Figure 10. *Enola Gay* on display *c*.1995.
© Smithsonian National Air and Space Museum.

space for twelve men. It is also a deadly machine: the B-29 bomber that was used to drop the atomic bomb—code-named 'Little Boy'—that would destroy Hiroshima on 6 August 1945.

The intention of the show, titled *The Crossroads: The End of World War II, the Atomic Bomb and the Cold War*, was to display the plane, to examine the creation of the bomb, and to reflect on the new era it introduced. Crucially, it would raise questions about its use. The *Enola Gay* was to be the centrepiece of a display that would discuss and debate the role of the atomic bomb in international affairs (see Figure 10). Little did those planning the exhibition anticipate just how explosive these intentions would turn out to be.

As plans developed in early 1993, the museum discussed them with various constituencies who might have a stake in the show. In so doing, a dispute was quickly set alight. Many of those consulted were worried that this was to be a revisionist history, which would be too sympathetic towards the Japanese and too condemnatory of what they understood as a necessary act. The military lobbying group, the Air Force Association (AFA), liaised with the museum, increasingly tersely, over the presentation of the show. The AFA's executive director, Monroe E. Hatch Jr, wrote to Martin Harwit, the museum director, complaining that the plan 'treats Japan and the United States . . . as if their participation in the war were morally equivalent. If anything, incredibly, it gives the benefit of opinion to Japan, which was the aggressor.'[65]

The Smithsonian was quickly accused of being 'anti-American' and of having 'highjacked history'. The American Legion, academics, journalists, and politicians became involved. The AFA mobilized Congress and wrote to President Bill Clinton, who aligned himself with these critics. The *Wall Street Journal* described the planned exhibition as a 'sneering look at aerial combat in World War II', blaming the Smithsonian for employing 'revisionist social scientists' who had 'overrun many university programs' to work as their curators.[66]

The dropping of the atomic bomb had always inspired debate, and curators anticipated disquiet—but they did not expect the ferocity of the reaction. After many discussions and meetings, commentary and editorials, the museum was forced to abandon the exhibit. In January 1995, somewhat bruised, they announced that the exhibition was to be replaced by a different, scaled-back display, with minimal historical context. The director, Martin Harwit, resigned in May.

There was a wider backdrop to these controversies. The late 1980s brought the eruption of what has become known as the 'culture wars': heated arguments between the advocates of values considered traditional or conservative and those advocating more liberal and progressive values, which has dominated politics from this time onwards. Ideological debates between opposing camps cut across the realms of politics and economics. Political debate moved away from being defined by social class and political affiliation, towards a focus on cultural or moral questions.

Previously moral, or private, issues, or those which were not the focus of narrow party politics, now became major questions for debate, such as arguments over race, identity, religion, and sexuality.[67]

How the past is interpreted has long inflamed passions. Museums display and present a version of various histories: therefore, what they show and how they show it will inevitably be the focus of disagreement. A museum display crystallizes and presents a point of view about the past, and in this case a reasonably recent one, by putting it on display. But the *Enola Gay* controversy took debates in museums into new arenas, pitched at a different level. Up until this point, reporting on what happened in museums was confined to the arts pages; the exhibitions were something for specialists to mull over, audiences to consider, and academics to discuss, but they were not the focus of major and national discussion. This event, by contrast, brought screaming headlines in major newspapers, the involvement of politicians, and ended with the resignation of a director.

From the late 1980s onwards, museum displays have been the focus of intense and high-profile controversies about the construction of history, and the representation of past events and people—although none had the intensity that surrounded the exhibit of the *Enola Gay*. In Canada, a row and boycott of *The Spirit Sings* at the Glenbow Museum in Calgary (1988) marked a turning point in the exhibition of indigenous peoples and artefacts. The first title for the show—*Forget Not My World: Exploring the Canadian Native Heritage*—was felt to relegate First Nation people to the past. Meanwhile, the corporate sponsor, Shell Oil, was simultaneously drilling on land that was the subject of disputes over land rights with the Lubicon Lake Cree Indian Nation. Two years later, in 1990, *Into the Heart of Africa* at the Royal Ontario Museum in Toronto drew attention to Canadian complicity in the colonization of Africa. It resulted in charges of racism and calls for a boycott.

The *Science in American Life* exhibition at the Smithsonian in Washington in 1994 set out to examine critically the relationship between science, technology, and culture. It aimed to stimulate questions about the purity of science and its ambiguous impact on society. Arguments exploded when the show was condemned as revisionist for questioning the idea of pure science. In a letter to the Smithsonian, Burton Richter, president of the Council of the American Physical Society, criticized the show as 'a portrayal of science that trivializes its accomplishments and exaggerates any negative consequences'.[68]

It didn't stop there, and the focus of the disputes was not confined to the representation of science or indigenous peoples. *Sensation: Young British Artists from the Saatchi Collection*, which was shown in 1999 at the Brooklyn Museum of Art, made headlines with the painting *The Holy Virgin Mary*. This painting, by Chris Ofili, depicted Mary as a black woman with a clump of elephant dung as one of her breasts. One group of complainants viewed the painting as blasphemous and perverted; another saw it as reflecting Ofili's ethnic and Catholic background; others saw it as essential freedom of expression. Street demonstrations ensued. The mayor became involved, and the media published a lot of copy.

The shift of the museum from temple of culture to forum for debate is of interest to our discussion. Today, when certain high-profile exhibitions are launched, there are wide-ranging debates that go beyond the arts features of newspapers and radio programmes, and into the news commentary. Steven Dubin, a scholar who has documented many of these controversies, notes: 'Virtually sacred spaces in the past, museums have become hotly contested battlegrounds.'[69] Indeed, this pattern is now so common that institutions anticipate reactions in their decisions about what and what not to show. Tate Britain cancelled plans to display John Latham's work *God Is Great* as part of the 2005 *British Art Displays* exhibition before it went ahead. *God Is Great* consists of a large sheet of glass and copies of the Bible, the Quran, and the Talmud that have been cut apart. Managers of the gallery were worried that it could upset

Muslims in the wake of London's 7 July bombings, even though there had been no complaints or protests.

The development of museums into such controversial spaces is not-able. The questions raised in these debates have a lot in common with those raised by repatriation claims: Who owns culture? Who decides what is put on display? What is the role of cultural institutions? These examples may not be claims for return, but they are demands that are made over what is shown and who writes the narrative of the past. And they indicate that it is not just excluded minorities, but conservatives, members of the air force, Republicans as well as Democrats, left-wingers and right-wingers, who can become involved in debating these concerns in dis-agreements over history, artefacts, and how they are represented.

While the 'Museum Wars' are recent, these arguments were prefigured by older controversies. One of the first big arguments over an exhibition surrounded *Harlem on My Mind: The Cultural Capital of Black America, 1900 to 1968*, held at the Metropolitan Museum in 1969. The exhibition at the Met set out to explore the cultural history of the black community in New York. In August 1968, Thomas P. F. Hoving, director of the Metro-politan Museum, explained:

> To me Harlem on My Mind is a discussion. It is a confrontation. It is education. It is a dialogue. And today we better have these things. Today there is a growing gap between people, and particularly between black people and white people. And this despite the efforts to do otherwise. There is little communication.[70]

The exhibition intended to challenge racial and aesthetic hierarchies. It was the first attempt to recognize black America in a museum and art gallery, and clearly trying to be critical and socially relevant. But there were two key problems with this exhibition. The first was the refusal to involve Harlem residents and artists in an exhibition that was ostensibly about them, and had been set up as a provocation about their lives and social position. Secondly, it treated black people as a culture to be understood—an ethnographic study—rather than as active agents and artists in their own right. As Bridget Cooks explains in *Exhibiting Blackness*: *African Americans and the American Art Museum*:

> Near the end of the Civil Rights Movement and the beginning of the Black Power Movement, Black culture emerged in the Metropolitan not as creative producer but as ethnographic study. The decisions to display African American people through oversized photo-murals and to dismiss their input and artwork as unworthy of being in the museum made Harlem on My Mind a site for racial politics and debates about artistic quality and art versus culture in the United States.[71]

The show consisted of multimedia work, paintings and etchings, photographs, and sound. Art critics were annoyed at the lack of fine art, and black artists felt ignored because there was no painting in the show. Various groups took offence at how they were depicted: Irish and Puerto Ricans, as well as some members of the Jewish community.

There was a profound shift in this period in the perception of identity and definitions of culture. The ideas about the particularities of culture, first advanced as far back as the Romantic thinkers, came to be seen by many as central to who we are. It is this, as much as the nationalism fingered by repatriation sceptics, that is fuelling claims on the basis of identity. Where previous eras assumed the individual was able to transcend difference, today he is presumed to be defined by it.[72] Ideas of high art, seen to be the product of an elite, were replaced by the more anthropological definition of culture, and museums and galleries were identified as places to display and recognize culture and identities. As we will see in our discussion of Identity Museums in Chapter 7, by the late 1990s this outlook had led to the establishment of museums for particular ethnic groups with special rights for those communities.

QUESTIONING FROM WITHIN

The social anthropologist Sharon Macdonald has tackled the political and contested nature of recent exhibitions. According to her thesis, the battles are predominantly the consequence of challenges brought by social movements that make demands regarding the representation of 'their culture'.[73] The sociologist Jan Marontate reaches similar conclusions: 'Tensions also arise in relations between museums and their "subjects" about ethics and ownership of cultural information or things.'[74] Marontate posits that museum professionals resist these challenges from their subjects because they still hold on to ideas of truth and objectivity:

> Museum professionals, many of them trained historians, often resist the notion that knowledge is socially constructed... This has concrete implications for museum practices. Demands for parity of representation or affirmative action for under-represented cultural groups is a common source of friction.[75]

For Marontate, controversies and claims over collections are created when audiences challenge the representation or ownership of their culture. Curators and managers withstand these challenges as they still feel their way of understanding the world holds firm: that the world has an objective reality discoverable by rational investigation, and that it retains its legitimacy.

But this is to miss an important dynamic. Yes, there have been social changes that have contributed to these demands, and many of these demands have been resisted by museum professionals; but the response of the profession is more divided than most theorists appreciate. There has in fact been a sustained attack levelled at the museum institution from *within*. Museums have become embattled and defensive as a consequence. Indeed, it would appear that these ideas have very much been taken on board. If we are to understand the rise in controversies in the museum and their increased significance, this dynamic needs to be appreciated.

By the time Martin Harwit became director of the Smithsonian National Air and Space Museum and began planning the *Enola Gay* exhibition, a number of museums at the Smithsonian Institution had already shifted in the direction of involving communities, rather than solely concentrating on the display of artefacts. Many of their curators were already convinced that museums could play a role in social change and the affirmation of identity. They had been inspired by a heightened commitment among history museums around the nation to offer alternative readings of American history to give a voice to groups that had been silenced, or forgotten by traditional museum exhibitions. As a consequence, Smithsonian museums had already begun to arrange provocative exhibits. Take, for example, an exhibition at the National Museum of American Art, *The West as America: Reinterpreting Images of the Frontier, 1820–1920* (15 March 1991–28 July 1991), which called into question the heroic myth of the American frontier and raised questions about the relationship between art and politics. Similar aims were at play in the exhibition *A More Perfect Union*, at the National Museum of American History (1 October 1987–11 January 2004), which dealt with the internment of Americans of Japanese ancestry during the Second World War.

Some of the loudest voices calling for changes in museums and their role have been museum professionals. This applies equally to the question of repatriation. There has been an intense internal debate within museum institutions about the role of the institution, and prominent advocates of repatriation are themselves from the museum world—this is often overlooked in analysing the debate over who owns culture.

At a two-day international conference on repatriation at Manchester University in 2010, papers were presented by academics and museum managers arguing, in various ways, the case for the restitution of artefacts and art to their countries of origin. Not one paper questioned repatriation; rather, the problems raised were in relation to the demands placed on those asking for return. Tristram Besterman, the former director of Manchester Museum and vocal campaigner for repatriation, advocated a system whereby the onus placed on proof of ownership and reason for return is shifted away from the claimants having to justify 'why?' to the museum having to justify 'why not?' Maurice Davies, deputy director of the Museums Association, agreed:

> Regarding decision making, perhaps the problem with restitution is that the museum is setting the criteria on its own values and prejudices? Instead of the museum assessing the fate of the object, could they look instead at the consequences of its actual return or retention?[76]

A poll conducted by the *Museums Journal* in 2012 asked its readers: 'Should the Parthenon Marbles be returned?' Seventy-three per cent answered in the affirmative.[77]

In early 2014, the Denver Museum of Nature and Science repatriated thirty memorial totem poles to the National Museums of Kenya. This act was initiated and funded by the Colorado institution itself. The material was acquired legally and legitimately; it had been received as a donation from two collectors—the actor Gene Hackman and the film producer Art Linson. But the staff at the museum were no longer comfortable holding these objects. One of the curators became 'convinced by the research that showed that the vigango [i.e. the totem poles] are communally owned property, and without the consent of the entire community they are by definition stolen'.[78]

The curator spent five years calling and sending letters to the Kenyan government, stating the museum's desire to return the objects. Chip Colwell-Chanthaphonh, the museum's curator of anthropology, explained: 'The process is often complicated, expensive and never straightforward ... But just because a museum is not legally required to return cultural property does not mean it lacks an ethical obligation to do so.'[79] He further stated that 'Collections should not come at the price of a source community's dignity and well-being.'[80] When the Kenyan government finally responded and gave its consent, the Denver Museum of Nature and Science paid the bill of over $10,000 to send the artefacts back.

A STOLEN WORLD

The Museum of World Culture in Gothenburg, Sweden, once held examples of the striking textiles known as the Paracas Collection. Discovered on the Paracas peninsula in Peru at the beginning of the twentieth century, they are over 2,000 years old. The people who gathered the wool, dyed, and stitched the cloth lived in the Ica Region of Peru. They were the first complex society to inhabit the south of Peru, in a period that is divided into two phases: the early Cavernas phase (*c.*400–100 BC) and the more developed phase of the Necropolis (*c.*100 BC–AD 300). They are a people who paved the way for later societies, including the Inca.

The textiles that used to be in the Museum of World Culture are thought to have been made in the second phase—that of the Necropolis—which has a distinctive style of its own. Made from cotton and llama wool, they are covered in strong patterns in bright colours. Human and animal figures—birds, serpents, and two-headed birds—are embroidered in red, orange, blue, and black, as are local plants and species. The people wear tall and elaborate headpieces and sport anklets around their legs. Other figures are part human and part animal. One person has a head of snake, another has whiskers. Stranger still, one man has the head of a killer whale and the fins of a shark. Elsewhere, long arms stretch out from the body of fish.

A number of the motifs woven on the textiles are understandable today. The serpent—a frequently used image—wriggling out of the human bodies is probably 'Amarau', believed to be able to foresee natural disasters and impending political events. One of the most commanding images is of a trophy head, which was also a common theme, and it is thought to have been associated with victory in war: (real) enemy heads were taken in (real) battle. But the meaning of many other motifs are lost in time.

What is fascinating is that the textiles were for the dead. It was the tradition of the Andean civilization to clothe their people upon their death with ponchos, cloaks, and hats that they would take with them to the afterlife. The materials were found on skeletons and are called mummy bundles. Large groups of the shrouded dead were discovered housed and hidden away in complexes in caves, sitting, wrapped up in the materials and feathered headdresses. It is these conditions—dry, dark, protected from the outside elements in the tombs—that ensured their survival.

It would have taken a great deal of time to construct a funerary bundle. The largest are 5 feet tall, comprising around 400 textiles which could have taken about 10,000 hours to construct, requiring the cooperation and hard work of many hands. The hard work required applies not only to the sewing, but also to the gathering of the material and the dyeing of it, before the hands turned to spinning, weaving, and needlework. It is probable then, that making the burial clothes would have been an important communal act, given the amount of time and energy required from so many.

The caves were first opened with the arrival of the Spanish conquistadors in the sixteenth century. Centuries later, excavations in the 1920s unearthed over 100 burial complexes of various sizes. One find—what came to be known as the Necropolis de Wari Kayan—housed 429 conical burials. Once discovered, the textiles were shipped all over the world. Many were smuggled out of Peru during the 1930s, a time of political instability. The striking colours and patterns attracted attention and the textiles ended up in museums and galleries, including the Museum of Fine Arts in Boston, the Brooklyn Museum of Art, the American Museum of Natural History, and the British Museum. The largest collection is in the Museo Nacional de Antropología, Arqueología e Historía in Lima, Peru, which has a large number of unopened funerary bundles. They are valued, not only because they are gorgeous and dramatic, but because they are from a period and a culture about which we know little, a time and place about which we hold no written records and few artefacts. These textiles therefore take on a greater importance as a small piece of evidence about these people.

About 100 textiles were donated to the Ethnographic Department of Gothenburg Museum, after being illegally exported (to use the term on the museum's own website) to Sweden between 1931 and 1933 by Sven Karell, Swedish consul in Peru. The materials he secretly brought over in his suitcase are thought to have come from the Necropolis de Wari Kayan complex. Four of the textiles have been radiocarbon-tested. The earliest dates from 400 to 200 BC—making it almost 2,300 years old.[81]

The Museum of World Culture in Gothenburg opened in 2004. The collection for the new museum was taken from that of an ethnographic museum that had closed in 2000. Like many institutions, its precursor was founded in the nineteenth century, in 1861, inspired by the museum building in the rest of Europe. The aim was that the new Museum of World Culture would distance itself from the old 'colonial style' of doing museum work. In contrast, it described its mission as follows:

> In dialogue with the surrounding world and through emotional and intellectual experiences the Museum of World Culture aims to be a meeting place that will make people feel at home across borders, build trust and take responsibility together for a shared global future, in a world in constant change.

In line with the new way of doing things, the exhibitions are designed to allow multiple voices, and to address contemporary issues. One exhibition dealt with AIDS, and another–*African Voices*–aimed to critique stereotypical images of Africa from a postcolonial perspective. In 2008, the museum held an exhibition of the Paracas textiles that departed from the traditional way of presenting the material. It was this exhibition that stimulated a repatriation request.

The exhibition was called *The Paracas Collection: A Stolen World* and ran from September 2008 to 2009. The title itself suggests that the materials on display and in the collection were stolen. And whilst this is true, it is unusual to advertise the fact. Not only does the promotional material of the show state that textiles were stolen, but so, it says, was a whole world. The catalogue (see Figure 11) opened with the following statement:

> Gothenburg has taken pride for 75 years in a material known for coming from tomb raiding. The hunting for objects we are referring to, seen in the past as an honourable adventure, now constitutes a problematical and uneasy reality...A world that belongs elsewhere.[82]

'A world that belongs elsewhere'; 'Stolen'; 'A Stolen World'; 'a problematical and uneasy reality'–the exhibition's title and text explicitly described the material as looted from tombs, and the catalogue discussed the problem of looting more broadly, showing pictures of grave robbers holding human skulls. It would be difficult not to draw the conclusion that the textiles should not be in Sweden, but in Peru.

The show opened at the end of September 2008. By December 2009, a formal request for repatriation had arrived from the foreign ministry of Peru, sent by the ambassador, Gilbert Chauny, which noted: 'The Peruvian Government recognises the transparency and veracity with which the World Culture Museum has presented the above-mentioned exhibition.' The letter continued: 'Particularly–as it is highlighted in the introduction of the exhibition's catalogue–because "Gothenburg has

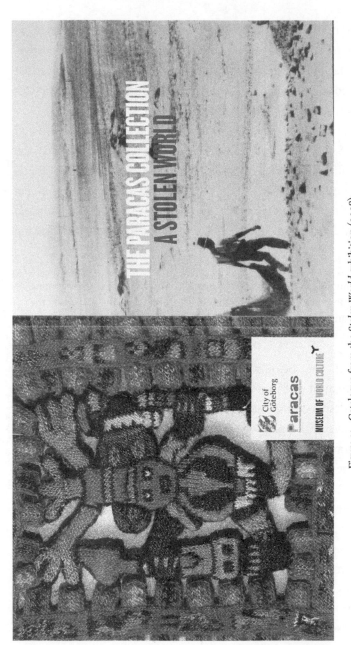

Figure 11. Catalogue from the *Stolen World* exhibition (2008). With thanks to © Richard J. Williams.

taken pride for 75 years in a material known for coming from tomb raiding."' The letter continued:

> Thus, by instructions of the Peruvian Government, this Embassy kindly requests to the Honourable Kingdom of Sweden the exercise of its good offices before the responsible Swedish authorities–specially [*sic*] those of the City of Gothenburg–, in order to return to Peru all the textiles, and other artefacts associated with the Paracas civilisation, which are currently kept by the city of Gothenburg and the World Culture Museum.[83]

The letter used the text of the exhibition as the evidence for the Peruvian government's claim for return, pointing out: 'The catalogue confirms that the textiles were looted from the Paracas cemetery known as "Necropolis de Wari Kayan."'

Before the exhibition, there had been no request for repatriation. Curators and experts from Peru worked with curators and experts in Sweden on the textiles. But once the exhibition opened, and was presented as 'stolen' from its rightful home and as belonging elsewhere, the Peruvian government became involved. National governments have additional and separate, political interests beyond caring for ancient material; and it could be argued that the Peruvian government could not ignore the presentation of the show and what it implied. It is certainly fair to say that in presenting this material as looted and problematic, the museum invited the claim for repatriation.

The repatriation request was successful. An ancient shroud and four other textiles were returned in 2014. Another eighty-five textiles are expected to be returned by 2021. I have no doubt that the textiles sent to Peru will be loved, cared for, and will yield interesting information to the world. My observation here is that, when museum curators promote the idea that their institutions house looted artefacts and that those artefacts 'belong' elsewhere, it should be of little surprise that requests are made for the return of that material.

6

Who Owns Culture?

 ⤜ ⦁ ⟨⦁⟩ ⦁ ⟨⦁⟩ ⦁ ⟩⦁⟨

Towards the end of 2012 Remzi Kazmaz, a lawyer from Istanbul, told the international media that thirty lawyers were acting on behalf of the Turkish Ministry of Culture and the town of Bodrum to request the return of ancient sculptures that once adorned the Mausoleum at Halicarnassus, now in the British Museum. Senior officials in Turkey suggested that they would take their case to the European Court of Human Rights—a first for such campaigns:

> We thank the British authorities and the British Museum for accommodating and preserving our historical and cultural heritage for the last years. However, the time has come for these assets to be returned to their place of origin . . . Preparations for formal requests are taking place now.[1]

The Mausoleum at Halicarnassus is a tomb built between 353 and 350 BC for Mausolus and his wife and sister Artemisia, who ruled as the overlords of Ionia in the ancient coastal region of Anatolia, in what is now southwest Turkey. Under Persian rule, prior to its conquest by Alexander the Great, Halicarnassus (which today is Bodrum) became a dynamic and beautiful city state.

The tomb was never finished, but it was much admired, designed by the greatest Greek architects of the time—Pythius of Priene and Satyros. It was massive, with a podium that the Roman writer Pliny the Elder records as 140 feet high, and a pyramid roof, crowned by a four-horsed chariot, the four sides made up of sculptural reliefs. The Greek poet Antipater of Sidon identified it as one of the Seven Wonders of the Ancient World.

The tomb became so renowned that Mausolus' name acquired a generic use in Latin: *mausōlēum*. But like many ancient works, over time it fell into disrepair and was abandoned. The stones were severely damaged by an earthquake in around the twelfth century. In the fifteenth century, the Western Christian military order the Knights of St John invaded the region. They used remaining blocks of green volcanic stone—which had made up the core of the mausoleum—marble sculptures, and reliefs to fortify their castle at Bodrum. Centuries later, the fortifications and random pieces of sculpture were all that was left. The once magnificent monument turned into a dilapidated ruin, covered in dust and earth.

The Mausoleum was rediscovered in the nineteenth century by Europeans who wanted to find the old world. Having read ancient accounts they started to look for what remained. The sculptures and fragments from the Mausoleum in the British Museum's collection were acquired in the mid-nineteenth century as a result of this search, after two British initiatives. They were all acquired with firmans that granted permission for the excavation of the site and removal of the material from the site and from Bodrum Castle to the British Museum. In 1846 slabs from the Amazonomachy frieze (which portrays the mythical battle between the ancient Greeks and the Amazons—a nation of female warriors) were recovered from Bodrum Castle by the British ambassador to the Ottoman Sublime Porte, Stratford Canning, and presented to the British Museum. The second lot of material that would end up in the museum came as a result of Charles Newton's excavations.

Charles Newton was initially employed by the British Museum as a trainee in the Department of Antiquities. After over a decade's work, he took a role in the Foreign Service as vice consul at Mytilene on the island of Lesbos. He intended to pursue archaeological interests whilst there, a plan approved and given some financial backing by the museum. Newton, who later became the museum's Keeper of Greek and Roman Antiquities, helped to locate the Mausoleum and directed the excavation—assisted by Robert Murdoch Smith, who went on to be director of the Edinburgh Museum of Science and Art, now the National Museum of Scotland.

They found the site after some difficulty. Before the digging could start they had to bargain with the locals for every plot, at prices Newton thought were inflated. But his determination was rewarded with a great discovery. His own accounts describe how the hindquarters of one of the horses was finally unearthed, together with the reaction of the people of Bodrum, who were apparently amazed by the sight:

> After being duly hauled out, he was placed on a sledge and dragged to the shore by 80 Turkish workmen. On the walls and house-tops as we went along sat the veiled ladies of Bodrum. They had never seen anything so big before, and the sight overcame the reserve imposed upon them by Turkish etiquette. The ladies of Troy gazing at the wooden horse as he entered the breach, could not have been more astonished.[2]

Sections of the Amazonomachy frieze, a few figures, statues, and reliefs, as well as fragments of the colossal marble four-horse chariot that once crowned the pyramid roof, now stand in Room 21 in the British Museum. But maybe not for much longer. One hundred and fifty years after the artefacts arrived in London, officials in Turkey have asked for them back. And that's not all.

A few months after the grand opening of the Department of Islamic Arts in the Louvre, newspaper headlines in Turkey's *Radikal* newspaper alleged that the Iznik tile panels on display in the new galleries were stolen goods, and reported that Turkey would be launching proceedings to ask for them back.[3] The article cited a Ministry of Culture and Tourism paper that suggests the panels could have been taken many years previously, in the nineteenth century, from Istanbul's Piyale Paşa mosque, built in 1573. The mosque was once decorated with striking tile panels. It now has bare walls.

The headlines in the press came as little surprise. Not because museum directors agreed that the tiles had been stolen—the Louvre is firm that they do not come from the Piyale Paşa mosque and that they were acquired legitimately—but because multiple requests for the return of artefacts have been made by senior officials in Turkey, with increasing passion and with some success.

That same year, the Turkish government wrote to the British Museum with a request for the Samsat Stele, a carved stone slab, dating from the first century BC. The stele is about 4 feet high and is carved with the figure of King Antiochus I Epiphanes greeting a nude Herakles-Verethragna. Born of a Persian father and a Greek Macedonian mother, Antiochus ruled what was the Kingdom of Commagene—the capital of which is Samsat, south-east Turkey—in 69–35 BC. The first recorded sight of the stele was much later, in 1882, when it was found near Samsat. It had been used as an olive press and a large hole was drilled right through the middle. This should remind us that these artefacts are not always considered museum pieces and have often been put to more immediate, practical use: they can take on a different life and meaning, used locally in a pragmatic and practical way.

A few years after it was rediscovered, the stele was bought by the archaeologist Leonard Woolley, who was digging in Carchemish with the permission of the Ottoman authorities. When the British Museum purchased it from the Carchemish Exploration Fund in 1927, the stele was being stored in Syria, which was then administered by the French, who gave permission for the sale. The shifting sands of who owns which object on whose land is, as is often the way, complicated; but the acquisition was all above board.

The Turkish government is also asking for the return of a third-century BC marble head of a child, representing Eros, in the V&A in London. It was removed from the Sidamara Sarcophagus, probably because it was portable, by archaeologist Charles Wilson, who discovered the entire sarcophagus in 1883. The sarcophagus is now in the Istanbul Archaeology Museum. The Turkish government is also claiming eighteen objects from the collection of the late Norbert Schimmel, a major collector of Mediterranean antiquities.

Had these antiquities been smuggled out of Turkey illegally, especially in recent decades, then it is possible they would be returned immediately: acts of return are common in such circumstances. For instance, in 2012 Boston's Museum of Fine Arts returned a 1,800-year-old statue, *Weary Hercules*, when they became aware that it had been stolen forty years previously. The Metropolitan Museum sent back what it discovered was an illicitly taken hoard of Lycian gold. The Dallas Museum of Art returned the Roman Orpheus Mosaic, thought to have been taken abroad by smugglers in the 1950s. And in 2011 the Serbian government gave up 1,485 coins and 379 small antiquities.

However, most of the artefacts that Turkey is claiming now were bought or excavated hundreds of years ago, and with permission. These antiquities are also well beyond the parameters of the UNESCO convention of 1970, signed by Turkey in 1983, which states that if a cultural object left the country in which it was produced before the year 1970, it is free to be bought and sold. But even where this does not apply, where it is not clear that they were removed illegally or since 1970, the requests are proving to be difficult to ignore. The request for the child's head from the Sidamara Sarcophagus has been met with a somewhat positive response from the V&A and negotiations are ongoing about a loan.[4] Berlin's Pergamon Museum returned a 3,500-year-old sphinx, one of two that were discovered by German archaeologists at the Hittite city of Boğazköy, which were sent to Berlin for restoration in 1917. One was returned in 1924. The other stayed in Germany, with the permission of the Ottoman Empire, according to museum directors (the documentation was destroyed in bombing raids on Berlin in the Second World War), and was built into an archway in the Pergamon Museum. In 2011, that old sphinx left Berlin to join the other in Turkey. Both are now on display at the Boğazköy Museum in the area of Hattushash, the ancient capital of the Hittites.

One of the reasons these requests are difficult to ignore is that Turkish museums have important artefacts to lend; thus they have bargaining power. The Turkish government has threatened to terminate loans until certain objects are returned. The Metropolitan Museum of Art in New York is organizing a major exhibition on the Seljuks, but it may have to do without loans from Turkey. When the British Museum asked to borrow thirty-five objects for a major show about the Hajj, Islam's holy pilgrimage, the museums agreed but the Turkish Ministry of Culture refused, and the British Museum had to do without.

The Mausoleum at Halicarnassus was built about 2,400 years ago; ancient Greek sculptors carved the sculptures in 350 BC. Given that it was built centuries ago, that it had been abandoned, that pieces were taken when nobody one else was interested in them, during the nineteenth century within an area that was then run by the Ottoman Empire, and given that they were removed with permission—who owns these objects? Where do they belong?

In recent times, more countries and groups within those countries have been claiming the return of artefacts. I now examine the various, often overlapping, arguments made for repatriation, exploring what is being said and why. Some of the arguments are questionable. In venturing that certain artefacts belong in a certain place, campaigners often impose national boundaries onto artefacts that rarely fit easily into these national categories. They fail to recognize the shifting ownership and meanings of such objects that have had long, multiple, and complex lives. Campaigners assert a causal relationship between those artefacts from ancient civilizations and people's sense of identity in the here and now, arguing that this identity is particular and exclusive; that owning the artefacts reinforces this identity, which is why they should be returned; and that their people relate to the objects in a way that nobody else can. In what follows, I engage with these arguments.

But just as there are limits to the arguments for repatriation, the arguments made in favour of retention also warrant scrutiny. Repatriation sceptics also challenge the national categories placed upon these artefacts, going on to claim that demands for repatriation are political, even dangerous, expressions of nationalism. While it is true that nation states have changed over time, those critiquing repatriation tend to underplay the historically specific context of the creation of cultural artefacts. They often fail to address the claim that cultural artefacts affirm identity. Most significantly, those resisting repatriation sometimes seek to defend a particular kind of museum—the encyclopaedic museums, which have artefacts from multiple cultures from all over the world—by claiming that such museums can help to foster a more tolerant world. In this way, the case against 'political' claims for repatriation itself draws on political and instrumental arguments, by stressing the need to build more encyclopaedic museums to counter a rising and dangerous nationalism.

Notably, the two 'sides' in this debate share a number of assumptions: in particular, the idea that objects and museums can contribute to shaping a certain kind of person or a certain kind of politics. After surveying the case both for and against repatriation as it is presented by the protagonists on each side, I suggest my own resolution to the thorny question of where objects belong, by focusing on the problem of the Elgin Marbles.

DOES CULTURE HAVE A HOMELAND?

'I wholeheartedly believe that each and every antiquity in any part of the world should eventually go back to its homeland,' declared Turkey's then minister of culture Ertuğrul Günay, when issuing claims for the repatriation of artefacts in 2012. 'Even if these objects are made of stone, just as people have souls, so do animals, plants and monuments. Taking a monument away destabilizes the world and is disrespectful to history.'[5]

Peru's president Alan García celebrated the return of artefacts from Yale University in 2011, saying that their return would 'strengthen [Peru's] national pride and self-esteem'. The artefacts had been taken (legally) following excavation by the explorer Hiram Bingham. 'They represent the dignity and pride of Peru because they are works done by our ancestors,' said García.[6]

After listing the various Egyptian artefacts in museums abroad that he wanted to have returned to Egypt, the Egyptologist Zahi Hawass, then minister of state for antiquities affairs, made the wish: 'I hope to one day see all these artefacts back in their motherland.'[7] Included on his list was the Rosetta Stone—'an icon of our Egyptian identity'.[8] Hawass never made an official request to the British Museum—many of his demands were aimed primarily at the media—but even so, these claims were a force to be reckoned with. However, Hawass was a casualty of the changing political regimes in Egypt; he no longer holds a prominent position and his campaigns for repatriation stalled.

Just as it is said that artefacts created centuries ago in what is now Turkey have a homeland and are vital for Turkish identity, that Peruvian artefacts belong in Peru and are central to being Peruvian, and that Egyptian artefacts are vital for the Egyptian people, it is said that the Elgin Marbles in the British Museum are integral to being Greek. Melina Mercouri, Greek minister of culture in the 1980s and 1990s, and a prominent advocate for the return of the Elgin Marbles, advanced the argument that the Parthenon and its sculptures embody the values of democracy and that they belong exclusively to the Greek people: 'We are asking only for something unique, something matchless, something specific to our identity.'[9] Similarly, the Elgin Marbles, according to the journalist Henry Porter, 'represent the core of Greek civilization, and they are the beating heart of modern Greek identity'.[10] Porter argued that there was something so 'Greek' about the Elgin Marbles that they belong only in Athens, and nowhere else. When in 2012 the Greek official Anastassis Mitsialis introduced a draft resolution before UNESCO, urging the return of cultural property to countries of origin, he too announced: 'Cultural heritage is the mirror of a country's history, thus lying within the very core of its existence, since it represents, not only specific values and traditions, but also a unique way a people perceives the world.'[11]

The idea that there is an exclusive relationship between objects and a particular national identity, and that those objects play a role in affirming that identity, is not confined to campaigners or governments. It is advanced by academics and in international law. 'Cultural property embodies the group's national identity. Specific cultural objects in every society bear the mark of that society's unique identity,' writes the historian Elazar Barkan, who continues:

> Demands for restitution of such objects as the Parthenon Marbles, the Benin Bronzes, and Mesoamerican treasures and of indigenous sites of cultural significance go beyond the economic value of the objects because the group's identity is invested in them.[12]

Likewise, according to the Convention on the Means of Prohibiting and Preventing the Illicit Import, Export and Transfer of Ownership of Cultural Property, adopted by the UNESCO General Conference in Paris in 1970:

> cultural property constitutes one of the basic elements of civilization and national culture, and . . . its true value can be appreciated only in relation to the fullest possible information regarding its origin, history and traditional setting . . . it is essential for every State to becoming increasingly alive to the moral obligations to respect its own cultural heritage

According to UNESCO, the cultural heritage of a state is that which was 'created by the individual or collective genius of nationals of the State' and includes artefacts 'found within the national territory'.[13] Laws and policies grant ownership of antiquities (defined as objects over 150 years old) in the state in which they are discovered, limiting their export on this basis. Furthermore, cultural property laws grant states power over the art and antiquity found within their borders. One agreement between the US and China has led to a ban on the import to America of objects created before the end of the Tang Dynasty, in AD 907. Italy, as a modern state, is less than 200 years old—but the state of Italy is aggressively pursuing the return of ancient artefacts in the discourse of a unique Italian identity, as expressed when it demanded special import restrictions by the US:

> These materials [covered by the request] are of cultural significance because they derive from cultures that developed autonomously in the region of present day Italy that attained a high degree of political, technological and artistic achievement... the cultural patrimony represented by these materials is a source of identity and esteem for the modern Italian nation.[14]

We have, then, three intertwined arguments to explore. The first is that cultural artefacts were created in a particular place and in a particular time. The second is that having those artefacts now does something for that particular people. The third is that the artefacts therefore belong in that particular place of origin, and that their identity gives them a special right to owning and understanding the meaning of the objects. Below, we look at these claims in order.

The countries that are demanding the return of ancient antiquities—Turkey, Greece, Nigeria, Peru, and Italy, to name the most prominent—are in many cases relatively recent formations in human history. The antiquity that is claimed by these states predates them. So, for example, when we consider the case of Turkey, it is by no means simple to argue that the antiquities claimed are 'Turkish'. The history of Anatolia is one of rich exchange of ancient cultures, of relations between East and West, of changing nations and tribes, of different religions and rulers, and of domination and empire. Prior to the control of the Ottoman Empire, it was under Roman rule. Constantinople (now Istanbul) was the capital city of the Eastern Roman Empire, better known as the Byzantine Empire. It is typified by regionalization but also regarded as the heartland of great cultures, which is reflected in the antiquity from these lands. Hittites, Greeks, Romans, and Byzantines all built palaces, amphitheatres, and monasteries in the region.

Under the Ottomans, the sultans were generous with the permission they gave to others to take away antique objects. Recall that it was the Ottoman Empire that gave Lord Elgin firmans to remove the Parthenon sculptures; they also gave many others firmans to remove artefacts. And as a colonizing power, the Ottomans not only permitted artefacts to leave in great quantities, they took treasures from others of the many lands under their rule. The objects that the British Museum desired for its Hajj exhibition had been removed from Mecca by the Ottoman authorities in the nineteenth century, when they ruled over the ancient pilgrimage site.

The Republic of Turkey, as we know it today, was founded in 1923 by Mustafa Kemal Atatürk, replacing the religious and dynastic Ottoman system. The parliamentary system is secular and democratic, and most of the population is Muslim. To say that Turkey is different now to how it was when the Mausoleum at Halicarnassus was built would be an understatement. The history is one of great variety within and outside relatively new borders; not a straightforward case of centuries of fixed Turkish culture.

The Istanbul Archaeology Museum, founded in 1846 as the Imperial Museum (Imparatorluk Müzesi), showcases this past of multiple influences and threads, in the display of artefacts from many cultures that have inhabited Anatolia, as well as those taken from further afield. The governors from the many different provinces were instructed to send in treasures and objects to the capital city, helping to create a great museum collection, which opened in 1891. The museum has a good collection of locally found artefacts that shows the history of the city. It also has objects from way beyond the local area: including pieces from Greece, Yugoslavia, Lebanon, and other regions where the Ottomans once ruled. The Istanbul Archaeology Museum also shows artefacts taken in the invasion of Cyprus in the 1970s.

Similarly, when the Rosetta Stone was discovered and removed by French engineers, there was no independent state of Egypt. It had not yet been formed. Its rulers granted Europeans permission to remove great monuments from their lands. The Egyptian people would come to be more interested in this ancient culture, but it took time. Indeed, even within ancient Egypt there were many different phases of pharaoh rule, where different kingdoms and generations destroyed or adulterated the cultural remains of those that preceded them. The description of 'ancient Egyptians' masks a rather more complicated history.

No one culture, or people, has ever been fixed throughout history. The idea presented in claims about a continued 'Turkishness' or 'Egyptian-ness', which ties together the ancient past and the people of the present, is selective. It ignores centuries of invasions, changing borders, and the mixing of peoples. This is particularly clear in the example of Greece.

Ancient Greece was a series of city states, and it was Athenians—not Greeks—who built the Parthenon. The Acropolis was not a symbol of democracy; and although democracy was born in Athens, it was very different to the democracy we know today—not least because Athens was a slave-owning society, and those slaves would have helped to build the Parthenon. A great deal of time has passed between now and then, and the people have not remained a static entity. Nomadic tribes, slavery, and colonizing adventures shaped the area, as did the movement of popula-tions. One might be forgiven for seeing the people of Athens and the people of Troy as uncomfortable bedfellows; yet modern Greece could claim them both as 'national' ancestors. The claims made for repatriation on the basis of the original location tend to ignore the fact that objects move and meanings change, conflating the geography of their origin with the people who live there today.

We might then ask: given that the Elgin Marbles have spent 200 years in the British Museum, what relationship do the visitors to the museum have to the Marbles, what relationship do the British have to the Elgin Marbles, how do these 'groups' relate to objects that have become part of the nation's cultural life? Could one not argue that the Marbles belong to the people of London, or to the British, on the grounds that they have become part of their identity? After all, the sculptures have been in this museum for two centuries: visited, written about, argued over, sketched, painted, referred to in Parliamentary Debates, and above all, revered. Surely, according to the logic of identity politics, they are also part of British history, as well as Greek history? The layered history of the Parthenon Marbles—what they have meant to whom over time—should indicate that these sculptures are not reducible to a fixed concept of belonging solely to a contemporary 'Greek' people, and meaning only one thing to one people.

Artefacts may have been created in one place with a specific purpose and meaning, but these change, often rapidly; and the artefacts go on to hold a meaning and influence beyond that which they had at the moment of creation. The influence of ancient Greek culture did not end at the borders of Athens, and nor does it end at the borders of present-day Greece. Ancient Romans embraced Greek culture and mod-elled their own society on it, as we can see in their attempts to replicate their sculpture. One towering monument where I live in Scotland is Edinburgh's Disgrace, which was modelled on the Parthenon. (It is a 'disgrace' only because it was never finished.) In the painting *The Vanilla Grove*, Gauguin depicts a man and a statuesque horse in what looks like a tropical environment. Gauguin was French and is well known for the influence of his observations from time spent in Tahiti on the Primitivist art movement; but the pose of the man and the horse was taken from a frieze on the Parthenon sculptures.

The visual aesthetic of the Benin Kingdom was formed in a specific historical period by a particular people, but it also developed in relation to outsiders. The people of Benin traded with European peoples—the Portuguese, Dutch, French, and British—and this shows in their artwork, both what they were about and what they were made out of. The Benin Bronzes were crafted from brass bracelets known as manillas, which were melted down and brought over by the Portuguese, to be traded for spices, ivory, or slaves—Benin did not sell its own citizens as slaves, but captives from neighbouring peoples. Many sculptures depict life in the kingdom, but one set of sculptures shows the presence of European traders kneeling at the foot of King Oba. These exchanges were not always straightforward or benign. One depicts a Portuguese figure with protective armour, who holds a gun and has a sword attached to his belt—a salutary reminder that there were serious power struggles at play. How are Portuguese people to relate to this figure? Can it be counted as 'theirs'?

The philosopher Kwame Anthony Appiah has scrutinized the concept of cultural patrimony used in these debates, where objects are understood to belong to a particular group, using the idea of Nigerian heritage. 'What does it mean, exactly,' he asks, 'for something to belong to a people?' He continues:

> Most of Nigeria's cultural patrimony was produced before the modern Nigerian state existed. We don't know whether the terra-cotta Nok sculptures, made sometime between 800 BC and AD 200, were commissioned by kings or commoners; we don't know whether the people who made them and the people who paid for them thought of them as belonging to the kingdom, to a man, to a lineage, or to the gods. One thing we know for sure, however, is they didn't make them for Nigeria.[15]

As Appiah concludes, Nigeria's material culture no more 'belongs' to the people of present-day Nigeria than to anyone else.

This is not to suggest that a group or a people do not feel a particular attachment to cultural artefacts from their locale. I admit to a tingle from seeing the Crosby Garrett Helmet, a copper Roman cavalry helmet found in Cumbria, partly because I know the area well. I have walked there, and sometimes feel that I have passed by the distant shadows of those who wore it. But my interest, here, is in the one-sided character of the arguments that are used—especially by politicians and campaigners—to support the claim of ownership.

Another such argument is the identity-affirming properties with which present-day campaigners endow cultural artefacts. When the academic Elazar Barkan writes that '[c]ultural property embodies the group's national identity', thereby implying that artefacts belong to that group, I would argue that things are not as simple as that. Whilst artefacts may embody and express certain ideas, it is unlikely that they can—or should—decisively affirm that more intangible sense of 'who we are'. This is particularly the case if the identity in need of affirming is already fragile, or lacking. Looking to the past as a solution to the uncertainty of identity today tends merely to impose today's uncertainty onto the past.

In any case, objects can inspire a range of responses, often prompting thoughts about others, rather than ourselves. When I look at the Crosby Garrett Helmet, it does not make me feel more British—it encourages me to think about Roman Britain and the lives of other people in a different time and place.

The potential flip side of the argument that a group's identity gives it ownership over a particular cultural object is that you can, or should, only like and understand 'your' culture: that other cultures are not for you. The logic of this way of thinking is that if you are, say, Nigerian, the Parthenon is not 'yours'; you were born in the wrong place to the wrong parents to relate to or understand ancient Greece. Equally, it would follow that someone in Athens today can relate to ancient Greek urns but that they do not really 'get' African art as they are not from Africa. But this is not the case.

The case for repatriation along national lines tends to obscure the universal nature of great art and artefacts. By appreciating these objects, we can abstract ourselves from our immediate circumstances and understand creations made by anybody, wherever they were from and whenever they were alive. Being white, middle-class, and female, living in Scotland in the twenty-first century, I have no lived experience of classical Athens, but I look at the sculptures from the Parthenon and see something of the time in which they were created. No doubt I do not see that something as the ancient Athenians did, or even as people did when the sculptures arrived in the British Museum. I probably do relate to these ancient sculptures in a similar way to other people living today in Athens, Bodrum, and Peru. In this regard—and many other ways—I have more in common with someone in Athens today than with someone from London in the nineteenth century; and despite the discourse of difference and unique identities, we would discuss the Marbles through a shared prism of understanding.

Nobody can experience ancient culture in the way people did when it was first created. Once that first generation has passed, the original intent of the artefacts is dispersed. But something remains in certain objects that, due to an exceptional, sometimes accidental, quality and set of circumstances—including, I would suggest, the response of different societies over time, which has kept it valued in our cultural memory—means they still appeal to us. And this is despite the fact that every generation since has reinterpreted the meaning of certain artefacts. Rather like Chinese whispers, as the message gets passed on it changes, with the receiver using their contemporary experience to decipher meaning. There is nothing wrong with this: it is the only way it can be.

Karl Marx once asked why we continue to gain pleasure from Greek art. The point of his question was to ask how people in particular circumstances can think themselves out of them:

> [T]he difficulty lies not in understanding that the Greek arts and epic are bound up with certain forms of social development. The difficulty is that they still afford us artistic pleasure and that in a certain respect they count as a norm and an unattainable model. A man cannot become a child again, or he becomes childish. But does he not find joy in the child's naiveté and must he himself not strive to reproduce its truth at a higher stage?[16]

Marx argued that we find Greek art of continued interest due to a consciousness of universal humanity and because Greek art prefigured later great art. (It would appear he wasn't as impressed with Greek art as others have been.) We respect that it was created by another person, and it is this aspect of us—the fact that we are social creatures—that ensures the durability of art and the fascination it continues to hold, long after the historical period of creation has passed. For Marx this ability to see beyond our own immediate lives, our own interests and circumstances, was also the basis for solidarity: a solidarity that could be the foundation for trying to make a better world.

We are capable of appreciating cultural artefacts and the civilizations that bore them, regardless of our present circumstances and nationalities, because most human beings try to understand what is beyond their everyday experience. We are all born in a particular moment, in a particular nation, and we are influenced by this; but we can also think ourselves out of these circumstances and into the lives of others. This, however, has become a deeply unfashionable opinion. Cultural policy specialist Munira Mirza outlines how the concept of universalism is commonly aligned with so-called 'imperialistic values' and 'dead white men', or taken to mean that we are all somehow the same. Mirza persuasively restates the case for universalism, arguing that it instead means something much more profound: we are all shaped and informed by our particular historic, geographical, ethnic, and cultural backgrounds and circumstances, but as human beings we have the capacity to use our imaginations, not merely to understand difference but also to transcend it.

'This simple quality, which distinguishes man from beast, is the basis of human culture,' writes Mirza.[17] We could add to this the words of Terence, the Roman dramatist, writing over 2,000 years ago: 'Nothing human is alien to me.'

THE POLITICAL MISUSE OF CULTURE

What lies behind the claims that one national identity is uniquely related to certain cultural artefacts, and that they therefore should be returned? While such claims focus on a particular object, their aim appears to be more about laying claim to a particular past, for reasons that lie firmly in the present day. Thus, artefacts are sometimes pawns in political positioning, played either for domestic reasons or for diplomatic purposes abroad.

Such claims on the past are not a recent development. Previous chapters detailed Napoleon's ambitions for antiquity: he wanted to use the achievements of ancient civilizations to suggest that he, and France, were following in the footsteps of the great leaders of the ancient world. Similarly, when Egypt became interested in its ancient heritage in the mid-nineteenth century, elements of this were driven by political concerns: Egyptian antiquity was employed in the argument advancing Egypt's separatist ambitions from the Ottoman Empire. Nationalists made the case that Egypt was older, more ancient, and more credible. In the nineteenth century, Britain's cultural and political elite, as well as the leaders of what was then a new Greek nation, associated themselves with the ancient Greek culture, praising and venerating its art and political values, in the hope that the association would rub off well on them.

In more recent times, one example of the multiple reasons behind repatriation claims is provided by the case of Turkey. Whilst making the requests, the Turkish economy was in a strong place, with record growth. Tourism creates massive revenues and the then culture minister, Ertuğrul Günay, planned to develop this. He also aimed to build 'the largest museum in the world... The museum that we are planning to build will not be the largest of [the] Middle East and Balkans but it will be the largest museum of the world.'[18] Arguably, as important a driver for Turkey's repatriation claims as the potential for tourism was international positioning. Turkey is not a member of the European Union (EU), but it has joined both the G20 and NATO, and it has influence in a region where the EU and the US need influence. As the claims were made, the country was considering how to reposition itself in the Middle East. The administration had been pro-Western in recent times, and appeared to want to be considered European. Cultural claims are one, relatively soft, way of asserting Turkey's presence and significance on the world stage. Such acts are a common strategy for emerging nations, which sometimes use culture as a display of civility and credibility, and ironically—given that it is often antiquity that is used in this process—to show that they are modern.

However, one narrative in particular has been presented in many of the museums. The ruling Justice and Development Party is keen to revisit Turkey's Ottoman heritage; religious conservatives claim it as their heritage, and the museums tend to reinforce Ottoman narratives. The creation by the Turkish prime minister, Recep Tayyip Erdoğan, of a Seljuk ('the first Turks') museum in Kayseri, underlines a nationalist narrative: so here we do have the political use of museums in a nationalist cause.

Andrew Finkle, author of *Turkey: What Everyone Needs to Know*, makes the point that the Samsat Stele in London's V&A Museum, and the focus of a repatriation claim, is not an object of national identification per se. What's important, Finkle suggests, 'is the political kudos that goes with being seen to be able to force the great powers to eat humble pie'.[19] The British Museum is a symbol of Britain; and making it bend and bow to Turkey is a way of showing that Turkey has power and influence. In addition, the repatriation of antiquities could strike a nationalist appeal with the electorate at home, which may be advantageous.

Finkle warns that these claims do not benefit artefacts and understanding: '[T]he effort and expense of fighting over long-lost objects in Britain would be better employed on improving the deplorable state of cultural management at home.' Furthermore:

> Instead of wallowing in cultural nationalism Turkey should be protecting its treasures and attracting all the foreign expertise it can. It does no good to refuse to lend an object to a foreign museum—particularly for an exhibition that is trying to further understanding between faiths.[20]

The case of China also suggests contemporary influences at play. With the emergence of China as a superpower, the Chinese are starting to show an interest in antiquity and art. One of the most prominent illustrations of this interest and the way it is framed was at the sale, in February 2009, by Christie's auction house of two bronze zodiac heads seized by British and French troops from the Summer Palace in 1860. The two heads were sold to an anonymous bidder for £14 million ($21 million). The bidder turned out to be the Chinese collector Cai Mingchao, an adviser to China's National Treasures Fund. He wanted to make a stand against the astronomical price of these artefacts, artefacts that had originally been looted from China. He had no intention of paying for the heads, Mingchao said, but had made the bid as a 'patriotic act'. 'I did this on behalf of the Chinese People,' he told a newspaper. 'Every Chinese would have liked to have done this at this moment... I am honoured to have had the chance.'[21] François Pinault, the French billionaire and owner of Christie's, returned the heads to China two years later.

Auction houses have subsequently been more careful with Chinese artefacts that have a dubious or uncertain provenance. In 2012, Bonhams in London intended to sell at auction two jades from the Qing era—a green jade hanging vase and lid, from the reign of Emperor Qianlong (1711–99), and a white jade disc from a slightly later period. Chinese officials suggested that these may have been taken from the Summer Palace in the 1860s, and that therefore they should not be on the market. Tan Ping, an official at China's State Administration of Cultural Heritage, complained, saying it went 'against the spirit of international conventions'.[22] Bonhams withdrew the items and apologized for causing any offence. The return of artefacts has caused trouble, even when they have been purchased for that purpose. In 2014 a real estate developer, Huang Nobo, made a large donation to a museum in Bergen, Norway; in return, the museum sent seven white marble columns from the Summer Palace, that were in their collection, back to China. But some argued that the columns should not have to be purchased to be returned; they should have been returned because this was the morally right thing to do. Yao Le, of the Jiangsu Provincial Academy of Social Science, told the *Global Times* newspaper: 'The recovery of relics should be a state action, which ought to be achieved by justice without paying for them.'[23]

The return of such artefacts is currently a relatively minor issue in China. If anything, China's Communist Party is more alert to the use of contemporary art in repositioning Chinese society as a modern player on the world stage. But this could change. Whilst active political Chinese nationalism is a minority interest, the Chinese identity, which is a subset of nationalism, is key to social stability. Chinese tradition is another way of showing how China is different, and in this regard the place of ancient antiquity could become more important. It could also be used by the state as a way of giving people a sense of China's place in history, as the country continues to develop and modernize. Mao destroyed thousands of historic sites, artefacts, and cultural products through philistine revolutionary acts—the present-day politicians could use heritage protection as a way of expressing its progressive rejection of Maoist extremism. We will have to wait and see how this question develops in China.

Claiming artefacts today gains a great deal of media attention, and that is often as important as succeeding in the claim. In this regard, the act of claiming has become important in its own right. Whilst there is no question that Turkish, Greek, and Chinese officials are sincere in their desire to have the figures from the Mausoleum at Halicarnassus, the Elgin Marbles, and the treasures from the Summer Palace returned to their respective countries, the very fact of demanding their return is nevertheless also a way of restating the importance of Turkey, Greece, and China in the present day.

THE PROBLEM WITH REPATRIATION SCEPTICISM

Culture is usually the product of different influences, a point emphasized by repatriation sceptics. For example, the writer Jason Farago argues that Turkey's claims for repatriation are based on a flawed concept of a nation state as being the same across time and history:

> That nationalistic statement puts Turkey in the vanguard of a troubling tendency, one seen everywhere from Israel to China: that the nation state has an infinite claim to a cultural heritage that may date back thousands of years before the state's foundation... Cultures are not ahistorical and immutable. They change all the time. And they certainly don't line up easily with the borders on our maps, to say nothing of the governments that delimit them.[24]

But repatriation sceptics tend to overstate this point, and to underplay the specificity of the creation of culture. And the kind of argument presented by Farago conflates the problem of 'nationalism' with the recognition that culture was created in a particular moment. This is a disingenuous and unhelpful elision. Saying that an artefact is from somewhere and some place is not—necessarily—'nationalistic'. What's more, the conclusions drawn from this conflation are problematic.

James Cuno, president and CEO of the J. Paul Getty Trust, has authored a number of books advancing a similar line of argument. Cuno puts a timely and well-argued case against repatriation and the cultural property laws that have been passed in the name of protecting antiquity, and his enthusiasm about museums and what they have to offer is inspiring and infectious. The argument he advances, however, is debatable.

Cuno contends that

> It is the nature of culture to be dynamic and ever changing. Yet national governments ignore this fact. They impose a national claim of distinction on culture, and they seek an ancient pedigree for that culture. They want to claim primacy as much as purity: ancient origins and uninterrupted identity. But this is only politics.[25]

'The real argument', he continues, 'is between museums and modern nation-states and their nationalist claims on that heritage.'[26] Nationalistic feelings, he warns, 'have also hardened into ideologies with roots in fear and hatred of the Other, often with racist affinities'.[27] Archaeologists, he alleges, 'encourage the institution of nationalist retentionist cultural property laws, believing them to be important to the protection of archaeological sites'.[28] They are used in the service, he says, of 'nationalist political purposes'.[29] Crucially, it is because of this problem—nationalism, inflamed by national museums and archaeologists—that his kind of 'encyclopaedic' museum is necessary:

> The encyclopaedic museum encourages a broad understanding and appreciation of the historical interrelatedness of the world's diverse cultures and promotes inquiry and tolerance. And in the process, it preserves our common artistic legacy in the public domain for the benefit of the curious public. This is the promise of museums.[30]

Cuno is not the only one making grand claims made for what encyclo-paedic museums can achieve. Soon after Neil MacGregor became dir-ector of the British Museum in 2002, the narratives about, and justifications for, the role of the museum subtly altered. His is a far less forceful and far more nuanced position than that presented by James Cuno. But it is interesting to look at how MacGregor repositioned the British Museum, and the museum in general. For example, the British Museum used to be described as 'universal', but now it is more com-monly described as 'encyclopaedic'—a linguistic shift that warrants reflection.

In December 2002, a group of museum directors issued the *Declar-ation on the Importance and Value of Universal Museums*. The Declar-ation defended the role of the museum as a space in which to understand artefacts from different cultures and historical periods, and argued that they should not be judged by their practices in the long-distant past, practices that should be appreciated as the product of different sensitiv-ities and values. It was seen as a call to arms against repatriation, and immediately condemned as an attempt to hold on to artefacts. Although the British Museum was not among the original signatories, the Declar-ation was circulated through the British Museum press office, and a furious reaction was unleashed in its direction from many within the museum world. Reporting in the *Art Newspaper*, the headline given to the initiative was: 'A George Bush approach to international relations'.[31] Quoted within, Geoffrey Lewis, chair of the International Council for Museums (ICOM), argued that the 'real purpose' of the Declaration was to 'establish a higher degree of immunity from claims for repatriation', and was simply a statement of 'self-interest'.[32]

Since that time, the British Museum is less often formally referred to as a 'universal museum'. Its publicity for touring exhibitions describes the institution as 'A museum of the world for the world' or an 'encyclopaedic museum'. MacGregor writes that the British Museum has surrendered its eighteenth-century definition of universality, it has developed a new identity as a collection of the cultures of the world, ancient and modern. The Museum remains a unique repository of the achievements of human endeavour, and there is no culture, past or present, that is not represented within its walls. It is truly the memory of mankind.[33]

This one case of a self-conscious distancing from the ideal of universality is notable. On one level, it can be accounted for by a change in the content of the collection—in the above quote, MacGregor is discussing the removal of the natural history collections, the paintings, and the books to other institutions. But in the wider context, the favouring of the term 'encyclopaedic' suggests a difficulty and defensiveness with the concept of universality. The term 'encyclopaedic' seems to be less charged, more descriptive and neutral. Furthermore, the significance of the shift, for the discussion in this book, is in the way that the 'encyclopaedic museum' has come to be characterized. The encyclopaedic museum is presented as playing a new kind of role—a social, verging on political, role, that furthers good relations in the present.

Writing in the British newspaper *The Guardian*, MacGregor argued that the display of objects from multiple civilizations, in the way that the British Museum today allows, encourages the visitor to address 'questions of contemporary politics and international relations'. That is, the museum plays a role—in MacGregor's words, as a 'weapon'—in understanding contemporary conflict. He elaborates:

A collection like that held in trust for the world by the British Museum is surely a powerful weapon in a conflict that may yet be mortal, unless we find means to free minds as well as bodies from oppression. World museums of this kind offer us a chance to forge the arguments that can hope to defeat the simplifying brutalities which disfigure politics all round the world. The British Museum must now reaffirm its worldwide civic purpose. That must be the goal that shapes our future plans. Where else can the world see so clearly that it is one?[34]

Among the strategies that come under this kind of socially aware activity is a programme of loans. One loan that has received some attention is that of the Cyrus Cylinder to the National Museum of Iran in Tehran, and latterly to America. The press release about this loan to the Museum of Iran stressed the independence of the institution from the national government, the multiplicity of meanings of the cylinder, and, crucially, the essential role the loan and the object could play in contributing to 'a better relationship based on dialogue, tolerance and understanding'.[35]

The work of the museum is characterized as being in the service of 'cultural diplomacy', although Neil MacGregor is careful not to use the actual term himself. A good example of this form of 'cultural diplomacy' is the loan of one of the Elgin Marbles to Russia in December 2014, when the British Museum sent a marble sculpture of a river god, thought to be Ilissos, from the west pediment of the Parthenon, to the State Hermitage Museum, St Petersburg, for six weeks, to mark the 250th anniversary of its foundation, triggering requests for loan of the Marbles to other museums. This was the first time the museum had allowed one of the Marbles to leave the UK; previously it had said such loans were not possible.

Relations between Russia and the Western world were fragile and deteriorating. This loan, this piece of old marble, could warm up those frosty relations, it was suggested, reinforce ideals about freedom, and inspire the people of Russia to rebel. A Leader in *The Times* newspaper, titled 'A Message in Marble', praised the act as 'cultural diplomacy at its most inspired', outlining that the marble piece sent a 'pointed message':

> This faintly mottled sculpture, 2,500 years old, depicts a river beside which Socrates and Phaedrus would ruminate on freedom and truth, twin pillars of the democracy that Vladimir Putin would rather stifle than unleash . . . Some of those who see Ilissos in the Hermitage will live under the odious dictatorships of Uzbekistan and Turkmenistan. It is uplifting to think that a few may be moved to wonder why they are denied the freedom that flourished 25 centuries ago in Athens, and may even be stirred to fight for them.[36]

Neil MacGregor wrote:

> I hope that Pericles would applaud the journey of Ilissos to Russia, where 'far away in foreign lands', this stone ambassador of the Greek golden age and European ideals will write ancient Athens's achievements—aesthetic, moral and political—in 'the minds of every man'. It is a message that Russia, and the whole world, need to hear and I am delighted that the British Museum has been able to lend such a remarkable object.[37]

But the loan was received with hostility in some quarters. Not just from those campaigners who would like to see the return of the Marbles to Greece; but also by arts commentators and those who usually support the retention of the Marbles. The blogger Grumpy Art Historian encapsulated the reaction, writing that the loan is 'not for an exhibition that will show it in a different context or add to our understanding' but is 'a profoundly patronising gesture about civilizing bad regimes'. 'The statue is a towering work of art, but it doesn't carry a message, however much you seek to impose one upon it.'[38]

It was evident to many commentators that this was an attempt by the museum to change the debate over the Marbles. As the cultural writer Peter Aspden remarked, in the *Financial Times*: 'To Russia With Love is as near as the British Museum gets to lifting an elegant middle finger to Greece.'[39] Indeed, *The Times* Leader asserted that 'The lending abroad of any of the Elgin Marbles tells the world that the British Museum does not intend to hoard them.'[40] This highlights one problem with such strategizing. Obvious to many was that this loan was carried out as much in the service of trying to relegitimize the museum and affirm its right to hold the Marbles, as it was in the service of diplomacy or even scholarship. The loan invited cynicism about the work of the museum that might not serve it well in the long term. It certainly was not about improving or enriching an understanding of the art objects.

OVER-PROMISING WHAT THE ENCYCLOPAEDIC
MUSEUM CAN DO

In *Museum Matters*, James Cuno is emphatic that encyclopaedic museums can play such a particular, political role:

> This I hold to be the promise of the encyclopaedic museums: that as liberal, cosmopolitan institutions, they encourage identification with others in the world, a shared sense of being human, of having in every meaningful way a common history, with a common future not only *at stake* but increasingly, in an age of resurgent nationalism and sectarian violence, *at risk*.[41]

Cuno argues for what he calls the 'cosmopolitan aspirations' of encyclo-paedic museums. By this he means not only collecting and showing work from different human civilizations, but also the use of collections for 'tactical and political purposes'. He suggests that museums can encour-age a broad understanding and appreciation of the interrelatedness of the world's cultures. He even ventures that we are at risk if there are no encyclopaedic museums in foreign lands: 'The collective, political risk of not having encyclopaedic museums everywhere possible—in Shanghai, Lagos, Cairo, Delhi, and all other major metropolises—is that culture becomes fixed *national* culture.'[42]

James Cuno, and to some extent Neil McGregor, argue that in the context of a world that is experiencing a dramatic resurgence in nation-alism and sectarian violence, encyclopaedic museums can help to bring about reconciliation. But the idea that museums can create tolerance in a world of conflict requires scrutiny. For a start, it is something of a contradictory position. The very same people have criticized those nation states that use antiquity for legitimacy and political gain. When address-ing the use of culture by nation states, Cuno—rightly, in my view—points out: 'Culture is poorly served by politics.'[43] Why should museum directors use their institutions for political purposes, if they are unhappy when nation states do so? Furthermore, in the quest to restate the value of the museum—why museums matter, in the words of the title to one of Cuno's books—the role of the museum is altered in important ways. Depending upon one's point of view, museums become either 'good' or 'bad' kinds of institutions (encyclopaedic versus national), operating above all in the service of interests external to them.

In this view, a global interpretation is ruled as the only interpretation that is valid. Local and national collections are reinterpreted as parochial. 'National museums are of local interest,' writes Cuno. 'They direct attention to a local culture, seeking to define and legitimize it for local peoples.' Encyclopaedic museums do something different and better, he claims:

> Encyclopaedic museums direct attention to distant cultures, asking visitors to respect the values of others and seek connections between cultures. Encyclopaedic museums promote the understanding of culture as always fluid, ever changing, ever influenced by new and strange things—evidence of the overlapping diversity of humankind.[44]

Well—maybe some do. Some cultures have been more open and influential than others that have been more closed, such as China. Are we only to explore those that were harmonious and fluid? Are we to look only at connections and not breakages between peoples? Are we only to have one prism through which to understand the past?

Cuno advances a remit for the (encyclopaedic) museum as one dedicated to 'the dissipation of ignorance and superstition, where the artefacts of one time and one culture can be seen next to those of other times and other cultures without prejudice'.[45] In fact, he argues, they should cover the globe: 'the promise of the encyclopaedic museum is an argument for their being everywhere, in both the developed and developing world'.[46] But this goes too far. Not only is the promise of national museums underappreciated in this analysis, the promise of encyclopaedic museums is wildly overstated.

Let us remember a number of crucial points. First, the visitor is not easily and directly influenced—a point Cuno makes elsewhere in *Museum Matters*, as we have seen. When people visit either kind of institution—a national museum or an encyclopaedic one—they bring their own thoughts, understanding, and imagination with them on their visit. They are not empty vessels waiting to be directed about what to think. What is more, there are distinct national and cultural traditions that we should try to understand. Most objects at their point of creation may have been subject to different influences from diverse peoples and will have gone on to mean something different to others, but they were all created somewhere at a certain time: and this specificity is somewhat overlooked in the response to claims for repatriation. National museums can be one way of appreciating this specificity, in a way that is both informative and enjoyable: the Parthenon was conceived and built in ancient Athens, and the Acropolis Museum helps to tell that story of origin.

Furthermore, the accusation that nationalism is 'caused' by museums is disputable. When Berlin's Pergamon Museum returned a 3,500-year-old sphinx to Turkey in 2011, there was no nationalist uprising. The Turkish people did not respond in a nationalist way to the newly returned artefact. It is perfectly possible to look at artefacts in a museum that collects local objects and not fall into a nationalistic frenzy. Whilst it is true that in Turkey the authorities are changing museums in their own political interests, this is not a case of museums creating nationalists: it is the case of nationalists using museums. Similarly, after winning power, the Hungarian prime minister Viktor Orban built up national institutions of heritage, history, and culture, renovating the Liszt Academy and creating four new research institutes of national history, intended to produce conservative (in an artistic sense) historical narratives that will please the regime and present their vision of a Hungarian identity. Eight new museums are planned for Budapest, including five that the government intends to build in the historic City Park by 2018, as part of a $741-million project to rebrand the park as a museum district. There appears to be a twin strategy at play here. As with Turkey, there is certainly an intention to encourage tourism, and the broader claims that culture can create an economic revival, with Bilbao cited as an exemplar, are important here. But the museums will also bring Hungarian achievements to the fore. So culture *is* being used here by nationalists, but, again, it is not a simple case of culture causing nationalists. There is a difference. And this development wouldn't be halted by an encyclopaedic museum no matter how great it was.

Cuno's argument is a scaremongering tactic of sorts; and it is also a little glib, considering the history of the encyclopaedic museums and the basis on which they continue to operate. As the legal scholar Tatiana Flessas wryly points out, the critique of nationalism levelled by Cuno and others is ironic given that nationalism has been at the core of many encyclopaedic museums in the past, and they continue to be national in terms of legal status and protection.[47] National and encyclopaedic museums can coexist and complement each other. They have done so for centuries and should continue to do so.

Overstated arguments for what encyclopaedic museums and their artefacts can do can give us a simplified approach to international relations. Conflicts of national interest and historical troubles are reduced to acts of misunderstanding that museums can demystify and help resolve. But no museum has it in its power to 'defeat' nationalism on its own. Such claims may, in the short term, help to legitimize the museum by making it seem vitally important to addressing social problems, but it will be set up in the expectation of achieving aims that it cannot realize. This is a strategy aimed at trying to 'big up' these kinds of museums—improve their reputations—which could backfire in the long run as too much will be expected of them, whilst at the same time the core roles they do perform (research and dissemination) will be undervalued.

We will not find the solution to present-day conflicts in museums. These institutions are not about to stimulate great social change in such a direct and casual way. Looking to old objects to resolve conflicts avoids dealing with contemporary international situations. It obscures the *current* reasons behind clashes of interest and ideology. And it encumbers culture by asking it to resolve serious problems of the present.

What is above all interesting is the way in which the position of some of those advancing the social role of the encyclopaedic museum echoes that of campaigners who argue for repatriation. All 'sides' in this battle increasingly advance an instrumental role for the museum and artefacts. Campaigns asking for the return of artefacts claim that this act will affirm their unique identity. Cuno, MacGregor, and other repatriation sceptics claim that their kind of museum will create tolerance and address nationalism. Another camp, discussed in the Chapter 7 on identity museums, suggests that the museums can shore up the identity of indigenous peoples. And as we shall see in Chapter 8, some campaigners argue that the repatriation of artefacts can make amends for the wrongs of colonization. All these arguments demand a great deal from museums and old objects in instrumental terms; they have great expectations of these institutions and treasures. But these expectations cannot possibly be fulfilled.

WHAT IS A UNIVERSAL MUSEUM?

In his defence of the encyclopaedic museum, and of the retention of objects in those museums, Philippe de Montebello, the former director of the Metropolitan Museum of Art, makes a relevant and revealing elision. Montebello opens a book chapter with an inspiring quote from the nineteenth-century American scholar George F. Comfort: 'True art is cosmopolitan.' Montebello quotes Comfort saying: 'It knows no country. It knows no age. Homer sang not for the Greeks alone but for all nations, and for all time.' This is a stirring opening, and I would agree; certain cultural artefacts take on a new life when they become detached from their moment of creation, and they speak to many people across time. Shakespeare's work has been dislodged from the writer's historical and geographical birth, touching and influencing many people across cultures and times centuries later—so much so that his work is universal. It says something about and beyond the moment in which he was writing, something that millions of people still appreciate to this day.

Montebello goes on to argue that, because of universality, 'An ideal museum must thus be cosmopolitan in its character and it must present the whole stream of our history and all nations and ages.'[48] But in this, he is mistaken. Universality does not amount to presenting every object from history, or from every different culture. Universality is not necessarily found in an encyclopaedic museum. Equally, a museum containing only artefacts from the immediate locality could quite easily, also, be regarded as 'universal'. The point is that the person—the visitor—can imagine themselves out of their moment in time to look at and appreciate an object from a different time and place. And, crucially, some artefacts, for complicated and sometimes almost mysterious reasons, are better adapted to this than others. Some objects remain of interest only to the people who made them and kept them for personal, private, or sentimental reasons, but not much beyond that. Other objects hold the interest of people beyond both that usefulness and sentiment—there is something about them that appears truthful or special to people who are unfamiliar with their original context. This is most obvious with artefacts that are technically brilliant or exceptional, but also sometimes with artefacts that show how human beings lived, loved, and understood their world, in a way that others can relate to.

The Parthenon Marbles are an example of artefacts with this universal appeal: both the set that resides in Athens and the Elgin Marbles in the British Museum. Universality is not about collecting objects from everywhere; it is a way of engaging with certain objects that requires both something from the viewer and something unique and special about an artefact.

THE IMPORTANCE OF SOVEREIGNTY

When artefacts are found today, within borders, where and to whom do they belong? In *Who Owns Antiquity?* James Cuno broaches this question, taking issue with the cultural property laws that mean nations keep artefacts found within their borders. Cuno is also critical of the international body UNESCO, which was ostensibly set up to promote international cooperation in the culture sector. UNESCO's attempts at protection and care have been ineffective, argues Cuno, pointing to its inability to prevent the Taliban from destroying the Bamiyan Buddhas and much of the Kabul Museum's collection. Cuno describes how heritage sites are being destroyed and lost. Wars, poverty, development, and theft threaten antiquity. The existing laws, he argues, do not work. On this, Cuno has a point. But solutions are not simple, and his particular solutions have serious limitations.

Cuno's passionate critique raises legitimate problems. 'I question the premise . . . that it is the right of sovereign nations to legislate the protection of and access to whatever they consider to be *their* cultural property,' he writes.[49] Not only do modern populations frequently bear no relation to the ancient objects that they are reclaiming, Cuno argues, but the drive to establish cultural property laws feeds nationalist movements and their excesses. Cuno recommends partage, a system developed in the first half of the twentieth century, by which objects excavated in archaeological digs are divided between the country of origin's cultural authority (usually the national museum) and the archaeologist's home institution. But, in freeing artefacts from the ownership of the state in which they were found, it seems as if he would remove state sovereignty. 'Why should state sovereignty determine ownership?', he argues, in the case of Turkey. 'Nationalized cultural property within the jurisdiction of the nation-state', he laments, 'is the state's to do with it as it pleases.'[50] As a solution, Cuno suggests that countries should instead cede control of all cultural goods to some kind of 'international trusteeship under the auspices of a nongovernmental agency'.[51]

Archaeologists suggest that Cuno misunderstands the true nature of the market in antiquities. Colin Renfrew argues that museum curators have a great deal more discretion than Cuno admits, and that looting continues to be a serious problem that needs to be addressed. The best way of doing so is to keep things as they are: with territorial authorities bearing the responsibility for protecting archaeological sites. Ethnicity is not the issue here, Renfrew suggests; the issue is how best to protect antiquity and the context in which it is found.[52] The trade in illicit antiquities is a problem, and there is something important in Renfrew's argument that the accusations of nationalism are a distraction from how to protect the artefacts. But there are further issues with Cuno's proposal.

Centrally, it is not clear who would sit on his proposed non-governmental agency, what power they would have, and on what basis. It is not clear to what country or people they would be accountable. Given the historical—and present-day—tendency for the West to compromise the sovereignty of other nations, often through non-governmental agencies which bypass national officials and institutions, this needs to be clarified. Because in these terms, Cuno's proposal sounds like a kind of supranationalism erected in the interests of artefacts; and as with any supranationalism, there are pitfalls and problems. The artefact may not morally 'belong' to the state in which it was found, it may not be 'theirs' in relation to a group identity to the exclusion of everyone else, and it will be of value to the whole of humanity, but to remove objects automatically to a non-governmental agency would have significant implications for state sovereignty way beyond the artefacts in question. In the cause of saving 'artefacts for humanity', important rights would be lost. Democracy, representative government, and the rule of law are all impossible if the sovereignty of these states is bypassed: and the perceived needs of cultural artefacts should surely not override these vital principles.

There are hints that in the name of protecting heritage, processes that could override sovereignty are already in play. The international community has been involved in the restoration and safeguarding of cultural heritage in societies marked by recent conflicts, including Cambodia, former Yugoslavia, East Timor, Iraq, and Afghanistan. This has entailed working with the invading armies to access heritage sites. The aims are understandable, but the assumptions and consequences are controversial.

In the case of Iraq, cultural professionals worked alongside the army, in an 'embedded' relationship, to try to stem looting and the destruction of heritage sites. Peter Stone, professor of heritage studies at Newcastle University in England, was approached by the UK Ministry of Defence to help identify archaeological sites in Iraq that required protection during the Second Gulf War, which raged from March 2003 to December 2011. His (albeit reluctant) involvement made the best of a bad situation, Stone explained: 'So long as you make the point that it is better not to go to war, then the next realistic step is to help mitigate the damage.'[53] Stone was convinced that permanently working with the military, rather than responding too late in urgent circumstances, was sensible: 'If we want to take protection seriously, we need to engage with the military, not as a kneejerk reaction, but continuously, to make sure they and politicians know the importance of cultural heritage.' It was also important, for Stone, that this relationship could be formalized: 'It shouldn't be about responding to a particular place. From day one, the military and senior

relevant government officials should be effectively trained in the importance of culture.'

Peter Stone's plans, to get archaeologists working with the army—a
body of armed men from one nation state, intervening in another
country—have been criticized by those who argue that this kind of
involvement militarizes archaeology. They warn that it amounts to an
endorsement of intervention and war, and that it is reminiscent of the
role archaeologists played in colonialist campaigns in the past. The
archaeologist Yannis Hamilakis is an opponent of heritage professionals'
involvement in war zones, arguing that 'It's about the loss of autonomy
and independence on the part of the specialist.' He writes:

> in situations like Iraq in 2003, assuming the formalized role of the military
> adviser once the conflict started and once the Western armies invaded the
> country, made these heritage specialists part of the structure of the
> occupation and colonization of the country, regardless of their personal
> opinion on the war.[54]

The consequence of such a relationship is, he warns, the legitimi-
zation of invasions and civilian casualties as a consequence of these
collaborations.[55]

The aim of embedded archaeology—to protect ancient antiquity—is
laudable. But it is difficult to see how archaeologists can be considered
separate or distant from a military intervention when they are working
alongside the army occupying a country in the midst of war.

There was a global howl of outrage in March 2015, when videos
emerged showing ISIS militants attacking not only artefacts in Mosul
Museum in northern Iraq but also a number of important archaeological
sites at Hatra and Nimrud. A few months later, in August, they blew up a
Roman theatre at the Palmyra World Heritage site in Syria.

James Cuno, rightly distraught, has recommended a number of measures that could be taken to safeguard antiquity from ISIS: putting UN

boots on the ground; safekeeping artefacts in museums around the world; policing the region's borders; and restoring partage.[56] I sympathize, greatly. But boots on the ground and policing the region's borders would mean unhelpfully politicizing antiquity further. It means endorsing military intervention, which raises ethical questions, and it is not clear that this strategy would defeat ISIS, which is what is ultimately required. As for safekeeping artefacts, by retaining them in museums that are not at risk from the political instability, looting, and destruction, there is some merit to this suggestion.

Until recently the UN Security Council Resolution 1483 (2003), obligated foreign countries to take 'appropriate steps to facilitate the safe return' to Iraqi institutions of property illegally removed from the Iraqi National Museum.[57] The intentions were understandable and admirable, and foreign countries have chosen to do the same with Syrian cultural property. But returning these objects to Iraq and Syria has meant putting them into harm's way. So in 2015, the US House of Representatives approved a bill that allows the president to waive this requirement and keep at-risk cultural objects in temporary custody of the federal government, or a cultural or educational institution in the US. Crucially, this is done at the request of the objects' foreign owners, and is a sensible measure. The bill should become law, and other nations should take similar steps. They already are: the British Museum is keeping and protecting an object found to be looted from Syria.

It is a strategy that may protect a very small amount of material in the West. But it will not protect material in museums in afflicted areas—where curators and scholars have valiantly tried to protect and safeguard antiquity, such as the renowned Syrian archaeologist Khaled al-Asaad, who was killed by ISIS after he bravely refused to tell them where treasures were hidden. Nor will it protect important archaeological sites.

It's vital to try and protect this heritage, by supporting scholars, and funding scholarship, but it is difficult to know what else can realistically be done. The one thing we can all do, and must do, is return to those artefacts housed in museums that we can easily visit, like the British Museum, the Louvre, the Met, the Museum of Fine Arts in Boston, and the Pergamon Museum in Berlin. It is here that we can understand the cultures that produced them and admire them. It is here that these artefacts also need to be studied and appreciated. ISIS may wish to wipe out humanity's history. But we must resist their attempts to estrange us from our shared past. We can do so by valuing and appreciating museums and the objects they care for.

WHERE DO 'THEIR' MARBLES BELONG?

One autumn, as I was writing this book, I stood inside the Acropolis Museum looking out through the windows up at the actual Acropolis, bathed in golden sunlight. Standing there, I was in no doubt that were the sculptures removed by Lord Thomas Elgin's agents ever returned to Athens, this museum would be a perfect home for them. But a week later, wandering around the Duveen Gallery in the British Museum, I was equally certain that the same sculptures are perfectly situated in the British Museum.

Standing in both the Acropolis Museum and the British Museum, I could hear arguments about where the Elgin Marbles belonged (see Figures 6, 12, and 13). In both contexts I could hear a case made for and against their return to Athens. These artefacts can embody a number of ideas, tensions, and disagreements about their meaning and ownership, the importance of particular histories, and the role of museums. That is quite something. These marble sculptures are caught up in debates about the British Empire; the significance and glories of ancient Greece; what it is to be Greek; what it is to be British; what culture does to and for people; what museums are for; and who museums are for.

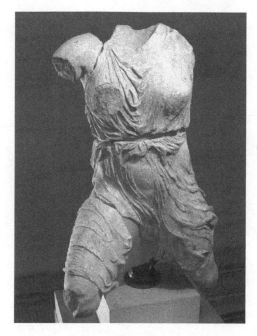

Figure 12. Figure of Iris from the west pediment of the Parthenon in the British Museum.
© The Trustees of the British Museum.

So where do these tremendous sculptures belong? They cannot go back to the original site, to the Parthenon on the Acropolis. Were this to be possible, there would be a case for doing so, but archaeologists agree that it is not safe to place them back on what remains of their birthplace. So the different parts will never be reunited where they were once placed by ancient Athenians. And even if they were, they would never look to us as they did to their first audience. Thousands of years ago, that location was part of a bustling centre, with other buildings surrounding it, in a powerful, boastful city state. It was not a ruin besieged by tourists. None of the Parthenon's sculptures even look how they did when they were first erected: they were brightly painted and covered in gilding, with metal belts on the figures and harnesses on the horses—not the bare white that they are today.

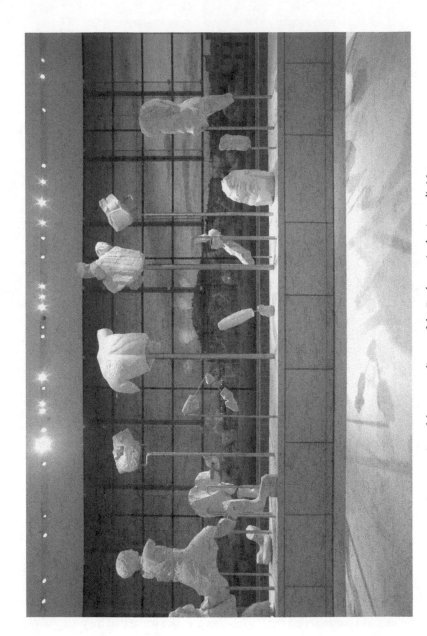

Figure 13. View of the west pediment of the Parthenon in the Acropolis Museum.
© Acropolis Museum.

But while they cannot be restored to the Parthenon on the Acropolis, the Elgin Marbles could go back to Athens, to a museum that has a special space for them. Doing so, would bring them together with other parts of the Parthenon already on show there, in the Acropolis Museum, which opened in Athens in 2009.

The Acropolis Museum is situated about a mile from the Acropolis. Through its windows you can see what remains of the Parthenon up on the hill. Thus, there is the potential to situate all the remaining sculptures together, close to the first site. But even this plan would not recreate the inceptive viewing experience. The Elgin Marbles could be reunited with the parts in the Acropolis Museum, but would not be presented as in the original setting vis-à-vis the spectator. The ancient Athenians would have found it difficult to see them, as they were made to be fixed 46 feet above the spectator's head. The metopes would only have been lit by light reflected from below, as they were out of the way of natural direct light. In the Acropolis Museum they are placed much lower down and everything is well lit.

But this arrangement would still convey a powerful sense of place and significance—it already does. The Acropolis Museum is rich in historical references to what preceded the sculptures. It holds a strong collection of pre-Classical sculpture, which helps to locate the Parthenon in time: where it came from, what came before it, and the break in style that it represented. As you walk through the galleries, before you reach the Parthenon sculptures on the top floor, where you can also see the Acropolis and remaining parts of the Parthenon through the windows, you see what came before them.

Half of the remaining Parthenon Sculptures are on display here. When the Acropolis Museum opened, the Greek president Karolos Papoulias restated the Greek claim for the return of the sculptures in the British Museum. 'Today the whole world can see the most important sculptures of the Parthenon assembled, but some are missing,' he said. 'Tragic fate has forced them apart but their creators meant them to be together.' With the opening of the new museum, it was 'time to heal the wounds of the monument with the return of the marbles which belong to it'.[58]

Bringing the different parts together is a plan with considerable support. The writer Christopher Hitchens argued that all the marbles should be reunited in his polemic *The Parthenon Marbles: The Case For Reunification*:

> Either all the marbles could be assembled in one museum in London, or they could be marshalled in a museum in Athens next to the Parthenon. But to keep them in two places, one of them quite sundered from the Parthenon and its context, seems bizarre and irrational as well as inartistic.[59]

In actual fact, Hitchens did not for one minute consider that the British Museum should house all the marbles. He urged that they be brought together in Greece.

Hitchens is far from the only one who argues that it is wrong that the Parthenon sculptures are separated. 'Fragmentary works divided among museums around the world deserve to be viewed and understood as elements of a whole,' asserts the art historian Malcolm Bell III, writing in favour of repatriation, which he argues 'is a form of restoration'. Bell points to these sculptures as a case in point:

> There are many examples of divided antiquities that could be returned to wholeness by intelligent, reciprocal exchanges. The most prominent among these are, of course, the dispersed component parts (in Latin, *disiecta membra*) of the greatest single work of classical antiquity, the temple of Athena on the Acropolis in Athens known to the world as the Parthenon.[60]

This argument is increasingly advanced by campaigners, such as, and including, the grandly titled British Committee for the Reunification of the Parthenon Marbles.

It is an argument that is both right and wrong. It is right, because there is no doubt that bringing together the dispersed component parts would strengthen the museum in Athens and its display. It already has a strong collection, and adding substantial amounts from the Parthenon—the Elgin Marbles—would complement that. Millions of people would benefit. At present the Acropolis Museum displays casts of the Elgin Marbles in place, made to look like casts; in order to emphasize their absence. And while some argue that this could be achieved by making the casts look less like casts (which is possible), in reality everybody—directors, sceptics, campaigners, visitors—wants to see the real thing, not a lookalike.

However, there are also good reasons for the continued separation of the two sets, and for the retention and display of the Elgin Marbles in the British Museum. This is why, for me, the argument for the 'reunification' of the sculptures is also wrong. That the Elgin Marbles are apart from the others has benefits. It is not possible to call any of the pieces from the Parthenon, when isolated from the others, inartistic. What is so interesting about them is that they are still magnificent when standing alone. And if you look at any artefact and monument in any museum, all have been removed from their original location. Just think of altarpieces, which were made for a religious context, for a particular position in a particular church. And yet in a gallery they are admired and analysed.

The placement of the Elgin Marbles in London, situated in the context of a museum with objects from all over the world, may not go so far as to improve international relations, but it does assist our understanding of how cultures have shaped each other. It brings benefits to our appreciation of the Parthenon Marbles, by furthering our understanding of ancient Greece and how that understanding has changed over time and influenced others.

At the British Museum, the placement of the Marbles draws out the inspiration for the Parthenon sculptures, and underlines what they, in turn, inspired. Walking through the different galleries of the British

Museum you can see how the civilizations of Egypt, Assyria, and Persia, the enemy of ancient Athens, contributed to the great accomplishment of Athens in the fifth century BC. You can see what came before the Parthenon Marbles and on what existing ideas and forms their creators drew, helping us to understand the major breakthroughs that the sculptors made. In turn, by looking at the similarities and differences between the artefacts from different cultures, it also becomes apparent that this great Greek art influenced sculpture from Turkey to India. It is also evident, in this context, the impact that Greek culture had on the Roman Empire. You can see the Roman statues, made with the Greek sculptures in mind, in the Roman Gallery. And in the Prints and Drawings Room of the British Museum, there are a number of drawings that suggest that the great Renaissance artists were inspired by the Roman copies of Greek sculptures.

The positioning of the Elgin Marbles in Bloomsbury also helps us to appreciate their impact on European society and beyond in the nineteenth society. It aids an understanding of how this ancient Greek art changed ideals of fine art, and displaced, for some time, other antiquity in our esteem. It shows us the legacy of the Marbles: what they have meant to people long after they were a twinkle in the sculptor Phidias' eye. These Marbles have had different lives, and meant different things; and their London story is a major part of that history. In this regard, their display in London helps explain their significance—what they mean and what they have meant, why and how.

So where do the Elgin Marbles belong, and how do we decide?

Some suggest that museums should repatriate objects through digital means—making available detailed images of artefacts, or by sending reproductions. I have nothing against these plans and would encourage them, but they sidestep the issue and are unlikely to end the debate. Thus far, nobody is really happy with the virtual or the cast instead of the real thing, and I cannot see the demand for the physical object, authenticity, and originality dissipating easily.

Others have suggested that museums should loan their artefacts more often, to get around questions of ownership by sharing them, and some museums including the British Museum already do just this—not just with their historic act to loan a sculpture from the Elgin Marbles to Russia. The British Museum boasts that it is the most generous lending collection in the world: over 5,000 objects from its collection travelled to 335 venues across the world in 2013–14.[61] The problem with this, however, is that loaning more artefacts fails to tackle the reasons for criticism of the museum—it evades and avoids these questions. Frantically loaning hundreds of precious artefacts is not the same thing as making an argument for the museum and its universal value.

The enthusiasm for loans is worrying for other reasons too—they are not automatically a good thing. Yes, more people get to see the work, but this comes at a cost. The dangers are obvious: transporting precious, unique, and fragile works around the world can mean damaging them. It's already happened. A few years ago a committee in the Scottish Parliament was considering whether to allow Glasgow's Burrell Collection to tour some of its treasures, against the will of the donor (something that may put off future donors). Nicholas Penny, director of the National Gallery in London, sent a letter to the committee, which was later accidentally posted on the Scottish Parliament's website, warning that 'moving works of art has led to several major accidents, incidents and damage to works, of which many have not come to public attention'.[62]

Still, there is a voracious appetite for international travelling shows. As one blockbuster opens, another is in preparation, whilst another closes, in some city or other around the world. Whilst there are undeniable advantages—certain works are brought together which assists our appreciation of them, there are also additional disadvantages: there are too many exhibitions for exhibition's sake, rather than for the artwork; for creating the impression of an event and media headlines, instead of scholarship or appreciation. It is a juggernaut infecting the art world with what the art critic Blake Gopnik has called 'Exhibitionitis'.[63] And this can impact negatively on the attention we pay to the permanent collection. No piece on its own is worth a look, it seems; it is only worth a visit if the paintings and sculptures are from somewhere else. 'What's coming next?' is the question everyone asks, not 'What is in the collection?'

Legal theorists have suggested that restitution claims could be considered by examining the contemporary reactions to a given case in order to establish how those taking contested items justified their actions and how they were protested at the time.[64] This is an interesting historical exercise, but it does not get to grips with why claims are being made now. Nor, I should point out, does it aim to—that is my aim. In my view, however, this approach runs into the danger of organizing the present around mores of the past, and we would again be fighting the battles of now through the lens of history. People have already trawled through the history of the acquisition of the Elgin Marbles and found arguments on both sides, including a Parliamentary Committee verdict to keep them; and yet fights continue over what was thought and how these actions were regarded. No document or argument from the past will ever be found that brooks *no* further argument.

It is up to us in the present to decide on what basis we want to organize a museum and their artefacts. In thinking how to approach that problem, the cultural property scholar John Henry Merryman suggests that a 'triad of regulatory imperatives' be invoked. Questions that should help prompt a decision about who owns culture and where it belongs pertain to questions about the 'preservation, truth, and access' to the material.[65] This is not a scientific test. Indeed, no policy could ever be formed to decide definitively who owns cultural artefacts, as there is not one 'right' answer. But I think the best way to decide is with regard for what is best

for the object, scholars, and the public: where the artefact is best preserved, best displayed, and best understood. This should stimulate questions such as: how will the object in question be best preserved? How can
the object and its context best serve knowledge? How is the object
available to scholars and the public? These questions seem far more
appropriate for deciding the fate of an artefact than accusations and
assertions about what objects do for us in the causes of identity formation
or in bringing about a tolerant world.

With these questions in mind, the present situation, with half of the
remains of the Parthenon Marbles in Athens and half in London, is good.
They can be seen and understood both in Athens, close to where they
were created, and in London, where they are seen in relation to a
different collection. Both have interested publics, are researched well by
scholars, and are well displayed.

With the case of the Parthenon sculptures, the most important questions are: Does any benefit derive from their being in two different
locations? And do they add value to the two different locations that
they are in? Clearly, the answer to both of these questions is 'yes'.
There *is* a benefit to the sculptures being *both* in Athens *and* in London.
That significant parts are in one museum and significant parts are in the
other furthers our understanding and appreciation of these artefacts. In
Athens, visitors can see one set of Marbles near to their original geographical location in a new, purpose-built museum. Audiences can gaze
out of the window to see where they once stood, and examine them next
to the pre-classical sculptures in the Acropolis Museum. They can better
imagine ancient Athens this way. In London, on the other hand, they can
see the influence that the sculptures and the ideal of ancient Athens had
on other cultures; what makes them so distinctive but also how they fit
into a wider world historical and cultural context.

London and Athens do not have to be the final place for either set.
I am not suggesting they should not go anywhere else ever again. They

could potentially go to China or Saudi Arabia, where new museums are being built at a great rate—but we would have to think seriously about the potential damage that could be caused to them with travel, and they have already suffered a fair amount. But museums do change, and they need not be imprisoned by the historical moment of ancient Athens or nineteenth-century northern Europe. At the moment, we have the advantage of being able to see two wonderful sets of sculptures in two wonderful museums. Both situations, together, display the birth and different lives of the Parthenon Marbles to great effect.

7

The Rise of Identity Museums

>–¦–◂▸•◦•◂▸¦–≺

Looking forward as well as backward, I have no doubt that the launching of the National Museum of the American Indian represents a fundamental turning point for the Smithsonian. It begins to correct a vast wrong, and all the myths and stereotypes with which we surrounded it in order to hide it—or at least not to confront it ourselves.[1]

So announced the Secretary of the Smithsonian, Robert McCormick Adams, as the American Congress established the National Museum of the American Indian. It would be a new kind of museum, McCormick Adams promised, one that 'envisions a partnership of a new and unprecedented kind—with those whose history and culture, once torn away from them, will now be represented only with their full complicity'. This partnership, he pledged,

creates a model of a dialogue with wider relevance than any in which we have participated, ending the separation between specialists as embodiments of authority and a passive audience, and leading in the direction of a museum without walls.

The National Museum of the American Indian (NMAI) opened on the National Mall in Washington DC, in 2004. Part of the prestigious Smithsonian Institution, the NMAI holds a world-renowned collection of 825,000 objects, spanning 12,000 years, encompassing the work of Native peoples from Tierra del Fuego at the tip of South America to the

Arctic Circle. The curvy, sandstone building is an attractive addition to the National Mall, sitting alongside eminent institutions that together tell the story of the nation: the National Museum of American History, the National Gallery of Art, together with the Washington Monument and the Capitol Building.

But the NMAI is a museum with a difference. It is at the forefront of new museums and policies that have been implemented since the 1990s, which make formal concessions to particular groups on the basis of their ethnicity. This devolving of authority applies to a range of activities, including who designs and builds the museum, who selects what is in the collection and how it is interpreted and presented, and who can see parts of the collection—if at all—as well as how artefacts are conserved and cared for.

The NMAI is not a private, community, or tribal museum, most of which were founded since the 1960s and number over 200 in Canada and America. It is a museum established by federal law. The enacting legislation, the National Museum of the American Indian Act of 1999, ruled that seventeen of the twenty-five governing trustees were to be Native Americans. The lawyer Richard West, a citizen of the Cheyenne and Arapaho Tribes of Oklahoma and Peace Chief of the Southern Cheyenne, was the founding director. The original design of the museum was by the Canadian architect Douglas Cardinal (of Blackfoot, Métis, and German heritage), who collaborated with Native design consultants Johnpaul Jones (Chereokee/Choctaw), Ramona Sakiestewa (Hopi), and Donna House (Navajo/Oneida), among others. Even the coffee in the Mitsitam Native Foods Cafe is grown by indigenous farmers and provided by the Eastern Band of Cherokee.

This is all done in the name of decolonization, self-determination, and self-definition for Native people. '[T]o decolonize the museum'—a priority today—'institutions need to develop long-term relationships with source communities built on trust,'[2] contends the museum scholar

Janet Marstine. 'Source communities' is the term for the group of people considered to be affiliated to the artefacts, and Marstine argues that they should control the interpretation of the past: how the artefacts are understood, presented, and stored in museums. The NMAI is an 'activist' museum, according to museum theorist Kylie Message, who describes it as 'a highly political and in many cases interventionist museum'.[3]

McCormick Adams, then, was correct in his opening address. The NMAI is indeed a departure from the traditional remit of a museum: that of acquiring, interpreting, and presenting collections—for everyone. The role of the NMAI is to pursue the perceived interests of particular groups and it has an explicitly political aim: to affirm and enliven Native cultures in the present.

The argument that one culture 'owns' a particular cultural heritage is having an impact within museums. As campaigners claim that certain countries such as Turkey, Italy, Peru, and Greece are the true owners of cultural artefacts because of their national identity, it is said that certain indigenous peoples—Native Americans, in the case of the NMAI—should be the sole arbitrators of their history and cultural artefacts. What is significant is just how many agree. Indeed, many museum professionals not only recognize that certain groups have privileges over others, but have enshrined this in practice. In many instances, in museums in America, Canada, and Australasia, certain groups benefit from privileged access and authority over the treatment, interpretation, and positioning of collections within museums.

Those resisting repatriation claims tend to concentrate on tackling the arguments that come from nation states, ignoring the demands from groups within nations. Critical examination of such claims is far weaker than that applied to the claims from nation states. But these arguments and practices express similar sentiments about who owns culture and why, as well as ideas about where knowledge comes from and who can access it, and so they also warrant scrutiny. Arguably, ideas about the exclusive rights of cultures within nations over material culture are more influential than the claims for repatriation from nations because, unlike the latter, they dominate both theory *and* practice in museums. In many institutions, exclusive privileges over the owning and interpreting of artefacts are asserted and granted on the basis of somebody's identity.

To understand where these identity museums came from and how they differ from the museums of the past, we need to begin by looking at how the material for them was originally collected.

GEORGE GUSTAV HEYE

The NMAI has its foundation in the passion of one portly, cigar-smoking man—George Gustav Heye, an eccentric amateur collector of the late nineteenth and early twentieth century. He was the son of Carl Friederich Gustav Heye, a German immigrant who earned his wealth in the petroleum industry, and Marie Antoinette Lawrence, who was from an old New York family and heiress to a cattle-trading fortune.

George Gustav had no background in collecting. He left Columbia College in 1896 with a degree in electrical engineering. But he grew up in an age when museums such as the American Museum of Natural History in New York and the Field Museum in Chicago were founded, and there was perhaps something in the air that fuelled his interest. Heye was on a railroad construction job, in Arizona in 1897, when he made his first acquisition—a Navajo deerskin shirt. 'I lived in a tent on the work and in the evenings used to wander about the Indians' quarters,' he recalled. One night:

> I noticed the wife of one of my Indian foremen biting on what seemed to be a piece of skin. Upon inquiry I found she was chewing some of the seams of her husband's deerskin shirt in order to kill the lice.

Heye took a liking to the shirt and bought it. Subsequently, he 'became interested in aboriginal customs and acquired other objects as opportunity offered':[4]

> I spent more time collecting Navajo costume pieces and trinkets than I did superintending roadbeds. The shirt was the start of my collection. Naturally when I had a shirt I wanted a rattle and moccasins. And then the collection bug seized me and I was lost.[5]

What started as a passing interest became a hobby. The hobby then became a full-time calling. Heye gave up his job as an engineer and went to work on Wall Street, but later gave that up as well, to pursue collecting full-time. He bought material from other collectors, snapping up whole collections, as well as buying from the commercial ethnologists at the Covert's Indian Store, then on Fifth Avenue in New York. Heye hired Mark Raymond Harrington, an archaeologist he met at Covert's, as a full-time collector for him, sourcing material on digs, visiting tribes, and acquiring a great number of artefacts.

Heye was not, of course, the first person to collect Native American material. Early collectors were European, mostly scientists, explorers, and traders, who started to collect objects 400 years earlier. In a published catalogue dated 1656, one of the most well-known cabinets of the seventeenth century—that of the Tradescants in London, which we encountered in Chapter 2—records twenty-nine items as likely to be from North America.[6] One of the first American collections assembled was from one of the early national reconnaissance surveys in 1804. It was sent to President Thomas Jefferson whose Philadelphia museum became a major repository for such material. Most American museums of natural history, many which were founded in the 1850s–70s, also had anthropological collections that included Native American material, and there was a vigorous period of collecting in the 1880s–1920s. The national collections of the Smithsonian were founded in 1846, but did not collect a significant amount of Native American material until the late 1870s.

Heye's collection, then, was a late start by a novice, but it grew exponentially, ending up as an extensive and important resource. In all, he acquired 58,000 objects. He funded—at times with his mother's support—archaeological and ethnographic expeditions in the US, as well as in Guatemala, Mexico, and Ecuador. His interest in Latin America predated the American Anthropological Association's interest in the area, but may have encouraged their identification, in 1907, of the region as a new priority. He bought huge swathes of archaeological material, a slightly different focus to the ethnological interest of the period. And on annual trips to Europe, made for this purpose, he purchased large collections from dealers and auctions in Paris and London. He demanded that the collections bought were no longer in use or found in communities. His 'Golden Rule' specified that the 'material *must* be old' and that there was to be 'NO TOURIST MATERIAL'.[7]

In 1916, he was offered a building site in New York between 155th Street and Broadway, for a museum that would join a new set of cultural organizations. It was here that the Museum of the American Indian was built, supported by his affluent friends. Heye was made director for life, and the museum opened to the public in 1922. The objective was 'the preservation of everything pertaining to our American tribes'. The founders hoped that it would mean 'the History of our primitive races may receive the attention that it deserves and that the proper facilities for the study of American anthropology may be presented to the scientist and general student in the proper way'.[8] Despite having a museum to manage, Heye continued to collect. Within four years of opening it was full, so a storage facility was built in the Bronx. But he did lose a couple of backers; this and the Depression meant that he had to slow down.

When Heye died in 1957, the collection held around 700,000 individual items which make up around 85 per cent of the current holdings in the NMAI. The collections were transferred to the Smithsonian in 1989 and formed the basis for the NMAI opening over a decade later.

Although there were other substantial private collections, George Gustav Heye's collection is the largest assemblage of Native American artefacts ever acquired by one person. He catalogued much of the material himself, making some mistakes on the way, and although he was much admired he never quite gained academic respectability. Marshall Saville, professor of archaeology and one of Heye's employees at the Museum of the American Indian, described him as having 'valuable magpie tendencies'.[9] Others just felt he was a little odd. This is partly because Heye took everything he could find rather than selecting the best or the most beautiful. His obsession drove his first wife away (their Madison Avenue apartment was the first point of storage), but his hoovering up of material would later prove useful.

Other collectors concentrated on acquiring what they considered to be highly attractive, unique, and decorative pieces. Heye bought every object he could, in one case accumulating around 5,000 moccasins. Many have intricate designs and are in fine condition. Others are worn out, frayed, and well used, and it is these that show us, not just how they were constructed and how lovely they were, but how they were worn, how, and for what. It is the size and scope of his collection that make it a treasure trove for the understanding and documenting of Native American cultures.

EXHIBITING LIVING INDIANS

In the period that Heye was actively collecting, the late nineteenth century and early twentieth century, the American frontier had closed. Relations between the settlers and the indigenous people were uneasy after the wars. Museums and their displays reflected the shifting and difficult relations between the United States and the Native people, and played a role in the positioning of America as a new nation.

The ideology of racism developed towards the end of the nineteenth century. A key rationalizing principle for colonization and imperialism was that subject peoples were racially distinct. A discourse of racial difference became the basis for which the denial of equality could be justified, as could the intervention of foreign powers and settlers. Those colonized were held to be incapable of self-government and in need of the rule of others: an outlook expressed in the poem 'White Man's Burden' by Rudyard Kipling, which describes one group of the colonized as 'new-caught, sullen peoples, | Half devil and half child'. The Chief Justice of the US Supreme Court in 1831, John Marshall, would describe the Indian tribes in a similar way, as 'domestic dependent nations' whose relation to the United States 'resembles that of a ward to his guardian'.[10]

With the ending of the wars between the settlers and the Native people, American society adopted what the anthropologist Ira Jacknis characterizes as 'a range of ambivalent attitudes' towards the indigenous people. The federal government pushed through policies designed to assimilate them into American society, demanding that they adopt 'habits of civilized life', which entailed the curbing of Native societies and the banning of certain religious practices.[11] At the same time as this attempt to assimilate and remove the Native cultures, and probably related to it, Jacknis identifies a rise in 'romantic nostalgia' for Indian cultures, which triggered a flurry of private collecting. The interest in non-Western cultures spread across the Western World, as evidenced in the art movement known as Primitivism, led by painters like Picasso and Gauguin, and as part of the Arts and Crafts movement, with its congruent interest in folk and handmade objects. Native American culture would not be part of an art gallery for some time, however. During this era it was more often part of history, natural history, and anthropology collections.

International expositions were held between 1876 and 1916, showing off manufacturing and commercial projects, and championing the economic strength of the nation and its artistic resources. This was part of the ordering of America, a display of the nation, a way of presenting what and who was important and why. The historian Robert Rydell describes how these fairs were infused with ideas of technological and national progress and how they presented and portrayed the different people of America in a way that was 'laced with scientific racism'.[12] Particular displays promoted the idea of a hierarchy of races, and contributed to legitimizing domestic and international policy in relation to the treatment of Native Americans and other non-European peoples abroad.[13]

The Smithsonian contributed to these scientific exhibits. Officials saw them as an important place for public education. A number of the fairs included anthropological material and this included living Indian people. Indians were on show, exhibited as if they too were objects. In some cases they were displayed as examples of America's past: Buffalo Bill's Wild West Show exhibited them as warriors who had to be fought and overcome. In other cases they were displayed as primitives in the evolution of human progress.

One such attraction in Atlanta was the Indian Village, where one exhibition recalled the recent events of the early 1890s, which had culminated in the last bloody battle of the American Indian Wars—the Wounded Knee massacre—in South Dakota. The very same Sioux Indians who had fought the United States troops in this battle were exhibited a few years later, living in a re-created village with replica lodges. Displayed for all to see were a woman and her young son who had been shot whilst they slept, at Wounded Knee. The little boy had in fact been shot twice. The director of publicity and official history, Walter G. Cooper, blithely observed: 'This boy, known as "Little Wound," seems to be no worse physically for this early taste of war, and during the Exposition, showed all the lively and mischievous tendencies of a robust urchin.'[14] The Smithsonian Museum's collection used to hold twenty-nine objects from the battle of Wounded Knee, including six Ghost Dance shirts— garments for warriors that were imbued with special powers—as well as moccasins, jackets, and caps. In 1998, they were returned to the descendants of those who took part in the battle.

The majority of what George Gustav Heye acquired was legally bought, but as we can see the background for this era is one characterized by a strained relationship between tribal peoples and the institutions of government. Their very way of life was under attack, or at best regulated and romanticized (as well, of course, as collected).

In 1922, Heye bought thirty-five masks and regalia from the Cranmer potlatch collection, paying what was then a huge sum, $435. The masks were part of a much larger collection that had been removed from the Kwakiuti people as they were celebrating a potlatch: an important gift-giving, ritual ceremony which could last for days and take years to prepare, which had taken place near Vancouver. The Canadian government had outlawed the potlatch in 1884 in the Indian Act. It was seen as unchristian, and officials thought that it took up too much time, which should be spent working. The Canadian Mounties seized the regalia at this potlatch, which was then exchanged for suspended sentences for the participants. The official account describes the removal of the material as benign and voluntary: 'As the Indians felt they would not have further use for this class of material, a large amount of it was obtained for the Museum, including several very unique mechanical masks, many head-dresses, rattles, besides utilitarian specimens.'[15]

The regalia was given to William Halliday, the local Indian agent, who sold them on to Heye, and others. Some of it ended up in the Canadian Museum of Civilization in Ottawa (which in 2013 was renamed the Canadian Museum of History) and the Royal Ontario Museum, and one of the masks was sent to the Cranmore Ethnographical Museum in Kent, in Britain. Items from this haul have since been repatriated to the U'mista Cultural Society in British Columbia, including, in 2002, sixteen pieces from the National Museum of the American Indian.

On one occasion George Gustav Heye, too, repatriated material. In North Dakota in 1907, a Presbyterian missionary who had been collecting for Heye bought a sacred shrine in which there was a medicine bundle with two skulls. This was an object that had been used in rituals to bring rain. In the 1930s a great drought struck the Great Plains. Leaders of the Hidatsa Water Buster clan negotiated with museum officials for the return of the bundles. Heye agreed to it, 'solely for the purpose of cementing the cordial relationship which had always existed between the Museum and the various Indian tribes'.[16] At a ceremony in 1938 George Gustav gave two Hidatsa elders, Drags Wolf and Foolish Bear, the medicine bundle (see Figure 14). In exchange they gave him a scared powder horn and war club. Soon after, it rained.

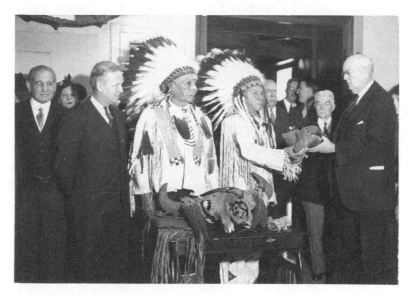

Figure 14. George Gustav Heye with Foolish Bear and Drags Wolf (1938).
Ceremony to return a medicine bundle from the collections to the leaders of the Water Buster clan.
© National Museum of the American Indian.

Forty years later, during the course of an inventory, a few pieces of that bundle were found stashed in a box. It appears that Heye had withheld some of the items and nobody had noticed. In 1977, a museum staff member travelled to North Dakota to return the rest.

THE RISE OF IDENTITY MUSEUMS

Heye's original collection was culturally specific. He was devoted to acquiring artefacts from a particular group of people: in the words of the Museum of the American Indian's mission statement, 'everything useful in illustrating and elucidating the anthropology of the aborigines of the Western Hemisphere'.[17] The museum that Heye founded—the Museum of the American Indian—and the National Museum of the American Indian, which opened in 2004, may, then, appear similar. Both were built around and house the very same collection of artefacts. But their purpose is not the same. What is different about the NMAI and other similar new museums today? What do the latter aim to do and how do they do it?

From the 1990s, new museums have been built for, and existing museums have been reoriented towards, particular groups on the basis of their ethnicity. Rather than being about the display of artefacts and the dissemination of knowledge, and aimed at the general public, these museums have an explicitly political role: the aim of improving the lives of those Native people.

In America, all museums are under pressure to proactively involve indigenous communities when planning exhibitions pertaining to Native American material or history. According to Amy Lonetree, a professor of Native American studies: 'If [museums] want to be part of the twenty-first-century museum world, they must produce their exhibitions with the full involvement of the Native communities they propose to represent and must involve them in all aspects of their development.'[18] The American Association of Museum Directors concurs. Its guidance recommends that all art museums routinely enter into negotiations with groups about the display of what is deemed their culture. 'Today, it is virtually unthinkable for a museum to create an exhibit about Native people without including Native people themselves in the planning and curatorial process,' explain art historian Janet Catherine Berlo and museum director Aldona Jonaitis.[19] So whereas the old Museum of the American Indian displayed Native American material for anybody to see and appreciate, regardless of their ethnicity, at the NMAI, people with particular identities decide who can see what—if at all—and how it is interpreted.

This practice is common beyond America, where there is a history of colonization or settler societies. In 1993, the Council of the Australian Museums Association endorsed a document entitled *Previous Possessions New Obligations*, which established new relationships between museums and indigenous peoples by compelling institutions to work collaboratively with indigenous groups on all aspects of running a museum. The Canadian Museums Association and the Assembly of First Nations said something similar in its 1992 policy *Turning the Page: Forging New Partnerships Between Museums and First Peoples*.

Te Papa in New Zealand operates in a similar way. It began as the Colonial Museum in Wellington in 1865, changing its name to the Dominion Museum in 1907, and became the National Museum in 1972. In 1992 the Museum rebranded itself as the Museum of New Zealand Te Papa Tongarewa. This followed the Museum of New Zealand Te Papa Tongarewa Act, which embodies the ideals of the Treaty of Waitangi, said to put the Maori people on an equal footing. Te Papa is formally bicultural. Seddon Bennington, a chief executive of the Museum of New Zealand, Te Papa Tongarewa, explained what this meant: 'My vision is Te Papa realizing the strengths that come from embracing two different ways of seeing the world.' He elaborated: 'There is a western way of seeing the world and a Matauranga Māori way. The rest of the world cannot tap into Māori wisdom.'

The premise of this way of working is that indigenous people should be the ones to tell their history. Native Americans only can speak for and tell the story of Native Americans; the Maori for the Maori; and Aboriginal groups for the Aboriginal past. Lissant Bolton, curator of the Pacific and Australian Collections at the British Museum, has put the point like this: 'In the Australian context, this means that any indigenous Australian is understood to have a greater right to speak about any Aboriginal object than any non-indigenous Australian.'[20]

It is important to ask: Who is indigenous? Who decides? And on what basis? In the US, it is not possible to separate Indian communities from federal policies and politics. Tribal entities are part of the product of historical negotiated settlements between the communities and the government. Historically, the federal government played a role in deciding, through consultation, which tribe was legitimate and who should speak for them, and this remains the case today: the federal government and museum institutions are involved in ruling on who is legitimately indigenous, and who is not. This has been criticized as being a pan-Indian approach, which sees all Indians as the same, when there are currently 600 different registered tribes. Furthermore, these policies tend to vest authority in anointed chiefs and elders. But how many and which tribal members need to subscribe to the traditional view for it to remain authoritative? What about those who disagree? And what about those who want to change this, or challenge it from within? Such strictures pertain to traditional indigenes and minorities, those now deemed to speak with one voice, but do they always do so? It becomes difficult for groups to modernize or change if they want to.

The motives are understandable, but these new identity museums are troubling on many levels. For a start, the suggestion is that researching and understanding history and material artefacts can only properly be done by someone of a particular race or religion; effectively knowing or understanding is something achieved due to birth or background. The idea promoted here is that knowledge and truth resides in blood or belief. This outlook resurrects racial ways of thinking about human groups, which should raise alarm bells among those who see identity museums as a way of challenging racism. And it follows, according to the logic of these institutions and their codes of practice, that those outside the culture cannot truly understand it because they have not experienced it. Such an approach creates barriers between people, and between people and artefacts. It advances the idea of impenetrable differences between fixed identities. At the new identity museums, cultures are separate, and irreconcilable. Far from tearing down walls between people, these institutions erect new ones.

The idea institutionalized here is that a particular identity owns history and decides how it is interpreted. But handing over the right to narrate history on the basis of ethnicity is not the way knowledge works. The pursuit of knowledge and the understanding of the past must be open to everybody, regardless of their class, their ethnicity, or their gender. That is how questions can be explored, and old forms of authority challenged.

When speaking to curators about this practice, some have argued that consultation with cultural groups can tell us more about the object. And, yes, people who may be close to the original manufacture and use of an artefact can reveal a great deal that is unknown about its creation, use, and meaning. It would be odd not to discuss practice with them, because they have valuable knowledge. But this is different to granting the final authority to people on the basis of their apparent cultural roots.

It is way of working that restricts who is permitted to see what and shuts down access for researchers or the public. Anointed groups decide how the material is to be shown, if at all. Exhibits are segregated and restricted if the objects are sacred or have ceremonial status. Some objects may only be seen by certain individuals in the tribe, or only by men. The anthropologist Ruth Phillips acknowledges that this is censorious, that these codes and policies 'set limits on classic methods of study' and that they 'erode the idea of universal access to knowledge'.[21] But the restrictions are justified, she argues, on the basis that 'the ethics and politics of pluralism require that museums and academic institutions attend seriously and respectfully to requests that render some objects non-visible'.[22] By 'non-visible', Phillips is referring to the way in which some objects have been removed from display, taken away from researchers, and hidden from the viewing public. As she notes, this has had a major effect:

> One of the most striking changes in ethnographic and art museum representations of Native North American peoples at the turn of the twenty-first century has been the disappearance from public display of object types long celebrated as canonical forms of art and material culture.[23]

Phillips elaborates:

> Coast Salish rattles and masks have been moved to restricted areas of museum storerooms, female museum staff have been asked to stop handling categories of Plains medicine objects specific to men, and research on human remains and associated burial objects has been curtailed.[24]

Removing objects from public display, and restricting access for researchers, is now common practice. As a result, there is less to see, less to learn about, and less to learn from.

The National Museum of Australia in Canberra keeps 'secret sacred' Aboriginal objects segregated from the rest of the collection so that only designated people are permitted to see them. The museum's director may not be permitted to know the contents of the secret sacred storage. Visitors to the Maori storeroom at the Museum of New Zealand Te Papa Tongarewa are given the choice not to enter if they are menstruating or pregnant. Te Papa explains that the advisory was given to protect women from the 'tapu', the sacredness of the objects. This practice alters how the artefacts are perceived—less as museum objects and more as objects of use, which can then be allowed to deteriorate. Harvard University's Peabody Museum chose to allow a historic set of photographs to disintegrate because the Navajo tribe objected to non-tribal members viewing the rituals that they depicted. The NMAI operates a policy on conservation whereby, if certain tribal leaders advise that the object should be allowed to deteriorate, it is.

It is appalling that objects have taken been off the shelves and hidden from view. At other museums, where there are artefacts on show that have a religious or particular, more private or special meaning for visitors, we can still all see and relate to those artefacts in ways of our own choosing. At the National Gallery in London, I have seen practising Catholics respond differently to me to a painting of the Virgin Mary— they cross themselves in front her; something I, an atheist, do not do. But we can both see her. The same applies to artefacts in the British Museum, which may mean something different to different visitors. At an ordinary museum our individual reactions to objects are not regulated, or controlled in the way they are at identity museums.

REDEFINING THE MISSION

According to Amanda Cobb-Greetham, professor of American studies at Oklahoma State University, the NMAI 'was expressly designed to celebrate—not to observe, study, or judge but to celebrate'.[25] The reason particular identities are privileged in these museums is in order to improve the lives of Native peoples today, as explicitly laid out in the mission statement:

> The National Museum of the American Indian shall recognize and affirm to Native communities and the non-Native public the historical and contemporary cultural achievements of the Native peoples of the Western Hemisphere.

It will 'protect, support, and enhance the development, maintenance, and perpetuation of Native culture and community'. In other words, the museum will advocate for the Native people today. It has a range of services specifically for Native communities, including artist residencies and community workshops and a strong outreach programme.

When I visited the NMAI, I enjoyed seeing many of the rich and colourful exhibits, but found that there was only minimal information available about them. The labels were often fairly non-specific, with plenty of generic statements about Native American peoples—statements that told me little about the particular people who made the objects and what they may have meant to them, or how the artefacts were used. I am far from the only person to have felt this way: the complaint that exhibitions are banal and celebratory, rather than informative and exploratory, has been commonly aired. Ed Rothstein, art critic of the *New York Times*, described the result as creating exhibitions that not only fail to ring true, but also do a disservice to history:

> Through a gauze of romance, th[e] museum portrays an impossibly peace-loving, harmonious, homogeneous, pastoral world that preceded the invasion of white people—a vision with far less detail and insight than the old natural history museums once provided.[26]

The historian Steven Conn suggests that the NMAI is akin to heritage: that is, it is an idealized version of the past, and one that never accounts for itself, as it cannot be questioned. The past on display at NMAI translates approximately as 'It's an Indian thing; you wouldn't understand', he writes.[27] The anthropologist Michael Brown makes similar observations, and explains that such practice will have serious, negative consequences for our understanding of the Native culture. Deciding who can access knowledge on the basis of ethnicity or belief hinders the understanding of the very people it claims to protect, because the effect is to make it difficult to pursue knowledge about past—and current—

indigenous life. Brown explains that descriptive facts, especially about religion, are now deemed 'culturally sensitive' and unsuitable for public discussion, leaving accounts of Native religion with little to report but 'generic spirituality'.[28]

Unfortunately, museums run like the NMAI curtail the pursuit of knowledge about past indigenous cultures; whereas it is the role of museums, Brown ventures, to create more knowledge about the past and let all of us access it. 'Don't institutions have a right, perhaps even a duty, to draw on their inherent strengths in the interest of promoting the widest possible public discussion on important social issues?' Brown asks.[29]

There are also big questions about the extent to which museums provide an effective way to improve the circumstances of particular communities in the present day. Suggesting to Native people that their problems can be resolved by controlling knowledge and exhibits in museums contains certain dubious assumptions: that indigenous people are formed by their past; and that control over the presentation of that past is where solutions to contemporary issues lie. This avoids tackling the deeper social problems of the here and now, and imagining solutions that could positively affect the circumstances of indigenous people today. Moreover, splitting people up into their ethnic groups encourages a mentality of segregation rather than solidarity, a solidarity that could be beneficial when demanding more from government—and other members of society.

FINDING THE RIGHT BALANCE

Two more museums are planned in the US organized around and for particular identities. A federal commission report to the US Congress endorsed the National Museum of the American Latino. The campaign launched by the museum's Friends plans to create a museum in our nation's capital to educate, inspire and encourage respect and understanding of the richness and diversity of the American Latino experience within the U.S. and its territories by highlighting the contributions made by Latino leaders, pioneers and communities to the American way of life.[30]

If opened, it will follow the Smithsonian National Museum of African American History and Culture, due to open on the National Mall in 2016.

With a planned Latino museum set to sit alongside the National Museum of the American Indian and a scheduled African American museum, the story of the American people may become segregated into separate buildings, each devoted to a particular ethnic category. There is a danger that American history is being fragmented into self-contained ghettos. But is this increased emphasis on ethnic identity, so constructed, really the best framework for understanding the past? Take, for example, the artist Diego Rivera. As a Mexican who was later to live in the US, he would be ripe for inclusion in the new Latino museum. But would he have considered himself a 'Latino' artist?

Rivera's work was influenced by Mexican folk art, but it was also deeply informed by his engagement with Spanish, French, and Italian art and artists. The core of his exchanges with his contemporaries was not Mexican: it was genres and meaning, musings on cubism, post-impressionism, and Renaissance frescoes. Indeed it was the Renaissance fresco that influenced his murals portraying the experiences of not only Mexican people but, crucially, an international working class. Rivera was occasionally excluded from the American mainstream. But this was due to his political stance, not his Latino heritage. Hence his mural *Man at the Crossroads*, begun in 1933 for the Rockefeller Center in New York City, was removed because it featured a portrait of the Russian Revolutionary leader Vladimir Lenin, which Rivera refused to erase.

Given these different cultural influences and his political commitments, is it fair to see Rivera as a Latino artist first and foremost? I do not think so. The wider present-day prism of identity can tend to rewrite the past and represent it as a monolithic struggle of 'empire' on the one hand versus 'race' on the other, when it may often have been a war *within* countries, or *across* nations.

America's story is of course one where race and ethnic categories have been very important. For some time society was formally organized along these lines. Nonetheless the question remains as to whether museums devoted to particular ethnic groups are the best way forward to understanding this past. At the Smithsonian's National History Museum of American History, there is a section of a Woolworths lunch counter, taken from an outlet in Greensboro, North Carolina. It is historically significant because in 1960 it served as the sit-in site for four black students to demonstrate against racial segregation—an act that helped to galvanize the civil-rights movement worldwide. It could also be said that this counter belongs in the new African American museum. But removing all the material from the American History museum that is relevant for the African American museum would leave the former as 'the white museum'. Taking away objects from current institutions because they are required to build a particular, ethnically constructed collection elsewhere would cause difficulties. In the attempt to include people, these actions could separate where there was no separation before.

Nonetheless, there is a case for specialist institutions that devote their time and energy to one people, to one time, or culture. In theory, a specific museum could tell a single ethnic group's story with rigour. This is especially the case in the US. Given the importance of this story to the American story, it would be a massive blind spot not to reflect on the experience of Black America. Lonnie Bunch, the director of the new National Museum of African American History and Culture, has tried to rebut the ghettoising claim by highlighting the museum's contribution to the story of America. He explains:

[The National Museum of African American History and Culture] is not being built as a museum by African-Americans for African-Americans... The notion that is so important here is that African-American culture is used as a lens to understand what it means to be an American.[31]

Bunch has a point. Race in America is too important, has been too central to the nation's past and present, for it not to have dedicated institutions reflecting on it. And campaigns for a museum devoted to the African American experience, developing in the 1970s when African Americans were excluded from the mainstream of American history, have a long and reputable history.

This brings us back to the kind of discussion we had about national museums. In many cases, there is an argument for studying the craft work and artefacts created in a confined time and location: the culture of a people is worthy of examination.

When, then, is it legitimate to study a particular people and their culture, and when is it questionable? Until recently, institutions that were devoted to understanding a culture and its artefacts would not have handed over the authority of interpretation and curation of the collection to that particular group of people on the basis of their identity. The American Swedish Museum, in Philadelphia, did not, and does not, specify that a certain proportion of Swedes have to be on the board, or that only those born in Sweden—or of Swedish ancestry—can curate 'their' history, or that if you are not Swedish you can have no say over that past. Nobody expects the Swedish Museum to make Swedish people feel better about their history or enliven their identity today. This is the difference: that culture can be studied in its particularity, confined to questions of geography and time, but such study should not be restricted to people on the basis of their identity.

Upon the establishment of the NMAI, Robert McCormick Adams said that he rejected 'the older image of the museum as a temple with its superior, self-governing priesthood'.[32] But here there is a new priesthood in the making, one that can only be joined on the basis of ethnicity. That is not a step forward for anybody. Today, as the telling of history on the basis of identity is legitimized, we are swapping old prejudices for new: exchanging historical myth-making for modern myths that cannot be contested. New hidden histories are being created.

8

Atonement

Making Amends for Past Wrongs

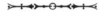

'It's time we lost our Marbles,' declared the British actor and com-mentator Stephen Fry, speaking for the motion 'The Parthenon Marbles Should Be Returned to Athens' at a debate in London.[1] Fry put the case that Lord Elgin's actions were 'little short of looting', and that the sculptures belong in Greece: 'the stone quarried from Mount Pentelikon, the dazzling white pentelic marble from which the Parthenon is made, is for Greece what the marble of Carrara was for Michelangelo and it belongs in his homeland, it expresses it'. He then proposed an additional reason, which was rewarded with a cheer from the audience. Return of the Marbles would 'redress a great wrong'; it would be an act of 'atonement'. In this way, by describing Elgin's historic actions as so heinous that they could and should be made right in the present, Stephen Fry drew on the increasingly popular concept of making reparations.

The repatriation of an object to the original location or people will, it is said, make amends for colonization, for the impact of settler societies, and for the harm that was done to conquered peoples hundreds of years ago. 'Cultural property turns out to be a particularly appropriate medium for negotiating historical injustices,' posits the historian Elazar Barkan.[2] In a similar vein, Richard Vernon, the professor of political science, advances:

Returning a prized object can be part of a process of acknowledging and publicly clarifying the past, in a way that changes (for the better) the relationship between the two parties. Beyond the intrinsic value of the object itself to its original possessor, the act of returning it expresses the end of a relationship of domination of one party over the other.[3]

The repatriation of cultural artefacts, advocates claim, can help to repair the past. But can it—or should it?

Explorers on the Voyages of Discovery in the seventeenth and eighteenth centuries returned with natural and artificial curiosities now held in museums all over the world. These adventures would lead to major breakthroughs in understanding the natural world, as well as different cultures—but the travellers paved the way for colonization and changed the lives of native people forever, and not always for the better. In the eighteenth and nineteenth centuries, European countries acquired fabulous treasures as a consequence of presumptive and destabilizing interventions and expeditions. Britain and France have great museum collections due in part to national and imperial rivalries; and as we have seen, the appropriation of many objects and monuments was occasionally the result of war, and often done to symbolize political triumph. Given our sensibilities today—the desire to distance ourselves from colonialism and imperialism; the recognition that many of these actions were morally questionable, even in those cases where they were legal and even when things turned out well—it is not surprising that we find ourselves wrestling with the question of whether the objects should now be returned to their original locations.

The concept of making reparations for past wrongs—returning an artefact to the original location or people, as a way of saying sorry for the circumstances of acquisition and an attempt to make amends—is an idea that emerged forcefully in the late 1980s, and is not confined to museums and galleries and what they do with their artefacts. Demands that states, churches, and individuals pay, or make some kind of atonement, have also been made. But despite its recent popularity, the concept of making reparations is one that is rarely analysed and engaged with, especially with regard to the debate over the repatriation of cultural artefacts. It is evoked in argument, but those on either side infrequently ask: what does this development mean and why has it appeared in a particular historical moment?

Let us now reflect on these questions; examine where the concept of reparations came from and how it emerged. This chapter asks: What forces are at work here? Why does this process occur now? What accounts for these claims? And above all, is the return of artefacts really, as Elazar Barkan contends, an 'appropriate medium for negotiating historical injustices'?

THE POLITICS OF REGRET

The notion of realpolitik—the idea that pragmatism, rather than ideology or ethics, should drive politics—was commonplace in international diplomacy in the imperialist period until the end of the Second World War, when coming to terms with the past became an urgent preoccupation, especially in post-war Germany. What had happened was so devastating that it was no longer possible to simply move on without recognizing formally what had taken place. The post-war German chancellor Konrad Adenauer described this process as *Wiedergutmachung*—'making good again'—and saw it as essential to the rehabilitation of Germany in the eyes of the international community. The philosopher Karl Jaspers suggested that there was a need formally to acknowledge the past, but not just for an instrumental political interest. In his work *Die Schuldfrage* (*The Question of German Guilt*), Jaspers argued that the German people should assume responsibility for the actions of the Nazis, making reparations in an attempt to forge a political and collective response to the crimes of National Socialism. Jaspers extended the concept of guilt from the Nazis to the German people.

Jaspers's student, the political philosopher Hannah Arendt, responded to the same problem in her work *The Origins of Totalitarianism*.[4] Arendt suggested that a relaxed attitude towards the past was no longer tenable. She engaged with the ideas advanced by the political philosopher Edmund Burke in his *Reflections on the Revolution in France*, published in 1790, who had taken a very different view. Burke argued against those who wanted to hold their countrymen to account for past injustices in the wake of revolution—doing so, he warned, would upset the present: '[W]ithout care it might be used to vitiate our minds and to destroy our happiness.'[5] Following the experience of totalitarian regimes, Arendt took exception with Burke's stance. 'We cannot afford to take that which was good in the past and simply call it our heritage, to discard the bad and simply think of it as a dead load which by itself time will bury in oblivion,' she wrote, warning: 'all efforts to escape from the grimness of the present into nostalgia for a still intact past, or into the anticipated oblivion of the future are in vein'.[6]

Karl Jaspers and Hannah Arendt were responding to a particular historical moment. What is important for our study is that this way of thinking—the need formally to acknowledge the past—has today become detached from the specific experience of the Second World War and the response to Nazism. It has become mainstream, commonplace in international relations and extended to multiple circumstances in different arenas.

The term 'reparations' was initially used in connection with fines exacted among states. It now refers to a broader project of making amends towards non-state groups and individuals, an expansion as part of what the sociologists Jeffrey Olick and Brenda Coughlin characterize as the 'the politics of regret'.[7] Under the framework of 'the politics of regret', Olick and Coughlin describe the rise of a variety of movements for redress that have won some form of financial or symbolic compensation, including the restitution of objects and art as well as criminal prosecutions and public apologies, all of which have become prominent. They describe this process as a 'proliferation of collective regret', and locate it as arising about forty years after the work of Arendt and Jaspers.[8]

In his important work *The Heritage Crusade and the Spoils of History*,[9] David Lowthenal identified a cultural turn towards the past dating from about 1980. He argued that much of this—a booming interest in the past from all sections of society, not just the elites, which itself was novel—was not history per se, but heritage: history is a record of the past, he posited; heritage is a celebration. Lowenthal argued the boom in heritage was driven by present-day problems. The past, as it was imagined, embodied lost but reassuring values. But the heritage industry was soon transformed from a nostalgic, celebratory outlook into one that was more negative, where the wrongs and ills of the past came to be blamed for contemporary problems.

In the late 1980s, the practice of making reparations went beyond those paid by the Germans to their Jewish victims, when it was extended to other groups for different historical wrongs. In a later study on the vogue for historical contrition, David Lowenthal identifies 1988 as the important turning point, when the American government distributed $1.6 billion to Japanese Americans who had been interned in camps during the Second World War, by way of compensation. Lowenthal documents several subsequent reparations campaigns all over the world, with claimants including groups in South Africa, Namibia, Argentina, Brazil, and Chile, as well as Australian Aborigines, Native Americans, Japanese, Americans, and African Americans.[10]

The historian Elazar Barkan locates the emergence of a new international moral order, based on apology for past acts, as emerging around the late 1990s. Barkan demonstrates that it was at this point that restitution for past victims became a major part of national politics and international diplomacy. He discusses what he describes as a 'performative guilt', where leaders theatrically say sorry for acts from the past for which they had no responsibility.[11] Today, the demand for apologies shows little sign of abating. One month after the British Conservative MP David Cameron became prime minister of a coalition government, in June 2010, he told the House of Commons: 'I am deeply sorry' for an event that took place when he was 5 years old. This was on the publication of the Saville Report on the Bloody Sunday massacre of 1972, when British paratroopers opened fire on crowds at a civil rights demonstration in Derry/Londonderry in Northern Ireland. Two years later, the prime minister was 'profoundly sorry' for the Hillsborough tragedy of 1989, where a series of failures by the police led to the deaths of ninety-six people, yet the authorities at the time attempted to blame football supporters for the tragedy.

The previous prime minister, Tony Blair, also issued a number of rhetorical statements of atonement for events that had taken place before his time in power—indeed, before he was even born. In 1997, soon after the election of the Labour government, Blair expressed his sorrow for the Irish Potato Famine that had occurred 150 years previously, resulting in the deaths of hundreds of thousands of Irish people. On the bicentenary of the abolition of slavery, Tony Blair again expressed his 'deep sorrow' for Britain's role in the slave trade.[12] Pope John Paul II apologized on over 100 different occasions. In 2000 he held a special Mass of the Millennium, asking God's forgiveness for the sins of Roman Catholics across history, including wrongs inflicted on women, Jews, and minorities. When Bill Clinton was president of the United States of America, he made many apologies, including apologizing to El Salvador for American policies. As queen of the United Kingdom, Elizabeth II formally apologized to the Maoris in New Zealand, and she said sorry to India for the massacre of Amritsar in 1919.

It is novel, Barkan writes, that political leaders draw attention to the wrongs committed by their societies in the past. Previously, society did not in general look back so much—or at least so regretfully. When it did look back, the tales it told of itself to itself tended to be myths of past greatness. Over the past 200 years, national myths about nations have tended to be based on heroic deeds and victory. The kings and great leaders would take centre stage and those that they governed were either portrayed as happy and grateful, or not mentioned at all. Those myths were one-sided; they celebrated the elite of a culture—the victors. The losers were brushed aside, forgotten. The new collective memory that is being forged, by contrast, is one more likely to recognize the heinous rather than the heroic, the victims over the victorious.

This turn is evident in some of the museums built in recent decades. In the past thirty years, more memorial museums have opened than in the previous 100 years.[13] These include the memorial museum of the 9/11 attacks; sixteen Holocaust museums in the US alone (with plans for more); and a museum dedicated to those who died and lost their loved ones in the bombing in Oklahoma City in 1995. There are scores of museums documenting slavery in America and genocide in Armenia, Rwanda, and the Balkans. Others show state repression in Eastern Europe; apartheid in South Africa; political 'disappearances' in Argentina; and massacres in China and Taiwan. Even within older institutions, such as the Natural History Museum in London, there is a memorial, alongside the natural history specimens and the old dinosaurs, to the lives lost in the 2006 tsunami, when an earthquake in the Indian Ocean caused a tsunami resulting in the deaths of around 300,000 people, including British people holidaying in Thailand.

The sociologist John Torpey has analysed the trends towards apologies, reparations, and repatriations, and is especially interested in explaining what he describes as the 'avalanche' of such activity that has taken place post-1989. Torpey suggests that the increasing efforts to make amends have arisen at the same time as forward-looking, future-oriented political movements have been in decline. In short, he argues that reparations thinking arose in the face of political defeat. It is, he writes, 'a substitute for expansive visions of an alternative human future of the kind that animated the socialist movements of the preceding century, which have been overwhelmingly discredited since the fall of the Berlin Wall in 1989'.[14] What he means is that developments that include the end of the Cold War and the collapse of an 'alternative' politics—by which he intends any form of socialist movement—have transformed contemporary politics, making it less about competing social visions for the future and more about accepting and managing the status quo.

John Torpey argues that it is difficult to overstate the significance of this change in outlook. Over the past two centuries, the big projects that captured the attention and focus of society were capitalism, socialism, and the idea of democracy. Even when people were at loggerheads, or at war—be that the Soviet Union against the USA, Capitalism versus Communism, battles over extending the franchise to wider sections of the population, or fights about extending democracy to new nations—Torpey posits that society was driven by visions of how things could be, or should be. They were future-orientated. Today, he contends, these aspirations have been found wanting and to a great extent, abandoned. Utopia is considered a dangerous aim.

From the 1970s onwards, political movements have weakened, and have mobilized fewer people. Political parties are losing supporters, and politics is increasingly run by career politicians, less interested in radical social change than were their predecessors. The slogan popularized by Conservative prime minister Margaret Thatcher to underline the defeat of the Soviet Union—that 'There Is No Alternative' to the free market and economic liberalism—is generally accepted. The competing political sides of 'Left' and 'Right', which were formed in the times of the French Revolution, now compete over centre ground. People continue to protest, and agitate for change, but in a way that is more inchoate, less directed, less effective, and less popular. And it is oriented far more around the process of the present day than around visions of the future.

In this post-ideological age, politics has become more a question of technocratic management than of social transformation, with the electorate increasingly disengaged from the parties that sit in Parliament. John Torpey argues that, as visions of a transformed future seem less plausible, people have turned away from fighting for competing visions of the good society. And in this context, the past has become a battleground. For Torpey, the desire to atone for past wrongs has come to supplant the search for a better tomorrow; the demand for reparations has supplanted the fight for a future. He recalls a phrase that was used with the socialist and labour movements—'Don't mourn, organize'—which, he notes, has been replaced by a sensibility that urges us instead to 'organize to mourn', ushering in what he calls the 'politics of tears'.[15] The political theorist Wendy Brown draws similar conclusions, characterizing the turn towards the recognition of victimhood—a key demand in reparations politics—as 'the language of unfreedom': 'its impulse to inscribe in the law and in other political registers its historical and present pain rather than conjure an imagined future of power to make itself'.[16] In this regard, it is argued, campaigners focus on reparations and the recognition of damage instead of shaping the life they would like to lead.

WHO BENEFITS?

Repatriation, restitution, and reparations are all often presented as positive for the victims of historic wrongs. It is often assumed that the people of the countries to which the objects would be returned to, or those who receive reparation, will benefit. But this assumption too deserves scrutiny.

When the historian Elazar Barkan documented the rise of restitution cases in the 1990s, he was intrigued that pressure for restitution and apology was more likely to come from the perceived perpetrators than from the victims. And the fact that political leaders seemed to be driving the process was of interest to him. Why would they invite such demands for reparations? Barkan thus explored the alleged perpetrators' willingness to engage with and accommodate the demands of the alleged victims'.[17] Especially from the 1990s onwards, he identified a 'new world opinion in which appearing compassionate and holding the moral high ground has become a good investment'.[18] Barkan concluded that reparations are acts that bring moral credibility to the elites of today, by drawing a contrast between the morally dubious actions of their predecessors. The political philosopher Jean Bethke Elshtain describes apologies from political leaders and institutions as 'contrition chic': 'a bargain-basement way to gain publicity, sympathy, and even absolution [that] now extends to entire nations'.[19] While these critics may seem a little harsh, there is no doubt that the processes they identify—making some kind of apologetic gesture—can act to secure legitimation for leaders.

Making reparations; apologizing can also be used as an excuse for not doing things today. Consider what energy and ideas are diverted away from imagining a better future when those who would have fought for it are now so distracted by finding the cause of present problems predominantly in the past. This is a point that the writer Marina Warner makes, in an essay on the ritual of public apologies: 'Yes, well, what are you doing about us now?'[20]

Even if we accept that today's political elites have something to gain from the rhetoric of reparations, is it not the case that the victims gain something too? Here, too, questions need to be asked. A number of theorists have raised concerns about the way people are conceptualized when their role is deemed to be simply that of the victim of historical wrongs. The one-sided presentation of the loser of a conflict as one whose life and that of their descendants is invariably damaged can rewrite the role that people actually played in the shaping of their circumstances. Those who fought and struggled, and whose actions had an impact, are recast in a passive role, as simply having being on the receiving end of violence and injustice. Elizabeth Willis, a curator at the Museum Victoria in Melbourne, Australia, has made this very observation, even though she broadly supports campaigns for reconciliation and the recognition of past wrongs by the repatriation of artefacts.[21] Willis's research into the case of Aboriginal populations has found that reparations, even repatriation claims, tend to ignore the agency of these people, simplifying and reducing the role they played. These claims 'can, unwittingly, diminish people', recasting people who fought as merely injured parties who suffered and failed.

Taking a similar critical stance, the anthropologist Gillian Cowlishaw questions much of the recent emphasis on the problems of Aboriginal history in Australia. Cowlishaw argues that rewriting of the past to highlight tragedy has ended up devaluing the achievements of older Aboriginal people. Far from being simply vulnerable and incapable, many fought back and overcame adversity—a side of the past that many now dismiss or sideline. Cowlishaw draws attention to the problem that foregrounding dispossession can decontextualize it. This development, she argues, has been encouraged by a young and urban intellectual elite, who claimed to respect but ultimately ignored the lived experience of older Aborigines, underestimating their agency and, in her view, degrading their achievements.[22] The anthropologist Sonya Atalay expresses similar qualms in relation to the National Museum of the American Indian: 'Native people were not simply passive receivers of colonial actions; they actively resisted repeated attempts of cultural, spiritual, and physical genocide and simultaneously had profound effects and influence upon colonial settler populations and governments.'[23]

As well as simplifying a more intricate history, the impact of emphasizing the victimhood of groups may have negative implications for how people are encouraged to view themselves today. People are presented, and asked to present themselves, as defined only by what horrible things were done to them, or their ancestors. They are identified as having a history of frailty, and as being now reliant on their conquerors to bestow upon them some kind of compensation. This fatalistic view sees the people of today as forever imprisoned by a past that predates their own existence, and encourages them to find refuge in enduring victimhood. In order to bid for reparations or compensation, different groups have to compete over how much they suffered, and this in turn helps to shape a culture of grievance. Indeed, some theorists have ventured that the logic of this culture means that Greece is better positioned as an iconic victim through its loss of the Elgin Marbles, than it would be should it succeed in getting the Marbles back.[24]

The movement for reparations is an example of a trend which relies on therapeutic measures, such as the recognition of historic ills through the movement of cultural artefacts, as a way to solve social problems. But in the process of making claims, groups and individuals have to enter a competition in which their wounds are evaluated. They cannot just ask for money, or demand material and political equality; rather, they have to prove how badly they have been affected. Because of this competitive dynamic, reparations are more likely to divide than reconcile. And because the process relies on supplication, with the victim asking the historical victor for a handout or a statement of recognition, power relations are not transformed, but reinforced.

Furthermore, we have to look at what the idea of reparations says about descendants of the so-called perpetrators of historical wrongs. People living today, most of whom were born way after the event in question, are held culpable for the past—not because of their own actions, but because of the particular national, religious, ethnic, or racial group to which they belong. Thus it is said that the British people today, and their institutions, are responsible for the suffering of those people conquered and subjected by the British Empire, and should assume a sense of collective guilt for the sins of imperialism. What is troubling is that this has uncomfortable echoes with old racializing discourse, which promoted notions about the biological inheritance of moral traits, and the culpability of whole populations or groups for the actions of their ancestors. Furthermore, by presenting the people of today as casualties of the past, the move towards reparations implicitly detaches responsibility for action in the *present*. By encouraging people to blame the past for today's troubles, rather than face up to the problems of the present and future, the all-important relationship between action and accountability becomes eroded.

REWRITING HISTORY

The American attorney Alan Audi states:

> From an anti-imperial perspective, I believe that the starting point must be restitution. Simply put, a wrongfully taken object should be returned, including objects taken by virtue of an imperial, exploitative apparatus that is widely abhorred today.[25]

The journalist Henry Porter ventures that for a similar reason, the Elgin Marbles should be sent back to Greece:

> To weigh the issue, you need only ask yourself if Elgin's behaviour would be acceptable today. Of course it wouldn't, and nor would we expect to keep the result of such looting. So why do we hold on to these ill-gotten sculptures now?[26]

Examining and reassessing the past is something that museums and history do all the time, and rightly so. But these commentators are calling for something quite different: an exercise in reading history backwards, judging it by a particular set of contemporary mores, and then taking action on the basis of how we—or rather, a number of influential commentators—feel about it now.

Attempting to undo history in this way erodes the differences between historical periods. Interpreting history through the eyes of the present contorts our understanding of what happened and why, and reduces what is always a more complex picture, in the interests of making us feel better. The first step in understanding the past is to appreciate that things have not always been the same; that many of the actions that appear unjust, even monstrous, to the present-day sensibility were accepted norms at the time. It is far better to try and get to grips with the past, and understand what gave rise to certain values and practices, than to embark on a futile project of trying to undo it.

Today, however, we don't seem to want to study what happened. The anthropologist Gillian Cowlishaw suggests, in relation to rewriting the past through the eyes of Aboriginal victims in Australia, that

> the White nation appears not to want to understand its [settler] forebears. Far easier to tar them with the same brush as the murderous Willshire or the eugenicist Neville, and disinherit them, than to try to unravel the uncomfortable fact that it was mostly reasonable and humane men and women who took park in the processes and policies that we now see as repugnant.[27]

If history can only be written by the victims, or if it can be rewritten to make them feel better, it will not be history. As Willis points out, 'Historians aim to write about the complexities of past interactions, rather than a simple two-dimensional account of the vanquished and the victor.'[28]

Besides, where would such actions stop? And who decides? History is long and untidy. It is always more complicated than the goodies versus the baddies. The ancient Athenians were not angels, but warriors. The Parthenon was a display of power and it was built by slaves; the enemies of the Athenian Empire would quite rightly have seen it as a monument to their humiliation. The glory of Benin was built on the slave trade: the contested Benin Bronzes were crafted from manillas, brought by European traders, traded for slaves, and melted down. A slave in 1506 cost around twelve to fifteen of these brass manillas; in 1517, the price had risen to fifty-seven; and at the peak of the slave trade, Benin provided

3,000 slaves a year.[29] In some instances, then, the very sculptures and plaques that some would like to see returned to Nigeria were made from the proceeds of slavery, exchanged for men and women. Are these artefacts tainted by how the material was acquired? We consider slavery wrong now, so should we also be making amends for these actions? This begs the further question—given the complexities of this past, to whom do the Benin Bronzes actually belong? Do they belong to the Portuguese who provided the manillas; to the ancestors of the slaves for whom they were sold; or the ancestors of the Benin king who was removed by the British army (see Figure 15)? 'Which victims—which memories—should have priority?' asks Tony Judt, in relation to the fall of communism:

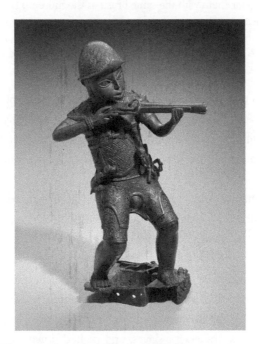

Figure 15. Portuguese rifleman, sixteenth century.
Benin kingdom, Edo peoples, Nigeria.
Robert Owen Lehman Collection © Museum of Fine Arts Boston.

'obscure Slovak or Hungarian peasants thrown off their property, or the Communist apparatchiks who ejected them but who themselves fell victim a few years later?'[30]

Judging the past though the eyes of the present does not change what happened. Nor will it aid our understanding of ancient Athens, nineteenth-century Europe, or Benin during its golden age. The best way to respect the lives of the people who came before us is to research history without such an agenda.

The philosopher Janna Thompson argues that we have a 'historical obligation' to take responsibility for the past by making reparations.[31] To the question of whether something can and should be done about historical wrongs today, I would answer: yes, quite possibly, but I do not believe that rewriting history is the right approach, and nor is moving objects from one museum to another. To address the issues that negatively affect people's lives in the present, we need to turn our attention to what should be, rather than what was. Moving artefacts about, and controlling the interpretation of the past by restricting it to certain groups over others, will not solve the problems of the present: it obscures these problems, and distracts from the search for solutions.

Throughout history, harm has been done; but it cannot be 'repaired', only studied and understood. The obsession with museums and their 'loot' can mean that we avoid engaging with the deeper forces that brought about war, colonization, and imperialism; we focus on objects and museums as the source of domination, rather than seeing them as institutions and artefacts that reflect wider political and social events of their times. In asking artefacts to atone for the past, we lose sight of their original meanings and purposes, viewing them only as objects of tragedy and apology. This hampers our appreciation of the artefacts: what they meant to their creators and owners, and what they say about their moment of origin.

9

Burying Knowledge

The Fate of Human Remains

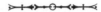

O ne display in the Pitt Rivers Museum in Oxford attracts considerable attention from visitors. Sitting behind the glass case are nine
small human heads with long, dark hair and very long eyelashes. Their
eyes and lips are ominously stitched shut. The label for the display reads:
'Treatment of Dead Enemies'. Not every object in a museum makes for a
pretty picture.

These are the shrunken heads—tsantsas—made by the Shuar and
Achuar peoples, two tribes from the Upper Amazon region of South
America between Peru and Ecuador. A tsantsa was constructed by skin-
ning the head of a murdered enemy and removing the skull and the
brain, letting the head deflate. It was then boiled and the cavity slowly
filled with hot sand so as to fill it out. Treating heads in this way was
believed to capture the souls of the people, harnessing their power, with
the mouth and eyes sewn up to prevent the vengeful soul escaping (see
Figure 16). When finished, the tsantsa was worn at three ritual feasts by
the man who had taken the life, after which it was thought that the soul
had been taken into the tribe and the head was traded or discarded.[1]

Shrinking heads in this way for ritual purposes is a practice that had
come to an end by the 1960s. It seems gruesome, but it is worth noting
that not altogether dissimilar actions have taken place elsewhere at

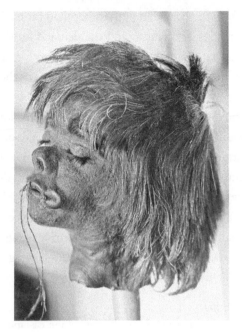

Figure 16. Shrunken head of a South American headhunter (1930). From an exhibit in a Paris museum.

© Mary Evans/Sueddeutsche Zeitung Photo.

different times. After the execution of Louis XVI, king of France, during the French Revolution, his guillotined head was held up in front of a cheering crowd. And historical accounts of the executions and beheadings at the Tower of London in the seventeenth century describe how traitors' heads were displayed out in the open on spikes—those belonging to Guy Fawkes and those of his co-conspirators were placed on London Bridge in this way after their execution.

The tsantsas on display at the Pitt Rivers Museum were collected between 1871 and 1936 by explorers and colonial officers. A couple were acquired by General Pitt Rivers, whose archaeological and anthropological collection was the basis for the museum—but one of these is made from the head of a sloth rather than from a human. There was a thriving market for tsantsas and the demand for shrunken heads became so great that the tribes manufactured them for sale, sometimes using monkeys, goats, and unclaimed bodies. Three of the heads in Pitt Rivers are fake heads of this kind; one cavity is filled with pages from a newspaper printed in 1935 in Quito, the capital of Ecuador.

Visitors arrive at the Pitt Rivers Museum through a door at the back of the Natural History Museum. This entails stepping out of the Natural History Museum, with all its specimens, crabs, and dinosaurs, and entering a very different space, which looks like something out of the Victorian age. Rows and rows of dark brown display cases with glass fronts are spread out in front of you. Boats, canoes, and spears hang above. It is an experience described well in the following extract from a poem by James Fenton:

> Entering
> You will find yourself in a climate of nut castanets,
> A musical whip
> From the Torres Straits, from Mirzapur a sistrum
> Called Jumka, used by aboriginal
> Tribes to attract small game
> On dark nights', a mute violin,
> Whistling arrows, coolie cigarettes
> And mask of Saagga, the Devil Doctor,
> The eyelids worked by strings.[2]

The collection includes objects from Johann and George Forster, whom we met in Chapter 1. It encompasses 150 items from their voyage with Captain Cook, as well as other objects from Cook's first voyage, brought back by Joseph Banks. The museum was founded in 1884 on the basis of a donation of a huge archaeological and anthropological collection belonging to Lieutenant General Augustus Henry Lane Fox Pitt Rivers, an influential figure in the development of archaeology and evolutionary anthropology. He had started out collecting firearms, but widened his interest to include assorted material from a great variety of cultures, as well as photographs and sound archives. Pitt Rivers amassed 22,092 artefacts in total. Since the museum opened, explorers and anthropologists including Beatrice Blackwood, the anthropologist who ran the Pitt Rivers in the 1940s and 1950s, and the traveller Wilfred Thesiger have donated objects and photographs acquired on their travels. Today, the museum holds around 312,686 artefacts and around 174,000 photographs.[3]

The collection is arranged typologically: objects from all over the world with the same or similar function are placed next to each other. Rather than having sections of the display space devoted to a particular culture, in the way that many museums present collections, you can see how different cultures all fashioned one kind of artefact, such as musical instruments or mourning clothing.

The origination of this display was fuelled by ideas that are deeply unfashionable now: that of evolution in different cultures. In placing artefacts with a similar purpose next to one another, the intention was to scrutinize the hierarchy of cultures. As General Pitt Rivers said:

> The objects are arranged in sequence with a view to show . . . the successive ideas by which the minds of men in a primitive condition of culture have progressed in the development of their arts from the simple to the complex, and from the homogeneous to the heterogeneous.[4]

Today the museum remains typologically organized; but this does not show the evolution of cultures. Despite its original intention, this arrangement points to similarities between cultures.

The tsantsas are some of the most popular exhibits in the Pitt Rivers Museum—but in early 2007 there were rumours that they were to be taken off display. One of the curators, the anthropologist Laura Peers, initiated an 'informal review' about their treatment and storage, because she questioned the ethics of keeping and exhibiting them. Peers was reported in a local newspaper saying that she was 'uncomfortable' about the display of the tsantsas: 'I personally would like to know more what the communities in Ecuador and Peru feel about it... We have never had a formal review of any particular display—this is an awkward area where personal views and professional training become mixed.'[5] Peers later wrote that she requested the review for a number of reasons: because indigenous groups have objected to displays of human remains in Western museums, largely since they were acquired through unequal power relations; because they have been used in the past as evidence for theories that suggest that Western societies are superior to indigenous societies; and because human remains, to many, are ancestors rather than specimens. All these reasons encouraged Peers to suggest that the display of human remains in general requires reflection, and that the display in Pitt Rivers Museum specifically warranted a review.[6]

When the local press heard of the plans to rethink the display of the tsantsas and maybe remove them from display, a media storm erupted. Visitors to the museum were reportedly furious. One letter stated:

> I am appalled at this news as the heads are one of the most distinctive and interesting exhibits and never fail to interest friends of mine from this country and abroad. Despite the fact that the heads are body parts they are a fascinating and integral part of the museum as the public see it and [to] remove them would be an unforgivable act of censorship. It seems that political correctness has gone mad and could deprive us Oxford residents of a much loved part of the City's culture.[7]

A spokesman for the Friends of Pitt Rivers Museum defended the display, pointing to their popularity, especially with the young. 'The children love them—they like being scared—and if they were removed the children would miss them.'[8] And it is true that one of the most popular events in the museum is held at night, in darkness, when children and their parents roam around the exhibits with a wind-up hand torch. All enjoy the effects of flashing the lights on the dead enemies encased in darkness.

Others commentators weighed into the debate. Philip Pullman, the author whose book *The Subtle Knife* includes a scene where Lyra, a central character, visits the Pitt Rivers Museum and the ancient skulls, argued that they should remain on display: 'The value of the shrunken heads is that they are real—you could replace them with plastic models but that would not be the same.' Pullman mused that they were too old to be traceable: 'It would be very hard to find the living relative.' And he praised the museum for putting them on show, for the glimpse of history that it gave: 'The great value of the Pitt Rivers Museum is the higgledy-piggledy nature of the displays, which itself is a window into the past, and the shrunken heads are part of that.'[9]

After reflection, managers at the Pitt Rivers Museum decided to keep the tsantsas on display. But the concern expressed here is not an isolated case. For centuries museums have held all kinds of human remains in their collections, but in the late 1980s this practice became controversial. Human remains in collections in Europe, the Nordic countries, North America, Canada, and Australasia became subject to activism from groups who agitate for the repatriation of human remains to what are considered to be affiliated communities. And in many cases, these demands have been met. From the 1990s onwards, thousands of human remains have been repatriated to communities deemed affiliated to them.

In 2001, members of the Tasmanian Aboriginal Centre (TAC)[10] wrote to the British Museum requesting the return of two animal skin bags containing human ash. The cremation bundles had been acquired in Australia by George Augustus Robinson, Chief Protector of Aborigines in Van Diemen's Land (Tasmania) between 1829 and 1838. His 'friendly mission', as it was termed, entailed persuading the Aborigines to leave Tasmania for Flinders Island because diseases, inadvertently transmitted by the colonizers, were decimating the Tasmanian Aboriginal people. It was a project that had limited success: the population of Aboriginal Tasmanians was nearly exterminated.

One passage in Robinson's diary records how he stumbled upon the making of a cremation bundle:

> In the course of my rounds this day and whilst passing through the sombre domain of the dead, I observed a native woman where a corpse of a male aboriginal had been burnt, clearing away the debris until nothing remained but the very finest ashes. I was not prepared for this and yet it was evident she had a purpose.[11]

Robinson watched as the woman made parcels of animal skin to hold the cremated ashes: 'I observed she went to her basket and took two circular pieces of kangaroo skin about thirteen inches in diameter having holes perforated on the outer edge.' She placed the ashes on the skin and sewed up the bundle. Then, she gave one to her sick husband to protect him.

The cremated remains in their bundle form were used as amulets. They were believed to accord the wearer protection against illness and disease. In an entry in his diary in May 1838, Robinson records how a women called Ellen wore an 'amulet parcel of ashes hung around her throat to alleviate the pain'[12] as well as a human bone suspended on her back. Robinson asked Ellen for the one on her back but she refused, pointing out that he already had one.

In 1882, two cremation bundles arrived in the collection of the British Museum, donated by the Royal College of Surgeons, which had acquired them from a private collector: Dr Barnard Davis, a Staffordshire surgeon and fellow of the Royal Society. They were originally collected by George Augustus Robinson. They are the only two bundles of their kind known to exist and offer an insight into ritual practices.

In 2001, the TAC had made a request for the return of the cremation bundles. It was the second request it had made; the first had been issued in 1985 and was refused. Robert Anderson, the director of the Museum, replied to the TAC with regard to its second request, explaining that return of the bundles was neither legally possible nor desirable:

> our collections are held under Act of Parliament which does not permit us to de-accession them: nor would we want to do so, because we are an international museum and resource devoted to preserving mankind's cultural heritage.[13]

The TAC wrote again in 2002 but without success. It wrote again in 2006, when the position—under a new director, Neil Macgregor—was reversed and the museum trustees agreed to the repatriation of the bundles. Writing in *The Guardian* newspaper, British Museum trustee and lawyer Helena Kennedy noted that it was a difficult decision to reach, because

> these are now the only two such bundles known anywhere in the world. That means they are the only surviving physical evidence of a whole system of belief and a social order that has since disappeared: precisely the kind of object the British Museum was established to keep and preserve.[14]

Kennedy explained that despite the research value of the cremation bundles, the trustees had decided that returning them was the right decision to take, because human remains are a special case; the bundles were taken at a time when the Aboriginal population was suffering from European settlement; the remains would probably have ultimately been laid to rest had they not been taken away; and the cultural and religious importance of the cremation bundles to the Tasmanian Aboriginal community outweighed the public benefit of retaining them in the museum.[15] The cremation bundles were sent to the TAC in 2006.

The period between the first request made by the TAC in 1985 and its last request in 2006 was crucial in shifting resistant attitudes both outside and inside the museum sector in Britain towards the repatriation of human remains. During this time vigorous campaigns for the return of human remains took place, and the issue also became prominent in the media. A government-appointed committee was established to examine the question. Following particular recommendations from the committee,[16] the law was relaxed to permit specific museums to deaccession human remains—and a number did so. This shift in attitude and law followed a similar pattern of events that had taken place in the US, Canada, and Australasia a decade earlier, where more widespread repatriation of human remains resulted, primarily because these countries have indigenous populations and campaigns were more forceful.

When I talk with friends and colleagues about repatriation out of museums, one area of concern that is raised is human remains. These 'objects', as you would expect, elicit strong feelings. Human remains were once people and thus require special care and consideration. At the same time, many hold unique *evidence* about past people—they contain information about human beings that cannot be found elsewhere in archaeological remains or the written record. And it is in part because of this—that human remains were once human beings and that they are also material essential for understanding past lives—that the claims for repatriation of this material have been so effective (and the debate over them so heated).

HUMAN REMAINS IN MUSEUM COLLECTIONS

There are tens of thousands of human remains in museum collections all over the world. Take, for example, those in English museums. A survey conducted in 2003 found 61,000 human remains across these collections. Roughly 15,000 of these human remains were from overseas; the remainder came from the British Isles. Sixty museums held human remains from overseas dating from between 1500 and 1947; sixty-one held human remains from overseas dating to pre-1500. One hundred and six institutions held human remains from the UK acquired through archaeological activity, and twenty-seven held human remains acquired for medical purposes.[17]

Many of the human remains in museum collections were initially acquired and exhibited in the eighteenth and nineteenth centuries, collected by explorers, colonial officers, and scientists on expeditions. Collecting was motivated at first by curiosity and later by a desire to preserve material from what was considered to be vanishing races. Human remains were taken in a variety of circumstances: in some recorded instances graves were exhumed against people's will, but many other human remains were freely given, purchased, or used in exchanges of goods.

The study of human remains is essential in order to understand where human beings came from. Scientists study them to chart human origins, and population diversity and distribution. Without this study, there would be no 'Out of Africa' theory'—the theory that modern humans originated in Africa.

The Natural History Museum in London, founded in 1881, is one of the most important research institutions in the world. It holds around 19,950 human remains, making it one of the largest collections there is. Some of the human remains date back many thousands of years. Just over half derive from the British Isles; the rest come from all over the world. Having such a large and diverse collection is vital for comparative research; for comparing human populations from different places and over a long period of time. It is a hive of scientific research for scholars from all over the globe who study human evolution and human origins. The collection has also been used to train anthropologists working on the identification of victims in mass graves, such as those in Bosnia.

One research finding in recent years is the radiocarbon dating of human remains used to create the first fully scientific estimate of the chronology of ancient Egypt. Up until this point, researchers had relied on traditional archaeological evidence, using the evolving styles of ceramics found at human burial sites to reach a chronology of events. Radiocarbon dating samples of bone, hair, and plants taken from key archaeological sites allowed researchers to develop a considerably more reliable timeline for the kings and queens who ruled over the Egyptian state between 4500 and 2800 BC.[18]

Scientists also study human remains to analyse diseases like osteoporosis, and people's lifestyle and diet. Research on human remains found in North America yielded the information that people suffered from tuberculosis before European contact in 1492. We thus know more about the infections people suffered, and that some of these were partly due to a diet that was overly dependent on corn.

CT scans and DNA studies have added to our knowledge of various ancient peoples. Scans taken of the mummy Rameses III by Albert Zink, a palaeopathologist at the 'Institute for Mummies and the Iceman' in Bolzano, Italy, showed a deep throat cut that could have caused his death. This information points to the possibility that he was assassinated. DNA tests of this mummy and an unidentified body of a young man, who was aged about 18 when he died, revealed that he was a blood relative of Rameses III, and likely to be the king's son, Pentawere. The British Museum has also used advances in computer technology to perform the 'virtual unwrapping' of mummies. In 2014, the museum ran the exhibition 'Ancient Lives, New Discoveries', which scanned eight of the 120 mummies in the collection, to analyse what lies beneath the wrapping. Scans revealed details about the mummifying process: amulets, a tattoo of St Michael on the thigh of a woman in Christianized Sudan, and the bread in one man's digestive tract, as well as medical conditions including a large dental abscess.

The study of human remains also sheds light on mortuary rituals and belief systems. The tsantsas in the Pitt Rivers Museum are far from the only human remains to do this. Of the objects in this museum, just over 2,000 are human remains, a fifth of which came from Europe. They have skulls that show trepanning—a surgical procedure that meant drilling into the skull in order to treat disease—which tells us something about the treatment of illness and injury. There are skull bowls from Tibet—cups made out of skulls, in which sacrificial offerings were placed, used in tantric Buddhist rituals. The Pitt Rivers Museum also has a male skull from Papua New Guinea that was subjected to headbinding—pressure applied to a baby's skull with cloth, bandages, and vine, to change the shape of the head permanently. This tells us something about what was considered attractive and how the body was modified to achieve this ideal.

REPATRIATING HUMAN REMAINS

Since the 1990s, human remains have been subject to extensive repatriation. Thousands and thousands of skeletons and body parts of varying ages have been repatriated, predominantly to communities in the US, Canada, and Australasia. These sometimes go to another museum, where they stay under the care and control of a particular tribe. But in many cases, particularly in America, the remains are buried.

In the US, in 1990, the Native American Graves Protection and Repatriation Act (NAGPRA) was passed. This law requires federal agencies, museums, and universities, to conduct an inventory and identify the geographical or cultural affiliation of remains in their collections with present-day tribes. The institution has to provide opportunities for federally recognized tribes to receive culturally affiliated Native American human remains and artefacts. It is a proactive programme. That is, museums and other institutions are obligated to research their collections and contact potentially related tribes about repatriation.

In the first decade after NAGPRA entered the statute book, over half a million sets of remains and artefacts were either returned or in the process of being returned. It should be pointed out that these are estimates—nobody is keeping track nationally. We do know that they are mostly buried, and by burying skeletons valuable scientific evidence is lost, as is the possibility to study them further if and when developments in technology permit.

Museum staff in Australia are also very active in this matter. Although there is no law, it is understood to be the ethical course of action. In the case of the National Museum of Australia, the process is guided by its policies on 'Aboriginal and Torres Strait Islander Human Remains', and on 'Secret/Sacred and Private Material': policies that suggest the immediate and unconditional return of human remains and secret/sacred objects to 'traditional owners' and custodians. External access to the remains collection is permitted only with the approval of the relevant community.

Mike Pickering, the director of the Aboriginal and Torres Strait Islander Program and Repatriation Program of the National Museum of Australia, and Phil Gordon from the Australian Museum, explain that research on indigenous remains 'is tightly controlled by the industry, institutional, and professional policies and protocols requiring community approval', and that 'no Australian museum will allow access to its holdings of Indigenous remains or secret/sacred objects without the approval of the socially associated community'.[19] They document that in the first seven years of the National Museum of Australia Repatriation Unit's operation, over 750 human remains were returned as well as over 400 sacred or secret objects.

Elsewhere, Te Papa in New Zealand has received 240 Maori ancestral remains from overseas institutions. Te Papa estimates that there are still 650 ancestral remains they would like to see returned to New Zealand, and most of these are in Europe.[20] In the case of New Zealand, human remains usually are held in a museum under the control of the relevant community.

Repatriation is celebrated as a victory for indigenous groups. Jack
F. Trope, the executive director of the Association on American Indian
Affairs, and Walter R. Echo-Hawk, a lawyer and tribal judge, have
described NAGPRA as the culmination of 'decades of struggle by Native
American tribal governments and people to protect against grave destruction, to repatriate thousands of dead relatives of ancestors, and to retrieve
stolen or improperly acquired religious and cultural property for Native
owners'.[21]

'Support for repatriation helps indigenous people understand how and
why these ancestors were taken and gives them the opportunity to
reunite with them physically and spiritually,' Arapata Hakiwai, the current Kaihautu (a senior position at the museum, one that means he is
guardian of the sacred treasures) at Te Papa Museum said on the return
of human remains to Te Papa from museums in Britain in 2013.[22] For
Laura Peers, the curator and anthropologist at Pitt Rivers Museum, the
return of human remains helps to affirm the identity of community
groups and distances them from historical practices under colonization.
It also lets them mourn their dead. As she writes:

> This reattachment of remains and social identity not only reasserts the
> group's own sense of identity and repudiates colonisers' categories of
> racial or ethnic identity or practices of anonymisation, but allows the
> living to mourn for and engage in social relations with the dead. In such
> cases, the reassertion of kinship and social identity has another implica-
> tion for the living as well: an assertion of their power to defy such
> problematic social and political relations and treatment, and to reinstate
> what they see as the proper patterns of social relations with the dead.[23]

WHOSE HUMAN REMAINS ARE THEY?

In many cases the human remains repatriated are hundreds, sometimes
even thousands, of years old. Only a very few have been repatriated that

are named human remains. In America, NAGPRA describes as 'Native American' any remains 'more than 500 years old'—that is, anyone in the New World before Christopher Columbus arrived. Human remains that are thousands of years old have been given to tribes and then buried, including the Buhl Women from Idaho (10,800 years old), and the Pelican Rapids woman found in Minnesota (7,800 years old). Some of these remains were from people who lived before the Pyramids were built and before any written human record. Any link to modern people is, to say the least, tenuous.

How, then, can these remains be considered as related to people living today? And how can a federal law work this out? It varies. Under NAGPRA, human remains (as well as funerary objects, sacred objects, or other cultural patrimony) are returned to what are deemed geographically and culturally affiliated Indian tribes. With anything so long ago, the question of who is deemed affiliated is decided through the accumulation of a broad range of evidence. Under NAGPRA it means a relationship of shared group identity that may be 'reasonably traced historically or prehistorically between a present-day Indian tribe or Native Hawaiian organisation and an identifiable earlier group'.[24] How do the officials that gather the evidence to adjudicate on cases 'reasonably trace' a connection between a group of people today to those from prehistory? They try to maintain rigour in their investigations, and there is an attempt to assess a preponderance of evidence, but ultimately the criteria are expanded to allow subjective categories, as it is not possible to prove lineage to anyone that long ago. Thus, under NAGPRA permissible lines of evidence are 'geographic, kinship, biological, archaeological, anthropological, linguistic, folkoric, oral tradition, historical, or other relevant information or expert opinion'.[25]

Indeed, repatriation laws in different states have decreased the proof asked of Native American tribes for repatriation claims. A yet to be implemented California law (CalNAGPRA) removed the requirement of federal recognition for Native American groups who are 'culturally affiliated' to obtain human remains. CalNAGPRA would allow as much weight to be given to Native Americans' 'oral histories' and 'tribal testimonies' as to forensic, geological, or other scientific evidence when determining affiliation. Elsewhere, in the case of the Buhl burial, the skeleton of a woman more than 10,000 years old, found in Idaho together with grave goods, was repatriated to the Shoshone-Bannock tribe and buried. Why? Because oral traditions held by the tribe claim that its ancestors have lived in the Americas since time immemorial.

But there are limits to using this kind of testimony as scientific fact. Oral history and tribal testimony may be revealing of something, but they should not be accepted unquestioningly as solid evidence of direct lineage. The claims for repatriation are based on ideas of biological or cultural descent that suggest we can biologically, or culturally, link one group to another. But human populations are not bounded through time in this way; they are more fluid than these strictures allow. The very idea of fixed groupings and cultural continuity over these many hundreds and thousands of years is unsound. People and geographical location remain stable for no more than a very small period of time. The human remains that are repatriated to communities today are the relatives of other people from long ago.

What happens to unaffiliated human remains—that is, the skeletons and body parts in the collections that no tribe has claimed or can be found that is considered to be affiliated—is instructive. The fate of unaffiliated human remains suggests that certain members of the museum sector in America have been so keen to be involved in repatriation that they do it even when there are no communities to which the bones can be sent 'home'.

Anthropologists in the Denver Museum of Nature and Science praised NAGPRA for 'redressing a historical imbalance of rights'.[26] But some felt that there was a problem with it: 'For nearly two decades, the Native

American Graves Protection and Repatriation Act of 1990 (NAGPRA) left unresolved a complex problem: the fate of human remains that could not be affiliated with federally recognized tribes.'[27] As a consequence, Chip Colwell-Chanthaphonh, Rachel Maxson, and Jami Powell, anthropologists at the museum, write: 'the unaffiliated remains of more than 115,000 individuals and nearly one million associated funerary objects have sat on museum shelves in legal purgatory.'[28]

Purgatory is a very emotive word here, coming from the museum anthropologists; but that is how they understand the condition of human remains in their collection that lack a tribe to claim them. The anthropologists feel that they have 'the obligation to proactively address' this problem. Most of these remains, they complain, 'came to the museum in discomforting circumstances—burials disturbed out of idle curiosity and skulls and scalps purchased at trading posts'; and the staff 'came to understand that it had an ethical duty to address the fate of these remains, even in the absence of legal obligations'.[29] So the anthropologists spent three years 'actively addressing' the unaffiliated remains in the museum's collection, paid for by three NAGPRA grants. They tried to find tribes that they thought could in any way be affiliated to the remains, and who might take them off their hands.

As consequence of their activism, and similar concerns expressed by other museum professionals, regulations passed in 2010 now require museums to compile inventories of remains that are not affiliated with any tribe, and to try and find them a new home with a tribe that is federally recognized: even though there is no evidence to suggest they could be affiliated in any way. The anthropologists from the Denver Museum of Nature and Science acknowledge the loss to knowledge but apparently do not lament this loss sufficiently to feel that it outweighs other considerations:

> the new rule does represent a loss of potential scientific data. But, this loss must be considered alongside the knowledge that the privilege of science is

not a license of absolute freedom. The human interest in science is limited—as it should be—by other human interests such as justice, religious freedom, promises made in treaties, respect for cultural differences, and basic human rights.[30]

Nancy B. Rosoff, a curator at the National Museum for the American Indian (NMAI), had a similar problem with human remains for which the museum could not find a community. She wanted to repatriate the material but could not find anyone to take it. In the end, staff at the NMAI buried the human remains themselves:

> The issue of what to do with undocumented and unaffiliated remains is also complicated. NMAI decided to bury a group of thirty-one such human remains...The museum's board of trustees took the position that these remains were entitled to a decent place of rest.[31]

Elizabeth Weiss, an associate professor of anthropology at San Jose State University, has examined the impact of NAGPRA on scientific research and is concerned that it is having a very negative effect.[32] Weiss describes how religion, animism, and the authority of present identities play the leading role in deciding who actually owns the bones. Scientists are beholden to those with the approved ethnicity and beliefs as to whether they can research historic remains, if at all. Weiss documents the cost of the effect of NAGPRA on her research. She points to the cost, first, in relation to monetary terms: large sums are now spent in museums, not on new acquisitions, or improving the presentation of the collections, or on education, but on researching what is in the museums in order to remove it. For example, in 2006 NAGPRA gave nearly $2.5 million in grants to Native American tribes to assist with the researching of remains. Such research takes a lot of time: many museums now have departments or offices devoted entirely to repatriation, whose job is to document and remove human remains from the collection. Anthropologists and archaeologists spend less time on researching the remains, and some are completely off limits. Amy Dansie of the Nevada State Museum notes that efforts to abide by NAGPRA have 'resulted in 10,000 hours spent over the past nine years of my life' and that NAGPRA work is 'sucking day after day, year after year, out of our careers'.[33]

Elizabeth Weiss's central concern is that the study of human remains to learn about the past, such as who were the first Americans—the people who lived long before Christopher Columbus—is curtailed. She warns that understanding the history of America before the settlers came is now impeded, if not blocked completely, and the evidence destroyed. There is a great deal about this period about which we know nothing. Scientists, Weiss believes, have an ethical obligation to understand and try to explain the world around us and what came before us, but this research has been curtailed. She concludes:

> But to me, the scariest aspect of repatriation and reburial is the loss of scientific freedom. Scientists should be able to investigate all sorts of questions about the world around them, a world that includes the past; and the attempt to answer these questions should not be hampered by political or religious sentiments. Scientific freedom is lost when tribal consultation or supervision is required. Tribes are not likely to allow the study of remains if they judge that the questions that the remains might answer are controversial or conflict with their creation myth.[34]

WHY DID HUMAN REMAINS BECOME A PROBLEM?

Fifty years ago there were few, if any, complaints about museums holding human remains. Today, the holding and treatment of human remains in museum collections is a major concern. How did this come to be such a heated issue? And are there benefits to repatriating human remains, despite the loss to knowledge? Unravelling the answers to these questions helps us to answer the problem posed throughout this book: why museums and cultural artefacts are the target of different claims and demands today.

In order to answer these questions, we start with the special nature of these objects and the symbolic potential of human remains. This helps to explain one reason why they have become the object of controversy and caught up in wider battles.

In an important study, the anthropologist Katherine Verdery outlined the way in which human remains have a number of qualities that mean they have salience as symbolic objects. She shows that dead bodies of various kinds and in various forms can serve as sites of political conflict and the reordering of political structures: for example, where the bodies of named rulers or religious figures, and nameless victims from the past, are exhumed or buried to legitimize new elites and associate them or distance them from the past. Verdery documents how human remains became symbolic political objects across Eastern Europe and Russia following the end of Communist rule. She describes how such remains, named and unnamed, were used in these particular political battles: to express social and cultural connections, but also to articulate opposition to particular regimes and institutions.

Verdery also suggests a number of reasons why human remains are uniquely useful symbolic objects. One reason, she suggests, is that human remains—unlike concepts or ideas—are physical objects, and can thus locate the ideas and values with which they are associated. They are also ambiguous: 'Remains are concrete, yet protean; they do not have a single meaning but are open to many different readings.'[35] This ambiguity is helpful for those who wish to use them as symbols, for they can be manipulated:

> Dead bodies have another great advantage as symbols: they don't talk much on their own (though they once did). Words can be put into their mouths . . . . It is thus easier to rewrite history with dead people than with other kinds of symbols that are speechless.[36]

Human remains suggest an authenticity that connotes a sacred meaning. They are not just any old symbols—they can evoke 'the awe, uncertainty, and fear associated with "cosmic" concerns, such as the meaning of life and death'.[37] Verdery argues that these are some of the reasons why human remains lend themselves particularly well to politics.

The dead bodies that Verdery examines as symbolic objects are associated with particular pasts and particular elites or publics. She writes:

> To understand any given case, one *might* find it helpful to ask what in present and past contexts gives what multiplicity of meanings to the résumé of that particular corpse: *How* does his complex biography make him a good instrument.[38]

In a similar way, looking at the emergence of the human remains controversy and the confluence of influences on it helps us to understand it. When, why, and how did the repatriation of human remains come to be a prominent issue? What did these campaigns come to represent, why, and for whom?[39]

In the early 1970s, a developing American Indian political movement and the Australian Aboriginal land rights movement gained broader political support and achieved legislation on questions of religious freedom and land rights. In this period, the type of claim voiced by these movements changed. Demands shifted from the more traditional agitation for land rights, political equality, and better material goods, to more cultural claims. As the anthropologist John Cove has observed, the Tasmanian Aboriginal rights movement formed in the 1970s, was preoccupied with asserting its rights over land, as were similar movements in America and Canada; but in the 1980s these claims over land transformed into demands directed at returning or transforming historic cultural heritage.[40]

In this period, Native Americans within American society started to talk less about integration, more about difference, and more about history. Ideas about the problems of indigenous groups became linked with wider debates about the importance of the past and the role of culture. The scholar and activist Vine Deloria Jr explains that the source of Native American activism during this time was 'urban Indians seeking an Indian identity and heritage' who, in searching for their tribal heritage, became 'the most militant of advocates for cultural renewal'.[41] The sociologist Joseph Tilden Rhea observes that stimulating the turn to the past were

> the identity needs of a generation of urban Indians who felt alienated from American culture and who turned to their Indian heritage for a better alternative. Reaching for a new sense of the past, they developed an active antagonism towards the mainstream representation of their history. Acutely aware of the connection between identity, history and political power, urban Indians became increasingly active in the reshaping of American collective memory.[42]

For some at this time, science came to be seen as a Western construct that had harmed native people. This outlook is evident in the writings of Vine Deloria Jr, in his work *Red Earth, White Lies: Native Americans and the Myths of Scientific Fact*. Science is only a myth, he argues, which has, at best, dismissed the theories of Native Americans:

> Regardless of what Indians have said concerning their origins, their migrations, their experiences with birds, animals, lands, water, mountains and other peoples, the scientists have maintained a stranglehold on the definitions of what respectable and reliable human experiences are.[43]

Vine Deloria Jr contends that science is responsible for the exclusion of Native American views in mainstream culture and their treatment as 'subhuman'.[44] Furthermore, he claims, Western science legitimized and encouraged the slaughter of Native Americans for experiments, and museums were involved: 'Some Eskimos staying at a New York museum to help the scientists were boiled down for further skeletal use instead of receiving a decent burial.'[45]

In this way, the past came to be seen as the reason for contemporary problems of indigenous communities. Science—and museums—came to be thought of as instruments of colonization and settler society. It is thought that rewriting the past might make a positive difference. 'There is a trauma of history,' the anthropologist and campaigner Russell Thornton argues, 'whereby groups must be healed from the wounds of traumatic events during their lives, if they are to achieve psychological well-being.'[46] The repatriation of human remains came to be seen as a way of making amends for this past:

> It is only now, through repatriation of ancestors and objects associated with these events that many Native American peoples may reconcile themselves as peoples with these histories. They will undoubtedly never forget them (nor probably should they), and scars surely will remain, but perhaps there will be no more open wounds and their collective mental health will improve.[47]

The campaign over human remains in Australia and America was initially an issue that concerned only a minority of indigenous people. When repatriation was debated in anthropology, archaeology, and museums in the mid-1980s, most tribes showed minimal interest in becoming involved. It was important for vocal indigenous activists and radical archaeologists, but more general interest amongst tribal people was limited, as is indicated in the initial take-up of offers from institutions for repatriation.

Anthropology professor Russell Thornton was working at the Smithsonian Institution when the museum first contacted tribes about repatriation. Most Native groups did not respond at first, Thornton notes, because they were 'generally focused on local issues'.[48] Museums had a hard job interesting communities. Barbara Isaac, from the Peabody Museum of Archaeology and Ethnology at Harvard University, documents that eighty out of the 117 notices sent out to tribes about repatriating human remains in 1995 received no response. With those that did respond, twelve decided they were not ready to act. In the end, the museum was only able to begin a consultation about repatriation with three tribes.[49]

In 1990, the co-ordinator of the Foundation for Aboriginal Islander Research Action, along with the president of the TAC, requested that the Pitt Rivers Museum return a jar of soft tissue and five skulls that originated from different parts of Australia. The supervising Committee of the Pitt Rivers Museum agreed, and the human remains were given to the Australian High Commission. The Australian authorities who received the remains then sent one skull to the Tiwi Land Council—the area from which they thought the human remains had originally been collected. But the council had not requested the skull and did not know the request for return had been made. Nor did it know to whom the skull should be returned; there was no information linking it to a family to a particular area. The chairman of the Land Trustees was dismayed, noting that it was 'considered a cultural offence to have body remains foisted upon a generation that had no knowledge of their origins and was being invited to invent some in order to dispose of the remains'.[50]

One of the most important factors in the emergence of the prominent concern with the holding of human remains in museums is the response to the issue from those within the museum sector. The indigenous campaigners demanding the repatriation of human remains met firm resistance from some museum professionals, anthropologists, and scientists, who wanted to retain what they saw as valuable research material. But, as we have seen, campaigners also met endorsement and agreement from many others in the museum sector and the related fields of anthropology and archaeology. It is this positive response from these professionals that helps to explain the success of repatriation campaigns. Anthropologists, archaeologists, and museum professionals, initially from North America, Australia, Canada, and Britain, have been significant participants in promoting the issue and securing the repatriation of human remains. Over time, their case—which tacitly accused museums of wrongdoing in the past, and suggested that such institutions could be a positive social force in the present—met with greater resonance than those arguing that museums should remain as research institutions and not repatriate human remains.

A significant moment in the rising prominence of the campaign for repatriation took place at the inaugural World Archaeological Congress (WAC)—a non-governmental body representing archaeologists—in 1986. In one conference session Jan Hammil, a representative of the organization American Indians Against Desecration, spoke about the problems of the desecration of sacred sites by archaeologists, how human remains were stored in museums, and how this affected American Indians. There was a rapid and enthusiastic response by the WAC Steering Committee to Hammil's concerns, after which she was co-opted onto the committee. The WAC subsequently campaigned for changes in how human remains were excavated and questioned whether they should be held in museums at all, lobbying the disciplines and the museum community in America, Australia, and Britain.

Museum professionals in the UK became concerned about holding and displaying human remains in museums in the late 1990s, when the debate over the rights and wrongs of repatriation gripped the sector. But even at the height of this debate, in England only thirteen out of sixty institutions holding human remains from overseas had received requests for return, amounting to thirty-three requests in all. Of these, a number were repeat claims from the same group, and some of the remains had already been returned. Even so, a report for the relevant government department on the issue stressed that the low number of claims did not mean that repatriation should be dismissed as an unimportant question:

> While the total number of requests for return perhaps seems low at first sight (and some of the claims repeat earlier claims), it is essential to recognise that in many cases the beliefs and emotions leading to individual claims are strong.[51]

The report argued that repatriation would make a significant impact to the lives of indigenous groups who were impeded from moving on by their past:

> Until this wrong is redressed, there will be no closure in respect of past injustices and an arguable enduring violation of fundamental human rights. The physical and psychological health, and indeed the social advancement, of indigenous communities are in consequence impaired.[52]

Whilst there has been strong activism from certain sections of some indigenous groups, some of the most prominent voices campaigning for repatriation—especially in Britain—have often been senior museum officials themselves, such as Tristram Besterman, former director of Manchester Museum. Writing in the *Museums Journal*, Besterman revealed that one reason why he endorsed repatriation was the responsibility the museum has to present-day communities:

> This concerns more than the remains of dead people. How the museum treats such claims speaks of its relationship with and obligations to living communities. But because it holds all the cards, it shames me as a colleague and as a UK citizen in the way it behaves.[53]

Whilst Manchester University Museum agreed to repatriate requested human remains in 1992 to the Aboriginal and Torres Strait Islander Commission, once the agreement was made no action was taken to retrieve the remains. In 2003 the museum was able to, in Besterman's words: 'revive' the issue.[54] When a representative of the Aboriginal and Torres Strait Islander Commission went to the UK to give evidence to a government committee, Besterman, at that time the museum's director, acted proactively to return the remains.

Why were some museum directors so keen to embrace repatriation? Museum professionals and activists cited the wrongs of colonialism as a primary reason for this, at a time when, in the 1990s and 2000s, human remains were being transferred to Australia from museums in Britain. In Besterman's words:

> These remains were removed during the colonial era at a time of great inequality of power. Their removal more than a century ago was carried out without the permission of the Aboriginal nations, and they have been held in the Manchester Museum ever since, in violation of the laws and beliefs of indigenous Australian people.[55]

Similarly, Maurice Davies, then deputy director of the Museums Association, stated in an editorial for the *Museums Journal*: 'Many UK museum collections were built up in the 19th and 20th centuries, a time when a certain set of political attitudes prevailed';[56] he went on to say that the bodies of indigenous groups still in these museums are 'a legacy of colonial collecting'. Davies concluded that UK museums should agree to return human remains. This standpoint extended the argument from the wrongs of acquiring material to the wrongs of the historical period, regardless of how material was collected. As the museologist and activist Moira Simpson makes explicit:

> The fact that material of human origin was acquired legally is often used as a defence against possible repatriation. However, the debate cannot ignore the colonial ancestry of the collections or the insensitivity of the methods by which many items were acquired.[57]

The British Museums Association commissioned Moira Simpson to undertake two research projects to determine its members' views about repatriation in general. The results are salutary. Simpson found the vast majority of respondents accepted the notion of repatriation: out of the 123 respondents, only three were categorically opposed. Significantly, of these respondents only seventeen institutions out of 164 had received enquiries or requests for repatriation. In other words: there was a widespread endorsement of repatriation, even when no demands for repatriation had been made.[58]

In Britain, where there are no indigenous communities,[59] the dynamic coming from within is stark. Human remains have become symbolic of the harm believed to have been caused by museums. This feeds into a wider questioning of the pursuit of knowledge and the role of the museum. In one case, museum professionals at Manchester University Museum covered up a number of Egyptian mummies on display. The unwrapped mummy of Asru (an elite female from Thebes, *c.*750–525 BC), a partially wrapped mummy of Khary (a priest from the temple of Karnak, *c.*750–330 BC), and a child mummy, were shielded with white sheets, in line with the museum's new policy on human remains. The officials were not responding to any demand or requests from the Egyptian people—or anyone, in fact—and their actions caused an outcry, similar to that expressed when the Pitt Rivers Museum raised the possibility of removing the shrunken heads. Nick Merriman, the director of Manchester Museum, who took over from Tristram Besterman, explained that the decision was taken in order to start a debate. 'We're asking the public what is the most respectful and appropriate way to display them. It's good practice rather than political correctness,' he stated. 'Is it appropriate to display them this way, given that they were originally wrapped, but then unwrapped in the 19th century to satisfy scientific and public curiosity? It's all part of the debate.'[60] Merriman received a stormy reaction, and Manchester Museum had to uncover the mummies a few months later.

In a revealing study, Hugh Kilmister, a curator at the Petrie Museum of Egyptian Archaeology in London, conducted research on the question of whether museums are becoming 'unduly sensitive' about the issues surrounding human remains. He interviewed museum visitors about their attitudes to display, and found that there was a 'very high proportion'—82.5 per cent of visitors surveyed—who believed that the museums should be allowed to display human remains in 'whatever way they see fit'.[61] Yet despite this interest and confidence from the public, Kilmister concluded that the display and treatment of human remains needed to change:

> Although not as contentious as the display of Aboriginal or Native American remains, the public is generally positive about the display of ancient Egyptian remains, but we perhaps need to look at the future re-display of these remains.[62]

Kilmister commented that the high level of public trust in professionals deciding the future of human remains is 'perhaps not justified'.

Surveys demonstrate that most people expect and want to see human remains on show in museums. In fact, they are big crowd-pullers. Around 90 per cent of respondents to an opinion poll of 1,000 people commissioned by English Heritage said they were comfortable with keeping prehistoric human remains in museums. Put mummies on show at any museum and the children and parents will follow.

This observation raises the question: what are the implications for the public of these battles over human remains? Many museums were originally built for the public, and collections are still held in their name. As we go forward, perhaps we should think of the interests of the millions of people who visit each day to find out a little bit and who trust museum curators to show them more about past human civilizations. It is surely time that museum professionals regained their confidence in this purpose—to explore and understand the past—rather than to try and make amends for it in the present.

Concluding Thoughts

A remarkable transformation is taking place on Saadiyat Island off the coast of Abu Dhabi, where a Cultural District is being built. Major museums and galleries, designed by top architects—Jean Nouvel, Frank Gehry, Tadao Ando, Norman Foster, and Zaha Hadid—are under construction. The Louvre Abu Dhabi, Zayed National Museum, and Guggenheim Abu Dhabi are opening soon.

The island is part of the Abu Dhabi government's vision for the Emirates. The Tourism Development and Investment Company, which is supervising the whole project, is working in relationship with—and paying significant sums to—Agence France-Muséums (a host of French cultural institutions including the Louvre and Quai Branly), the British Museum, and the Solomon R. Guggenheim Foundation. Substantial work has already taken place making plans, constructing the buildings, and acquiring art and artefacts. But unlike the nineteenth century, political leaders and archaeologists will not explore, excavate, nor invade other countries for artefacts to furnish these new cultural palaces. These new institutions will acquire their objects via the marketplace: money has replaced might.

These ambitious plans are about more than just nurturing tourism, although that is important. They are about nation-building. As nations rise, and countries become more powerful, culture can be a way that subtly demonstrates that rise. The Louvre Abu Dhabi and the Guggenheim Abu Dhabi will showcase great artistic achievements. The Zayed

National Museum will tell the story of the history of the United Arab Emirates (UAE), the Sheikh Zayed bin Sultan Al Nahyan, and the region. The National Museum, designed by Norman Foster, has distinctive towers, intended to recall the wing tips of the falcon—a unifying symbol of the nation (see Figure 17). A statement by His Highness Sheikh Khalifa bin Zayed Al Nahyan, president of the UAE, on the launch of the Zayed National Museum, explained:

> As a fitting memorial and a national institution, the museum will serve as a symbol of our historic cultural roots and of the many achievements of our country, providing us with an incentive to continue building our country with the same will and determination.[1]

The key partner in this project, from the everyday issues of how to train museum staff to what goes in the collection and how it will be displayed, is the British Museum. The British Museum, which once gave a visual

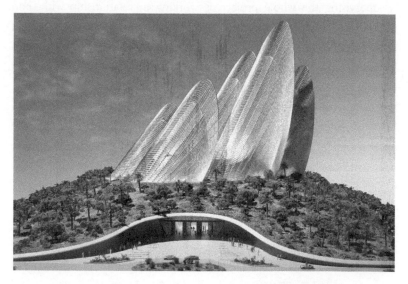

Figure 17. Zayed National Museum architectural drawing (2012).
© Foster + Partners.

form to the British nation, is now assisting the Zayed National Museum in presenting the history of the Emirates.

On the other side of the world, the China News Service estimates that around 100 new museums are opened in China every year. Shan Jixiang, the curator of the Palace Museum in Beijing, known as the imperial Forbidden City, has pledged to make the museum one of the 'best in the world', alongside the Louvre, St Petersburg's State Hermitage, the Met, and the British Museum.[2]

In Egypt, a colossus of Ramses II, which once adorned central Cairo, was put into to storage in 2006 and awaits a new home—the Grand Egyptian Museum, scheduled to partially open in 2018, though the political troubles may cause some delay. The collections of the Grand Egyptian Museum will include the Tutankhamen collection, currently in the Egyptian Museum in Cairo, and the Solar Boat, which is housed beside the Pyramids. The architectural competition, won by the firm Heneghan Peng from Dublin, have mapped out plans for a complex of activities devoted to Egyptology, with exhibition space that will take up four football fields in size. The new building will be in the shape of a triangle and will sit at the end of a desert plateau between the Pyramids and Cairo.

Museums, then, continue to be built. And objects of all kinds continue to be used implicitly to illustrate the rise of nations. It is partly because they are meaningful to people and associated with particular pasts, as well as ideas about being civilized and modern, that objects become caught up in broader social and political developments and uses from which they cannot easily be isolated. In one respect, then, if we go by the continuing expanding rate of museums, and the continued purchasing of artefacts, the future of museums appears to be assured.

But the threat to the future of museums discussed in this book is not about the number of museums being built or objects sold. My concern is with the destabilizing consequences of the shifting expectations that we hold for museums and collections. We have lost sight of what museums can do, whilst explicitly expecting them to achieve far more than is possible. The repatriation issue is not simply an argument, as it is often presented and understood, between old-fashioned museum directors and aggrieved campaigners. At its heart, it concerns the idea of what a museum is and who it is for.

Museums have always reflected the ideas of the time in which they are situated. But in the past forty or fifty years in particular, they have been challenged in ways that have proved destructive. They have been presented both as the cause of, and the solution to, all sorts of social ills. These trends threaten the museum by making it less free to pursue scholarship, and obliged to pursue social outcomes that it cannot possibly achieve. These challenges to the museum and shifts in their purpose have influenced the debate over repatriation. A crisis in the foundational authority of the museum—primarily, the questioning of the pursuit of knowledge—has intersected with the politicization of culture. In this context, claims for repatriation have greater purchase both within and outside the institution. The museum is no longer seen as a neutral space, but one that is threatening. At the same time, museums have been charged with changing society and have reoriented their mission towards making social impacts in the present. No wonder the content of exhibitions has become politically charged and the institution has evolved into a site of controversy.

As the accusations about past wrongs and claims that artefacts belong to one people instead of another grow louder, and are taken more seriously, we hear less about the objects that are at the heart of the dispute and of the people that once created and used them. Instead, these objects become the pawns of wider social and political tussles amidst which they are lost. In certain cases, with the rise of identity museums and the repatriation of human remains, knowledge of the past is restricted to certain groups, curtailed and even buried—sent to rot underground.

The contemporary preoccupation with the sometimes grubby stories of how artefacts came to be where they are, the idea that particular cultures connect to some artefacts instead of others, and that retention or repatriation will either repair the deleterious impact of imperialism or address contemporary conflicts, has become so powerful that they pose a threat both to the museum and to our understanding of civilizations past.

It is time to stop revelling in the wrongs of the past, to stop the recriminations. Political grievances cannot be overcome through the manipulation of objects. Attempts to do so are naive, and will have a detrimental impact on our understanding and appreciation of culture and history. Cultural artefacts can tell us a great deal about the past, and they are meaningful, but they are not the source of our national or ethnic identities and they will not bring about world peace.

Artefacts in museums have arrived via a number of routes. Now they are here, we should work out where they belong on the basis of where the artefact can best 'speak' about its varied history to scholars and audiences of all cultures, as well as being guided by practical—but important—questions such as how easy or risky is it to move the object. This will not result in one answer for all time, or one museum over all others. But these are the questions that should guide us.

We need to turn away from cultural institutions—and the past—as somewhere and something that can solve our very real present-day problems, because museums, objects, and history can only accomplish so much. I would like to see the struggles for a better present and future directed outside the museum, and more realistic expectations of what we ask of treasures from the past and the museums that house them.

There is so much about which to be curious, but too many have lost sight of the simple purpose of museums: to research and display what artefacts can tell us about past human civilizations, in order to understand other peoples, their lives, and their creations. The future for museums should be one that places objects, research, and the general public at their centre. That will benefit audiences and scholars everywhere. And by museums I mean both national and encyclopaedic: let us have both kinds of museums and more across the globe, not because they will create a harmonious world, but because museums are a good place to present and understand interesting objects from the past.

The mission of museums should be to acquire, conserve, research, and display their collections to all. That is all and that is enough. At present, the debate over objects and museums is too much about us: what culture can do for you and me today. It is not enough about *them*, and *then*. The object should be at the centre of the museum, not you and me. The questions that should be at the heart of museums are these: who came before us, how did they live, what did they believe, what did they make, how did they make it, and what did these treasures mean?

NOTES

Introduction to the Paperback Edition

1. 'Jesus votes in cockerel row', *Varsity*, 18 February 2016. <https://www.varsity.co.uk/news/9877>.
2. 'Benin Bronze "permanently removed" from Jesus Hall', *The Cambridge Student*, 9 March, 2016.
3. Cambridge college's bronze cockerel must go back to Nigeria, students say, the *Guardian*, 21 February, 2016.
4. 'Cambridge University agrees to remove Benin Bronze cockerel from the dining hall at Jesus College after students complained about its links to Britain's colonial past', *Daily Mail*, 8 March, 2016.
5. Cited in *'The Founder: Cecil Rhodes and the Pursuit of Power*, Robert L. Rotberg, (Oxford University Press, 1998) pg 225.
6. Rhodes statue removed in Cape Town as crowd celebrates, BBC News, 8 April, 2015. <http://www.bbc.com/news/world-africa-32236922>.
7. 'The Cecil Rhodes statue is not the problem', Kenan Malik, Aljazerra, 11 January 2016. <http://www.aljazeera.com/indepth/opinion/2016/01/cecil-rhodes-oxford-problem-160110061336569.html>.
8. Learning in public: An open letter on Sam Durant's *Scaffold*. Olga Visco, 25 May, 2016 <https://walkerart.org/magazine/learning-in-public-an-open-letter-on-sam-durants-scaffold>.

Introduction

1. I call the sculptures that Elgin acquired and sold and which are in the British Museum the Elgin Marbles, in order to distinguish them from the Parthenon Marbles in the Acropolis Museum in Athens, and because, upon acquisition by the British Museum, this was their given name. It is also normal nomenclature– *Madonna Litta*, *Medici Venus*, etc.
2. The definitive work on the acquisition of the Marbles is that by William St Clair, *Lord Elgin and the Marbles* (Oxford: Oxford University Press, 1998).
3. Lord Byron, *The Complete Poetical Works*, ii. *Childe Harold's Pilgrimage*, ed. J. McGann (Oxford: Clarendon Press, 1980), 100–1.
4. 'Nigeria Wants Museum of Fine Arts, Boston to Return Trove of Benin Artefacts', *New York Times* (23 July 2012).
5. 'Briton Returns Benin Artefacts After 177 Yrs', *Star Africa* (21 June 2014).

6. 'Sweden Forced to Return Looted Polynesian Human Remains', *HK Standard* (24 December 2012).
7. See, for example, John Torpey, *Making Whole What Has Been Smashed: On Reparations Politics* (Cambridge, Mass.: Harvard University Press, 2006); Todd Gitlin, *The Twilight of Common Dreams: Why America is Wracked by the Culture Wars* (New York: Owl Books, 1997).
8. Michael Ames, 'Biculturalism in Exhibitions', *Museum Anthropology*, 15/2 (1991), 13.
9. See, for example, Barbara Hoffman (ed.), *Art and Cultural Heritage: Law, Policy, and Practice* (Cambridge: Cambridge University Press, 2006); John Henry Merryman (ed.), *Thinking About the Elgin Marbles: Critical Essays on Cultural Property, Art and Law* (The Hague, London, and Boston: Kluwer Law International Ltd, 2000).
10. John Henry Merryman, 'The Nation and the Object', *International Journal of Cultural Property*, 3/1 (1994), 61–7.

Chapter 1. Great Explorers and Curious Collectors

1. In the spring of 2016, New Zealand's National Museum Te Papa Tongarewa long-term loaned the cape and helmet to the Bernice Pauahi Bishop Museum in Honolulu.
2. Adrienne Lois Kaeppler, *Artificial Curiosities: Being an Exposition of Native Manufacturers Collected on the Three Pacific Voyages of Captain James Cook, R.N., at the Bernice Pauahi Bishop Museum, January 18, 1978–August 31, 1978, on the Occasion of the Bicentennial of the European Discovery of the Hawaiian Islands by Captain Cook, January 18, 1778* (Honolulu: Bernice P. Bishop Museum, 1978).
3. *Selected Philosophical Works by Francis Bacon*, ed. Rose-Mary Sargent (Indianapolis, Ind.: Hackett Publishing Co., 1999), 119.
4. Quoted in Vanessa Smith, *Intimate Strangers: Friendship, Exchange and Pacific Encounters* (Cambridge and New York: Cambridge University Press, 2010), 195.
5. Neil Chalmers, *Sir Joseph Banks and the British Museum: The World of Collecting 1720–1830* (London: Pickering and Chatto, 2007), 9.
6. *Journal of the Right Hon. Sir Joseph Banks Bart., K.B., P.R.S.*, ed. Joseph Dalton Hooker (Cambridge: Cambridge University Press, 2011), 282.
7. Rashleigh Holt-White, *The Life and Letters of Gilbert White of Selborne* (London: John Murray, 1901), 211–12.
8. Holt-White, *The Life and Letters of Gilbert White of Selborne*, 211–12.
9. Holt-White, *The Life and Letters of Gilbert White of Selborne*, 211–12.
10. Holt-White, *The Life and Letters of Gilbert White of Selborne*, 211–12.
11. Joseph Banks to Ingenhousz, 31 May 1782, Papers of Sir Joseph Banks, State Library, New South Wales, Series 74.03.
12. Edward Miller, *That Noble Cabinet: A History of the British Museum* (London: Andre Deutsch, 1973), 75.

13. Edward Miller, *That Noble Cabinet: A History of the British Museum*, 75.
14. *The Yale Edition of Horace Walpole's Correspondence*, ed. W. S. Lewis, 48 vols (New Haven: Yale University Press, 1937–83), xxx. 114.
15. Margaret Cavendish Bentinck, Duchess of Portland, *A Catalogue of a Very Valuable Collection of Cameos, Intaglios, and Precious Stones, and other Curiosities… Many out of the Arundel Collection; Which will be Sold by Auction by Mr. Skinner and Co.… the 8th of June, 1786… Late the Property of the Duchess Dowager of Portland, Deceased* (London: n.p., 1786).
16. Mary Delany to Mary Dewes, 3 September 1769, in *The Autobiography and Correspondence of Mary Granville, Mrs. Delany; with Interesting Reminiscences of King George the Third and Queen Charlotte*, ed. Augusta Hall Landover (London: Richard Bentley, 1862), 238–9.
17. Alexandra Cook, 'Botanical Exchanges: Jean-Jacques Rousseau and the Duchess of Portland', *History of European Ideas*, 33 (2007), 142–56.
18. Margaret Cavendish Bentinck, Duchess of Portland, *A Marked Catalogue, containing the lots, what each respectively sold for, and the names of the purchasers of the four thousand two hundred and sixty-three articles. Which constituted the Portland Museum; late the property of the Duchess of the Dowager of Portland, deceased. Which was sold by auction by Mr Skinner and Co., etc.* (London: Kearsley, 1786).
19. *The Resolution Journal of Johann Reinhold Forster: 1772–1775*, ed. Michael E. Hoare (London: Hakluyt Society, 1982), 555–7.
20. Letter received by Banks from Daniel Solander (14 August 1775), in Papers of Sir Joseph Banks, State Library, New South Wales, Series 72.181. Available online: http://www2.sl.nsw.gov.au/banks/series_72/72_181.cfm.
21. This quote is in a letter received by Banks from Daniel Solander (14 August 1775), in Papers of Sir Joseph Banks, Series 72.181.
22. Quoted in Kaeppler, *Artificial Curiosities*, 45.
23. *The Endeavour Journal of Sir Joseph Banks 1768–1771*, ii, ed. Timothy Holmes Beaglehole (Sydney: Angus and Robertson Ltd, 1962), 133.
24. Michelle Hetherington, *Cook & Omai: The Cult of the South Seas* (Canberra: National Library of Australia in association with the Humanities Research Centre, Australian National University, 2001), 38.
25. Quoted in David Samwell, *A Narrative of the Death of Captain James Cook* (San Francisco: David Magee, 1957).
26. Jenny Newell, 'Irresistible Objects: Collecting in the Pacific and Australia in the Reign of George III', in Kim Sloan (ed.), *Enlightenment: Collecting the World in the Eighteenth Century* (London: British Museum Press, 2003), 246–57.
27. Anne D'Alleva, 'Continuity and Change in Decorated Barkcloth from Bligh's Second Breadfruit Voyage, 1791–1793', *Pacific Arts*, 11–12 (1995), 29–42.

28. Dorinda Outram, *The Enlightenment: New Approaches to European History* (Cambridge: Cambridge University Press, 2005), 53.

29. Journal of Lieutenant James King, in *The Journals of Captain James Cook on His Voyages of Discovery*, iii/1. *The Voyage of the* Resolution *and* Discovery, *1776–1780*, ed J. C. Beaglehole (Cambridge: Hakluyt Society, 1967), 512.

30. Adrienne Kaeppler (ed.), *Cook Voyage Artefacts in Leningrad, Berne and Florence Museums* (Bernice P. Bishop Museum Special Publication No. 66; Honolulu: Bishop Museum Press, 1978), 1–186.

31. Beth Fowkes Tobin, 'Acquiring Pacific Shells: Collectors, Dealers, and Cook's Voyages' (Draft MS, 2010), 17.

32. James Cook, *A Voyage to the Pacific Ocean; Undertaken by Command of his Majesty, for Making Discoveries in the Northern Hemisphere; Performed Under the Direction of Captains Cook, Clerke, and Gore, in the Years 1776, 1777, 1778, 1778, and 1780* (London: John Fielding, 1785), p. xxxviii.

33. Chalmers, *Joseph Banks and the British Museum*, 16.

34. Chris D. Paulin, 'Māori Fishhooks in European Museums', *Tuhinga*, 21 (Museum of Te Papa Tongarewa, 2010), 21.

Chapter 2. The Birth of the Public Museum

1. Paula Findlen, 'The Museum: Its Classical Etymology and Renaissance Genealogy', *Journal of the History of Collections*, 1/1 (1989), 59–78.

2. Luciano Berti, *Il principe dello studiolo: Francesco I dei Medici e la fine del Rinascimiento fiorentino* (Florence: Editrice Edam, 1967), 66.

3. See Michael Rinehart, 'A Document for the Studiolo of Franceso I', in Moshe Baraschi, Lucy Freeman Sandler, and Patricia Egan (eds), *Art, The Ape of Nature* (New York: Harry N. Abrams, 1981), 275–89.

4. Peter Burke, *The Italian Renaissance: Culture and Society in Italy* (New York: Polity Press, 1986).

5. Eilean Hooper-Greenhill, *Museums and the Shaping of Knowledge* (London and New York: Routledge, 1992).

6. Quoted in William Eamon, *Science and the Secrets of Nature: Books of Secrets in Medieval and Early Modern Culture* (Princeton: Princeton University Press, 1994), 224.

7. Hooper-Greenhill, *Museums and the Shaping of Knowledge*, 78.

8. Paula Findlen, *Possessing Nature: Museums, Collecting, and Scientific Culture in Early Modern Italy* (Berkeley and Los Angeles: University of California Press, 1994), 4.

9. Giuseppe Olmi, 'Science-Honour-Metaphor: Italian Cabinets of the Sixteenth and Seventeenth Centuries', in Oliver Impey and Arthur MacGregor (eds), *The Origins of Museums: The Cabinet of Curiosities in Sixteenth and Seventeenth Century Europe* (Oxford: Clarendon Press, 1985; 2nd edn, London: The House of Stratus, 2001), 10.

10. Thomas DaCosta Kaufmann, 'Remarks on the Collections of Rudolf II: The Kunstkammer as a Form of Representatio', in Donald Preziosi and Claire Farago (eds), *Grasping the World: The Idea of the Museum* (Aldershot: Ashgate, 2004), 527.

11. Quoted in Kaufmann, 'Remarks on the Collections of Rudolf II', 526-37.

12. Ken Arnold, *Cabinets for the Curious: Looking Back at Early English Museums* (Aldershot: Ashgate, 2006), 13.

13. Charles Hoole, *A New Discovery of the Old Art of Teaching School, in Four Small Treatises* (1660; London: Herman Hager, 1912), 284-5.

14. John Tradescant, *Musaeum Tradescantianum: Or, a Collection of Rarities, preserved at South-Lambeth neer London* (1656; London, 1980), preface, quoted in Marjorie Swann, *Curiosities and Texts: The Culture of Collecting in Early Modern England* (Philadelphia: University of Pennsylvania Press, 2001), 44-5.

15. Michael Hunter, 'The Royal Society's "Repository" and Its Background', in Impey and MacGregor (eds), *The Origins of Museums*, 226-7.

16. Frances Bacon, *Gesta Grayorum* (1594), cited in Impey and MacGregor (eds), *The Origins of Museums*, p. xvii.

17. Arnold, *Cabinets for the Curious*, 30.

18. Quoted in Swann, *Curiosities and Texts*, 89.

19. *The Yale Edition of Horace Walpole's Correspondence*, xx. *With Sir Horace Mann*, ed. Wilmarth Sheldon Lewis and George L. Lam (London: Oxford University Press; New Haven: Yale University Press, 1954), 358-9.

20. Sir William Jardine Bart, *The Naturalist's Library, Mammalia*, v. *Pachydermes* (Edinburgh: W. H. Lizars, 1836), 61.

21. Quoted in Tony Rice, *Voyages of Discovery: Three Centuries of Natural History Exploration* (London: Scriptum Editions and the Natural History Museum, 1999).

22. Barbara M. Benedict, 'Collecting Trouble: Sir Hans Sloane's Literary Reputation in Eighteenth-Century Britain', *Eighteenth Century Life*, 36/2 (Spring 2012), 111-42.

23. Benedict, 'Collecting Trouble', 111-42.

24. Benedict, 'Collecting Trouble', 111-42.

25. Benedict, 'Collecting Trouble', 128.

26. David M. Wilson, *The British Museum: A History* (London: British Museum Press, 2002), 19.

27. Derek Gillman, *The Idea of Cultural Heritage* (Cambridge: Cambridge University Press, 2010).

28. Paula Findlen, *Possessing Nature: Museums, Collecting, and Scientific Culture in Early Modern Italy* (Berkeley and Los Angeles: University of California Press, 1994), 396.

29. Quoted in Arnold, *Cabinets for the Curious*, 227.

30. Quoted in Marjorie Caygill, 'Sloane's Will and the Establishment of the British Museum', in MacGregor (ed.), *Sir Hans Sloane*, 47.
31. Quoted in Kim Sloan, *Enlightenment: Discovering the World in the Eighteenth Century* (London: British Museum Press, 2004), 17.
32. John Melton, *The Rise of the Public in Enlightenment Europe* (Cambridge: Cambridge University Press, 2001), 2.
33. Melton, *The Rise of the Public in Enlightenment Europe*, 2.
34. British Museum, *Annual Report* (London: British Museum, 2010), 11.
35. Quoted in Edward Miller, *That Noble Cabinet: A History of the British Museum* (London: Andre Deutsch, 1973), 44.
36. Wilson, *The British Museum*, 19.
37. From *Statues and Rules Relating to…British Museum*, quoted in Miller, *That Noble Cabinet*, 61.
38. Carl Philip Moritz, *Journeys of a German in England: A Walking-Tour of England in 1782* (Bath: Chivers Press, 1987), 52, 51.
39. Letter of Miss C. Talbot, 1767, British Library, Add. MS 39311, fo. 83.
40. Quoted in Arthur MacGregor, *Tradescant's Rarities: Essays on the Foundation of the Ashmolean Museum 1693* (Oxford: Oxford University Press, 1983), 62.
41. Letter of Miss C. Talbot, 1767, fo. 83.
42. Quoted in Andrew McClennan, *Inventing the Louvre: Art, Politics and the Origins of the Modern Museum in Eighteenth-Century Paris* (Berkeley and Los Angeles: University of California Press, 1999), 91.
43. Quoted in McClennan, *Inventing the Louvre*, 91–2.
44. Quoted in Stanley J. Idzerda, 'Iconoclasm during the French Revolution', *American Historical Review*, 60/1 (1954), 13–26.
45. Margaret Miles, *Art as Plunder: The Ancient Origins of Debate About Cultural Property* (New York and Cambridge: Cambridge University Press, 2008), 317–18.
46. Quoted in McClennan, *Inventing the Louvre*, 98.
47. Bette W. Oliver, *From Royal to National: The Louvre Museum and the Bibliothèque Nationale* (Lanham, Md.: Lexington Books, 2007).
48. Carol Duncan and Alan Wallach, 'The Universal Survey Museum', *Art History*, 3 (1980), 448–69.
49. Felicity Bodenstein, 'National Museums in France', in Peter Aronsson and Gabriella Elgenius (eds), *Building National Museums in Europe 1750–2010*, Conference proceedings from EuNaMus, *European National Museums: Identity Politics, the Uses of the Past and the European Citizen*, Bologna 28–30 April 2011, EuNaMus Report No. 1, published by Linköping University Electronic Press: http://www.ep.liu.se/ecp_home/index.en.aspx?issue=064.
50. Quoted in Peter Bailey, *Leisure and Class in Victorian England: Rational Recreation and the Contest for Control* (New York: Routledge, 1987), 58.

51. Juliet Steyn, 'The Complexities of Assimilation in the 1906 Whitechapel Art Gallery Exhibition "Jewish Art and Antiquities"', *Oxford Art Journal*, 13/2 (1990), 44.
52. John Ruskin, *The Complete Works of John Ruskin* (New York: T. Y. Crowell & Co., 1885), 71.
53. Quoted in Francis Michael Longstreth Thompson, *The Cambridge Social History of Britain, 1750-1950*, ii (Cambridge: Cambridge University Press, 1990), 322.
54. See online at http://www.sil.si.edu/Exhibitions/Smithson-to-Smithsonian/intro.html.
55. See online at http://www.metmuseum.org/about-the-museum/mission-statement.
56. George Brown Goode, *A Memorial of George Brown Goode, Together with a Selection of His Papers of Museums and on the History of Science in America* (Washington, DC: Government Printing Office, 1901), 8, 293.

Chapter 3. Antiquity Fever

1. Reilly Conor, *Athanasius Kircher S.J.: Master of a Hundred Arts 1602-1680* (Studia Kircheriana, 1; Wiesbaden and Rome: Edizioni del Mondo, 1974), 38.
2. *Letters and Documents of Napoleon*, selected and translated by John Eldred Howard, i (London: Cresset Press, 1961), 1999.
3. Quoted in David A. Bell, *The First Total War: Napoleon's Europe and the Birth of Warfare as We Know It* (Boston: Houghton Mifflin Harcourt, 2007), 212.
4. Quoted in Juan Cole, *Napoleon's Egypt: Invading the Middle East* (New York: Palgrave Macmillan, 2008), 17.
5. *Letters and Documents of Napoleon*, selected and translated by Howard, i. 269-70.
6. *Abd al Rahman al-Jabarti History of Egypt*, ed. Thomas Philipp and Moshe Perlmann (Stuttgart: Franz Steiner, 1994), 32.
7. *Abd al Rahman al-Jabarti History of Egypt*, ed Philipp and Perlmann, 93.
8. *Abd al Rahman al-Jabarti History of Egypt*, ed. Philipp and Perlmann, 29.
9. *Abd al Rahman al-Jabarti History of Egypt*, ed. Philipp and Perlmann, 33.
10. *Abd al Rahman al-Jabarti History of Egypt*, ed. Philipp and Perlmann, 398-400.
11. *Abd al Rahman al-Jabarti History of Egypt*, ed. Philipp and Perlmann, 398-400.
12. Florence Nightingale, *Letters from Egypt: A Journal on the Nile 1849-1950* (New York: Barrie and Jenkins, 1987), 33.
13. Donald Reid, *Whose Pharaohs?: Archaeology, Museums, and Egyptian National Identity from Napoleon to World War I* (Berkeley and Los Angeles: University of California Press, 2003), 54.
14. Reid, *Whose Pharaohs?*, 56.
15. See Reid, *Whose Pharaohs?*, 56.

16. Richard Parkinson, *Cracking Codes: The Rosetta Stone and Decipherment* (Berkeley and Los Angeles: University of California Press; London: British Museum Press, 1999), 21.
17. Sir Robert Thomas Wilson, *History of the British Expedition to Egypt* (London: printed by C. Roworth, 1803), 351.
18. See http://www.sal.org.uk/history/.
19. Holger Hook, *Empires of the Imagination: Politics, Wars, and the Arts in the British World, 1750–1850* (London: Profile Books, 2010), 223.
20. Alexander Wood, *Thomas Young: Natural Philosopher* (Cambridge: Cambridge University Press, 2011), 222.
21. Edward W. Said, *Orientalism* (London: Routledge and Kegan Paul, 1978), 84.
22. Salt to Banks, 20 June 1815, British Museum, CE 3/10 2617.
23. Ivor Noel Hume, *Belzoni: The Giant Archaeologists Love to Hate* (Charlottesville, Va.: University of Virginia Press, 2011).
24. Quoted in Brian M. Fagan, *The Rape of the Nile* (New York: Basic Books, 2004), 82.
25. Giovanni Belzoni, *Belzoni's Travels: Narrative of the Operations and Recent Discoveries in Egypt and Nubia*, ed. Alberto Siliotti (London: British Museum Press, 2001), 32.
26. Quoted in Deborah Manley and Peta Rée, *Henry Salt: Artist, Traveller, Diplomat, Egyptologist* (London: Libri Publications, 2001), 133.
27. 'Pharaoh Seto 1's Tomb Bigger Than Thought', *National Geographic News* (17 April 2008).
28. Manley and Rée, *Henry Salt*, 134.
29. John Timbs, *Walks and Talks About London* (London: Lockwood, 1865), 149.
30. Jacob Rothenberg, *Descensus Ad Terram: Acquisition and Reception of the Elgin Marbles* (New York: Garland Publishing Incorporated, 1977), 1.
31. Ian Jenkins, *Archaeologists and Aesthetes in the Sculpture Galleries of the British Museum, 1800–1939* (London: British Museum Press, 1992), 9.
32. *The Yale Edition of Horace Walpole's Correspondence*, vol. xviii. *With Sir Horace Mann*, ed. Wilmarth Sheldon Lewis and George L. Lam (London: Oxford University Press; New Haven: Yale University Press, 1954), 211.
33. Joshua Reynolds, Edmond Malone, and Joseph Farington, *The Literary Works of Sir Joshua Reynolds, Kt. Late President of the Royal Academy; Containing His Discourses, Papers in The Idler, the Journal of a Tour Through Flanders and Holland, and Also His Commentary on Du Fresnoy's Art of Painting*, (London: T. Cadell and W. Davies: 1819), 18.
34. Joseph Banks, *The Letters of Sir Joseph Banks: A Selection, 1768–1820*, ed. Neil Chambers (London: Imperial College Press, 2000), 249.
35. J. J. Winckelmann, *Winckelmann: Writings on Art*, ed. David Irwin (London: Phaidon, 1972), 72.
36. *Winckelmann: Writings on Art*, ed. Irwin, 107.

37. *Winckelmann: Writings on Art*, ed. Irwin, 113.
38. Jenkins, *The Parthenon Frieze* (London, British Museum Press, 1994). This is disputed by Joan Breton Connelly who argues that it is the scene of preliminaries to a human sacrifice. Joan Breton Connelly, *The Parthenon Enigma* (New York: Alfred A. Knopf, a division of Random House LLC, 2014).
39. Melina Mercouri, Speech to the Oxford Union (June 1986).
40. *Report from the Select Committee on the Earl of Elgin's Collection of Sculptured Marbles* (London: House of Commons, 1816), 20.
41. See Arthur Hamilton Smith, 'Lord Elgin and His Collection', *Journal of Hellenic Studies*, 36 (1916), 190, for this quote from Hunt. This is an extensive account of the acquisition of the Marbles.
42. *Report from the Select Committee on the Earl of Elgin's Collection of Sculptured Marbles*, 41.
43. *Report from the Select Committee on the Earl of Elgin's Collection of Sculptured Marbles*, 40.
44. William St Clair, *Lord Elgin & the Marbles: The Controversial History of the Parthenon Sculptures* (Oxford: Oxford University Press, 1998), 89.
45. St Clair, *Lord Elgin & the Marbles*, 89.
46. Mary Bruce, *Letters of Mary Nisbet of Dirleton, Countess of Elgin*, arranged by Nisbet Hamilton Grant (London: John Murray, 1926), 97–8.
47. Hamilton Smith, 'Lord Elgin and His Collection', 197.
48. Hamilton Smith, 'Lord Elgin and His Collection', 198.
49. St Clair *Lord Elgin & the Marbles*, 99.
50. Rothenberg, *Descensus Ad Terram*, 158–9.
51. Hamilton Smith, 'Lord Elgin and His Collection', 232.
52. Edward Daniel Clarke LLD, *Travel in Various Countries of Europe, Asia, and Africa* (London: T. Cadell and W. Davies, Strand, 1817), 224.
53. Rothenberg, *Descensus Ad Terram*, 178.
54. Rothenberg, *Descensus Ad Terram*, 164.
55. Rothenberg, *Descensus Ad Terram*, 164.
56. William Miller, *Memorandum on the Subject of the Earl of Elgin's Pursuits in Greece* (London: printed for William Miller, 1811), 39–41.
57. John Henry Merryman, 'Thinking About the Elgin Marbles', in Merryman, *Thinking About the Elgin Marbles: Critical Essays on Cultural Property, Art and Law* (The Hague, London, and Boston: Kluwer Law International, 2000), 39, 62, 42–3.
58. Mary Beard, *The Parthenon* (2002; London: Profile Books, 2010), 101.
59. Quoted in Beard, *The Parthenon*, 100.
60. Hamilton Smith, 'Lord Elgin and His Collection', 294.
61. Quoted in St Clair *Lord Elgin & the Marbles*, 164.

62. Adolf Michaelis, *Ancient Marbles in Great Britain* (Cambridge: Cambridge University Press, 1882), 138.

63. Michaelis, *Ancient Marbles in Great Britain*, 139.

64. Rothenberg, *Descensus Ad Terram*, 217.

65. Byron, *Selected Poetry of Lord Byron* (New York: Modern Library, Inc: 2002), 322.

66. Byron, *The Complete Poetical Works*, ii. *Childe Harold's Pilgrimage*, ed. J. McGann (Oxford: Clarendon Press, 1980), 100–1. See Roger Luckhurst, *The Mummy's Curse: The True History of a Dark Fantasy* (Oxford: Oxford University Press, 2012), for an exploration of the myth of the mummies' curse, especially in relation to excavations in Egypt.

67. Rothenberg, *Descensus Ad Terram*, 227.

68. Hamilton Smith, 'Lord Elgin and His Collection', 301.

69. Charles Bell, *Letters of Charles Bell to His Brother George Joseph Bell* (London: John Murray, 1870), 124.

70. Hamilton Smith, 'Lord Elgin and His Collection', 325.

71. Michaelis, *Ancient Marbles in Great Britain*, 146.

72. *Report from the Select Committee on the Earl of Elgin's Collection of Sculptured Marbles*, 1.

73. *Report from the Select Committee on the Earl of Elgin's Collection of Sculptured Marbles*, 30.

74. *Report from the Select Committee on the Earl of Elgin's Collection of Sculptured Marbles*, 70–1.

75. *Report from the Select Committee on the Earl of Elgin's Collection of Sculptured Marbles*, 000.

76. *Report from the Select Committee on the Earl of Elgin's Collection of Sculptured Marbles*, 74.

77. *Report from the Select Committee on the Earl of Elgin's Collection of Sculptured Marbles*, p. v.

78. *Report from the Select Committee on the Earl of Elgin's Collection of Sculptured Marbles*, 12.

79. Quoted in James M. Garrett, *Wordsworth and the Writing of the Nation* (London: Ashgate Publishing, 2008), 174.

80. *Hansard*, 1st ser., 34 (1816) 1028.

81. *Hansard*, 1st ser., 34 (1816) 1031–3.

82. *Hansard*, 1st ser., 34 (1816) 1031.

83. Jenkins, *Archaeologists and Aesthetes in the Sculpture Galleries of the British Museum*, 19.

84. *The Statues of the United Kingdom of Great Britain and Ireland*, vol. 24 (London: House of Commons, 1816), 974.

85. Hamilton Smith, 'Lord Elgin and His Collection', 351.

86. Quoted in Beth Cohen, 'Deconstructing the Acropolis', *American Journal of Archaeology*, 114/4 (October 2010), 745–54.

87. See Jenkins, *Archaeologists and Aesthetes in the Sculpture Galleries of the British Museum* for a detailed discussion of their aesthetic arrangement and history.

88. Ian Jenkins makes the point that most scholarship has concentrated on the acquisition of the marbles, leaving their history at an end in 1816. His work *Archaeologists and Aesthetes* continues the story.

89. Vaughn Emerson Crawford, Prudence Oliver Harper, and Holly Pittmann, *Assyrian Reliefs and Ivories in the Metropolitan Museum of Art* (New York: Metropolitan Museum, 1980), 10.

90. Crawford, Harper, and Pittmann, *Assyrian Reliefs and Ivories in the Metropolitan Museum of Art*, 34.

91. Crawford, Harper, and Pittmann, *Assyrian Reliefs and Ivories in the Metropolitan Museum of Art*, 34.

92. Quoted in Shawn Malley, 'Shipping the Bull: Staging Assyria in the British Museum', *Nineteenth-Century Contexts: An Interdisciplinary Journal*, 31/1 (March 2004), 16.

93. Quoted in Malley, 'Shipping the Bull', 25.

94. Austen Henry Layard, *Nineveh and Its Remains*, ed. Henry William Frederick Saggs (London: Routledge & K. Paul, 1970), 50.

95. Layard, *Nineveh and Its Remains*, ed. Saggs, 70.

96. Layard, *Nineveh and Its Remains*, ed. Saggs, 76.

97. Quoted in John Malcolm Russell, *From Nineveh to New York: Strange Story of the Assyrian Reliefs in the Metropolitan Museum and the Hidden Masterpiece of Canford School* (New Haven: Yale University Press, 1997), 37.

98. Quoted in Russell, *From Nineveh to New York*, 37.

99. Quoted in Russell, *From Nineveh to New York*, 37.

100. Quoted in Russell, *From Nineveh to New York*, 37.

101. Quoted in Russell, *From Nineveh to New York*, 37.

102. Quoted in Russell, *From Nineveh to New York*, 38.

103. Erner Alfred Wallis Budge, *The Rise and Progress of Assyriology* (London: Martin Hopkinson, 1925), 106–19.

Chapter 4. Cases of Loot

1. Cicero, *Selected Works*, trans. Michael Grant (Harmondsworth: Penguin Classics, 2004), 41.

2. Cicero, *Selected Works*, trans. Grant, 42.

3. See Mary Beard, *The Roman Triumph* (Cambridge, Mass.: Belknap Press of Harvard University Press, 2007), for an exploration of the ancient ceremonies.

4. Margaret Miles, *Art as Plunder: The Ancient Origins of Debate About Cultural Property* (New York and Cambridge: Cambridge University Press, 2008), 1.

5. Cecil Gould, *Trophy of Conquest: The Musée Napoleon and the Creation of the Louvre* (London: Faber and Faber, 1965).
6. Quoted in Gould, *Trophy of Conquest*, 40.
7. Quoted in Andrew McClellan, *Inventing the Louvre: Art Politics and the Origins of the Modern Museum in Eighteenth-Century Paris* (Berkeley and Los Angeles: University of California Press, 1999), 116.
8. Quoted in John Henry Merryman and Albert E. Elsen, *Law, Ethics and the Visual Arts* (The Hague, London, and Boston: Kluwer Law International; 4th rev. edn, 2002), 3.
9. Quoted in Noah Charney, *Stealing the Mystic Lamb* (New York: Public Affairs, 2012), 89.
10. *Letters and Documents of Napoleon*, selected and translated by John Eldred Howard, i (London: Cresset Press, 1961), 111.
11. David P. Jordon, *Napoleon and the Revolution* (Houndmills and New York: Palgrave Macmillan, 2012), 39.
12. Quoted in McClellan, *Inventing the Louvre*, 123.
13. Francis Haskell and Nicholas Penny, *Taste and the Antique: Lure of Classical Sculpture, 1500–1900* (New Haven: Yale University Press, 1982), 108.
14. Quoted in Patricia Mainardi, 'Assuring the Empire of the Future: The 1789 Fête de la Liberté', *Art Journal* (Summer 1989), 156.
15. Haskell and Penny, *Taste and the Antique*, 110.
16. Haskell and Penny, *Taste and the Antique*, 110.
17. Quoted in David Gilks, 'Art and Politics During the "First" Directory: Artists' Petitions and the Quarrel over the Confiscation of Works of Art from Italy in 1796', *French History Journal*, 26/1 (2012), 59.
18. Quoted in Gilks, 'Art and Politics During the "First" Directory', 69.
19. Gould, *Trophy of Conquest*, 131–5.
20. Quoted in Christopher M. S. Johns, *Antonio Canova and the Politics of Patronage in Revolutionary and Napoleonic Europe* (Berkeley and Los Angeles: University of California Press, 1998), 177.
21. Gould, *Trophy of Conquest*, 121.
22. Gould, *Trophy of Conquest*, 121.
23. Quoted in Johns, *Antonio Canova and the Politics of Patronage*, 177.
24. Miles, *Art as Plunder*, 341.
25. Bette W. Cooper, *From Royal to National: The Louvre Museum and the Bibliothèque Nationale* (Lanham, Md.: Lexington Books, 2006), 167.
26. Philip A. Igbafe, 'The Fall of Benin: A Reassessment', *Journal of African History*, 11/3 (1970), 385–400.
27. Felix Roth, 'Diary of a Surgeon with the Benin Punitive Expedition', in Henry Ling Roth, *Great Benin: Its Customs, Art and Horrors* (Halifax: England F. King & Sons, 1903), p. x.

28. Roth, 'Diary of a Surgeon with the Benin Punitive Expedition', p. ix.
29. Ian Hernon, *Britain's Forgotten Wars: Colonial Campaigns of the Nineteenth Century* (London: The History Press, 2003), 421.
30. Hernon, *Britain's Forgotten Wars* 421.
31. Henry Ling Roth, *Great Benin: Its Customs, Art and Horrors* (Halifax, England: F. King & Sons, 1903), p. vi.
32. Quoted in the BBC Radio 4 programme, *A History of the World in 100 Objects* (http://www.bbc.co.uk/ahistoryoftheworld/about/transcripts/episode77/), episode 77.
33. Victor Hugo, 'The Sack of the Summer Palace', *UNESCO Courier* (November 1985).
34. *Letters and Journals of James, Eighth Earl of Elgin*, ed. Theodore Walrond (Boston: IndyPublish, 2006), 127–30.
35. Hugo, 'The Sack of the Summer Palace'.
36. Viscount General Garnet Wolseley, *Narrative of the war with China in 1860: To which is added the account of a short residence with the Tai-ping rebels at Nankin and a voyage from thence to Hankow* (London: Longman, Green, Longman, and Roberts, 1862), 227.
37. *Letters and Journals of James, Eighth Earl of Elgin*, ed. Walrond, 127–30.
38. Robert Swinhoe, *Narrative of the North China Campaign of 1860: Containing Personal Experiences of Chinese Character, and of the Moral and Social Condition of the Country; Together with a Description of the Interior of Pekin* (London: Smith, Elder and Co., 1861).
39. Demetrius Charles Boulger, *The Life of General Gordon* (London: Nelson, 1896), 71–2.
40. *Letters and Journals of James, Eighth Earl of Elgin*, ed. Walrond, 365–7.
41. *Letters and Journals of James, Eighth Earl of Elgin*, ed. Walrond, 365–7.
42. Henry Knollys, *Incidents in the China War of 1860 Compiled from the Private Journals of General Sir Hope Grant* (London & Edinburgh: William Blackwood and Sons, 1873), 226–7.
43. General Joseph Wolseley, *Narrative of the War With China in 1860* (Wilmington, Del.: Scholarly Resources Inc., 1972), 224.
44. Greg Thomas, 'The Looting of Yuanming and the Translation of Chinese Art in Europe', *Nineteenth Century Art Worldwide*, 7/2 (2008), http://www.19thc-artworldwide.org/autumn08/38-autumn08/autumn08article/93-the-looting-of-yuanming-and-the-translation-of-chinese-art-in-europe, accessed September 2015.
45. Captain J. H. Lawrence-Archer, 'Chinese Porcelain, Particularly that of the Ta Ming Dynasty', *Art Journal* (London, 1875), 241.
46. Wayne Sandholtz, *Prohibiting Plunder: How Norms Change* (Oxford: Oxford University Press, 2007).

47. Milbry Polk and Angela M. H. Schuster, *The Looting of the Iraq Museum, Baghdad: The Lost Legacy of Ancient Mesopotamia* (New York: Abrams, 2005), 2.
48. See Neil Brodie, Jenny Doole, and Colin Renfrew (eds), *Trade in Illicit Antiquities: The Destruction of the World's Archaeological Heritage* (Cambridge: McDonald Institute for Archaeological Research, University of Cambridge, 2001); David Gill's blog http://lootingmatters.blogspot.co.uk/ as well as Derek Fincham's http://illicitculturalproperty.com/ for up-to-date material.
49. 'Stolen Artefacts Returned to the National Museum of Afghanistan in Kabul', British Museum Press Release (July 2012).
50. Kaya Burgess, 'British Museum Guarding Antiquity Looted in Syria', *The Times* (5 June 2015), http://www.thetimes.co.uk/tto/news/uk/article4460896.ece.
51. Tatiana Flessas, *The End of the Museum* (LSE Law, Society and Economy Working Papers 14/2013; London: LSE, 2013).
52. Jason Felch and Ralph Frammolino, *Chasing Aphrodite: The Hunt for Looted Antiquities at the World's Richest Museum* (Boston and New York: Houghton Mifflin Harcourt), 321.
53. Rosella Lorenzi, 'Tut Family Mummies Damaged in Egypt Riots?', *Discovery News* (4 February 2011).
54. Felch and Frammolino, *Chasing Aphrodite*, 1.
55. Felch and Frammolino, *Chasing Aphrodite*, 5.
56. Miles, *Art as Plunder*, 2.

Chapter 5. Museum Wars

1. Professor Richard Lane, 'Why Paraguay?', interview with *BBC News Online* (11 November 2010), http://news.bbc.co.uk/earth/hi/earth_news/newsid_9179000/9179669.stm.
2. Letter by Glauser (2010), copy available via a link on www.guardian.co.uk/world/2010/nov/08/natural-history-museum-paraguay-tribes.
3. Quoted in Isaiah Berlin, *Vico and Herder: Two Studies in the History of Ideas* (London: Chatto and Windus, 1980), 182.
4. Isaiah Berlin, *Three Critics of the Enlightenment: Vico, Hamann, Herder* (London: Pimlico, 2000), 223.
5. David Hume, *An Enquiry Concerning Human Understanding* (1748; Chicago: Open Court, 1988), 61.
6. Quoted in Isaiah Berlin, *The Proper Study of Mankind: An Anthology of Essays* (London: Chatto & Windus, 1997), 415.
7. Max Horkheimer and Theodor W. Adorno, *Dialectic of Enlightenment* (New York: Herder and Herder, 1971).
8. John Gray, *Straw Dogs: Thoughts on Humans and Other Animals* (London: Granta Books, 2004), 96.

9. Terry Eagleton, *After Theory* (New York: Basic Books, 2003), 13.
10. Zygmunt Bauman, *Legislators and Interpreters: On Modernity, Post-Modernity and Intellectuals* (London: Polity Press, 1989), 120.
11. Eilean Hooper-Greenhill, *Museums and the Shaping of Knowledge* (London and New York: Routledge, 1992), 2.
12. Peter Vergo (ed.), *The New Museology* (London: Reaktion, 1989).
13. See, for example, Alma Wittlin, *Museums in Search of a Useable Future* (Cambridge, Mass.: MIT Press 1970), for an earlier example of these ideas. Similarly, the interest in neighbourhood museums in the US in the 1970s.
14. Ralph Starn, 'A Historian's Brief Guide to New Museum Studies', *American Historical Review*, 110/1 (2005), 68-98.
15. Pierre Bourdieu and Alain Darbel, *The Love of Art: European Art Museums and Their Public* (Stanford, Calif.: Stanford University Press, 1991), 14.
16. Pierre Bourdieu, *Distinction: A Social Critique of the Judgment of Taste* (Cambridge, Mass., Harvard University Press; repr. edn, 1987).
17. Bourdieu and Darbel, *The Love of Art*.
18. John Berger, *Ways of Seeing* (Harmondsworth: Penguin Classics, 2008).
19. Munira Mirza, *The Politics of Culture: The Case for Universalism* (Houndmills: Palgrave MacMillan, 2011).
20. Gordon Fyfe, *Sociology and the Social Aspects of Museums*, in Sharon Macdonald (ed.), *A Companion to Museum Studies* (Malden, Mass. and Oxford: Blackwell Publishing, 2006).
21. Moira Simpson, *Making Representations: Museums in the Post-Colonial Era* (London: Routledge, 1996), 1.
22. Carol Duncan, *Civilizing Rituals: Inside Public Art Museums* (London: Psychology Press, 1995), 6.
23. Gilane Tawadros, 'Is the Past a Foreign Country?', *Museums Journal*, 9 (1990), 30-1.
24. Mark O'Neill, 'The Good Enough Visitor', in Richard Sandell (ed.), *Museums, Society, Inequality* (London: Routledge, 2002), 29.
25. Sonya Atalay, 'No Sense of the Struggle: Creating a Context for Survivance at the NMAI', *American Indian Quarterly*, 30/3-4 (2006), 597.
26. Moira Simpson, 'Revealing and Concealing: Aboriginal Australia', in Janet Marstine (ed.), *New Museum Theory and Practice: An Introduction* (Malden, Mass., and Oxford: Blackwell Publishing, 2006), 153.
27. Moira Simpson, 'Burying the Past', *Museums Journal* (July 1994), 31.
28. Catherine Bell, 'Repatriation of Cultural Material to First Nations in Canada: Legal and Ethical Justifications', in James A. R. Nafziger and Ann M. Nicgorski (eds), *Cultural Heritage Issues: The Legacy of Conquest, Colonisation, and Commerce* (Leiden: Martinus Nijhoff, 2009), 81-106.
29. Marstine (ed.), *New Museum Theory and Practice*, 14.

30. Marstine (ed.), *New Museum Theory and Practice*, 14.
31. Marstine (ed.), *New Museum Theory and Practice*, 14.
32. Marstine (ed.), *New Museum Theory and Practice*, 14.
33. Stuart Hall, *Modernity and Difference* (London: Institute of International Visual Arts, 2001), 23.
34. Hall, *Modernity and Difference*, 22.
35. Tony Bennett, 'The Political Rationality of the Museum', *Australian Journal of Media & Culture*, 3/1 (1990), 33–55.
36. Eilean Hooper-Greenhill, *Museums and the Interpretation of Visual Culture (Museum Meanings)* (London: Routledge, 2000), 152.
37. James Clifford, 'Of Other Peoples: Beyond the "Salvage" Paradigm', in Hal Foster (ed.), *Discussions in Contemporary Culture* (Seattle: Bay Press, 1987), 121–30, and *The Predicament of Culture: Twentieth-century Ethnography, Literature, and Art* (Cambridge, Mass.: Harvard University Press, 1988).
38. James Cuno, *Museum Matters: In Praise of the Encyclopaedic Museum* (Chicago: University of Chicago Press, 2011).
39. Bennett, 'The Political Rationality of the Museum', 33–55.
40. Cuno, *Museum Matters*, 43.
41. Cuno, *Museum Matters*, 45.
42. Cuno, *Museum Matters*, 45.
43. Hilde S. Hein, *The Museum in Transition: A Philosophical Perspective* (Washington: Smithsonian Books, 2000), 142.
44. Andreas Huyssen, *Twilight Memories: Marking Time in a Culture of Amnesia* (London: Routledge, 1995).
45. Patty Gerstenblith, 'Acquistition and Deacquisition of Museum Collections and the Fiduciary Obligations of Museums to the Public', *Cardozo Journal of International and Comparative Law*, 409/11 (2003), 414.
46. Nick Prior, 'Having One's Tate and Eating It: Transformation of the Museum in a Hyper-Modern Era', in Andrew McClellan (ed.) *Art and Its Publics: Museum Studies at the Millennium* (Oxford: Blackwell, 2003), 63. See also 'Postmodern Restructurings', in Sharon Macdonald (ed.), *A Companion to Museum Studies* (London: Blackwell, 2006).
47. Tony Bennett, 'Putting Policy into Cultural Studies', in Lawrence Grossberg, Cary Nelson, and Paula Treichler, *Cultural Studies* (New York: Routledge, 1992).
48. Marstine (ed.), *New Museum Theory and Practice*, 19.
49. Nancy Fraser, 'From Redistribution to Recognition? Dilemmas of Justice in a "Post-Socialist" Age', *New Left Review*, 1/212 (July–August 1995).
50. Iris Marion Young, *Justice and the Politics of Difference* (Princeton: University of Princeton, 1990), 174.
51. See Hilde S. Hein, *The Museum in Transition: A Philosophical Perspective* (Washington: Smithsonian Books, 2000) for a thoughtful account of these trends.

52. The conference was '(Re)Presenting America': Are Culturally Specific Museums a Good Thing?, held at the National Museum of the American Indian in Washington, 25 April 2012.

53. Museums Association, Museums Change Lives (London: Museums Association, 2013), 2.

54. Museums Association, Museums Change Lives, 6.

55. Fraser, 'From Redistribution to Recognition?'

56. Kwame Anthony Appiah, 'Whose Culture Is It?', in James Cuno (ed.), Whose Culture? The Promise of Museums and the Debate Over Antiquities (Princeton: Princeton University Press, 2009), 78.

57. Lois Silverman, 'The Therapeutic Potential of Museums', in Richard Sandell (ed.), Museums, Society, Inequality (London: Routledge, 2002), 77.

58. Stuart Hall, 'The Emergence of Cultural Studies and the Crisis of the Humanities', October, 53 (1990), 11–90; emphasis in the original.

59. Terry Eagleton, The Idea of Culture (Oxford: Blackwell Publishers Ltd, 2000).

60. Steven Conn, Do Museums Still Need Objects? (Pennsylvania: University of Pennsylvania Press, 2010), 15.

61. Steven Weil, 'From Being About Something to Being for Somebody: The Ongoing Transformation of the American Museum', Daedalus, 128/3 (1999), 229–58.

62. Sandell (ed.), Museums, Society, Inequality, p. xvii.

63. Sandell (ed.), Museums, Society, Inequality, 3.

64. Geraldine Kendal, 'Mark Taylor, Museums Are Not a Place to Come and Worship in Silence', Museums Association News (9 January 2013).

65. Quoted in Edward Linenthal, 'Anatomy of a Controversy', in Edward T. Linenthal and Tom Engelhardt (eds), History Wars: The Enola Gay and Other Battles for the American Past (New York: Owl Books, 1996), 35.

66. 'Snoopy at the Smithsonian', Wall Street Journal (25 October 1994).

67. James Davison Hunter, Culture Wars: The Struggle to Control The Family, Art, Education, Law, and Politics in America (New York: Basic Books: 1992).

68. Quoted in 'Controversy Over Smithsonian Exhibits on American Science and Atomic Bombs', American Institute of Physics History Newsletter, 27/1 (Spring 1995), https://www.aip.org/history/newsletter/spr95/smiths.htm, accessed September 2015.

69. Steven Dubin, Displays of Power: Controversy in the American Museum from the Enola Gay to Sensation! (New York: NYU Press, 2001), 2.

70. Quoted in Bridget R. Cooks, Exhibiting Blackness: African Americans and the American Art Museum, (Amherst, Mass.: University of Massachusetts Press, 2011), 45.

71. Cooks, Exhibiting Blackness, 45.

72. Adam Kuper, Culture: The Anthropologists Account (Cambridge, Mass.: Harvard University Press, 1999).

73. Sharon Macdonald (ed.), *The Politics of Display: Museums, Science, Culture* (London: Routledge, 1998), 118–38. See also, Macdonald, *Behind the Scenes at the Science Museum* (Oxford and New York: Berg, 2002).

74. Jan Marontate, 'Museums and the Constitution of Culture', in Mark Jacobs and Nancy Weiss Hanrahan (eds), *The Blackwell Companion to the Sociology of Culture* (Malden, Mass. and Oxford: Blackwell Publishing, 2005), 289.

75. Marontate, 'Museums and the Constitution of Culture', 289.

76. See the Institute for Cultural Practices, Manchester University for a write-up of the event here: http://culturalpractice.wordpress.com/?s=repatriation.

77. 'Should the Parthenon Marbles be Returned?', *Museums Journal* (31 May 2012).

78. Julia Halperin and Javier Pes, 'About-Face on Restitution', *Art Newspaper* (February 2014).

79. Tom Masberg, 'Sending Artworks Home, But to Whom? Denver Museum to Return Totems to Kenyan Museum', *New York Times* (30 January 2014).

80. Masberg, 'Sending Artworks Home, But to Whom?'.

81. Anna Javér, 'Textiles for the Afterlife', *Hali* (Winter, 2010), 56.

82. *The Paracas Collection: A Stolen World*, exhibition catalogue (Museum of World Culture, City of Gothenburg, 2008), 4.

83. Bjorn Sandmark, *Letter from the Embassy of Peru*, no. 83/2009 (15 December 2009).

Chapter 6. Who Owns Culture?

1. Quoted in Dalya Alberge, 'Turkey Turns to Human Rights Law to Reclaim British Museum Sculptures', *The Observer* (8 December 2012).

2. Charles T. Newton, *Travels and Discoveries in the Levant*, ii (London: Day & Son, 1865), 110.

3. '"Louvre'a suçüstü" haberi için Radikal'e teşekkür eden Kültür ve Turizm Bakanı Ertuğrul Günay, Türkiye'den çalınmış çinileri geri getirmek için çalışma başlattıklarını açıkladı', *Radikal* (29 October 2012).

4. 'Turkish Tomb Could Regain Long-Lost Head', *Art Newspaper* (May 2014), 18.

5. Quoted in 'Turkey's Cultural Ambitions: Of Marbles and Men', *The Economist* (19 May 2012).

6. Quoted in 'Yale to return all Machu Picchu artefacts by December 2012', *Peruvian Times* (31 May 2011).

7. Zahi Hawass, *Secrets from the Sand: My Search for Egypt's Past* (New York: Harry N. Abrams, Inc., 2011), 251.

8. See Zahi Hawass's website, http://www.drhawass.com/.

9. Her speech is available here: http://www.uk.digiserve.com/mentor/marbles/speech.htm.

10. Henry Porter, 'The Greeks Gave us the Olympics: Let Them Have Their Marbles', *The Observer* (20 May 2012).

11. Nicky Mariam Onti, 'Greece Pushes UNESCO on Cultural Heritage', *Greek Reporter* (13 December 2012).
12. Elazar Barkan, *The Guilt of Nations: Restitution and Negotiating Historical Injustices* (Baltimore: Johns Hopkins University Press, 2001), p. xxxiv.
13. UNESCO, Convention on the Means of Prohibiting and Preventing the Illicit Import, Export and Transfer of Ownership of Cultural Property 1970, full text available at http://www.unesco.org/new/en/culture/themes/illicit-trafficking-of-cultural-property/1970-convention/text-of-the-convention/.
14. Quoted in James Cuno, *Who Owns Antiquity? Museums and the Battle Over Our Ancient Heritage* (Princeton: Princeton University Press, 2008), 33–4.
15. Kwame Anthony Appiah, 'Whose Culture Is It?', in James Cuno (ed.), *Whose Culture? The Promise of Museums and the Debate Over Antiquities* (Princeton: Princeton University Press, 2009), 74.
16. Karl Marx, 'The Grundrisse', in Robert C. Tucker (ed), *The Marx-Engels Reader* (London and New York: W.W. Norton & Company, 1978), 246. I am grateful to Munira Mirza for drawing my attention to this passage.
17. Munira Mirza, *The Politics of Culture: The Case for Universalism* (Basingstoke: Palgrave Macmillan, 2011), p. x.
18. 'Ankara Welcomes New Civilisations Museum', *Hurriyet Daily News* (23 January 2012). Building great museums with fabulous artefacts will create a draw for tourists.
19. Email exchange between the author and Andrew Finkle, October 2012.
20. Email exchange between the author and Andrew Finkle, October 2012.
21. Bill Schiller, 'Art Dealer Honored to Sabotage Auction', *The Star* (3 March 2009).
22. 'China's Global Antique Auction Squeeze to Boost Contemporary Art', *Jing Daily* (5 November 2012).
23. 'Recovery of China's Lost Marbles Stirs Debate', *South China Morning Post* (20 February 2014).
24. Jason Farago, 'Turkey's Restitution Dispute with the Met Challenges the "Universal Museum" *Comment is Free*', *The Guardian* (Sunday, 7 October 2012), http://www.theguardian.com/commentisfree/2012/oct/07/turkey-restitution-dispute-met.
25. Cuno, *Whose Culture?*, 28.
26. Cuno, *Who Owns Antiquity?*, p. xviii.
27. Cuno, *Who Owns Antiquity?*, 132.
28. Cuno, *Who Owns Antiquity?*, p. xviii.
29. Cuno, *Who Owns Antiquity?*, p. xviii.
30. Cuno, *Whose Culture?*, p. ix.
31. Martin Bailey, 'A George Bush Approach to International Relations', *Art Newspaper*, 133 (February 2003), 7.
32. G. Lewis, 'The Universal Museum: A Special Case?' *ICOM News*, 1 (2004), 3.

33. Neil MacGregor, 'Preface', in Kim Sloane and Andrew Burnett (eds), *Enlightenment: Discovering the World in the Eighteenth Century* (London: British Museum Press, 2003), 6.
34. Neil MacGregor, 'The World in Our Hands', *The Guardian* (24 July 2004).
35. 'The British Museum Lends the Cyrus Cylinder to the National Museum of Iran', British Museum Press Release (10 September 2010).
36. 'A Message in Marble', *The Times* (5 December 2014).
37. Neil MacGregor, 'Loan of a Parthenon Sculpture to the Hermitage: A Marble Ambassador of a European Ideal', *British Museum blog* (5 December 2014).
38. 'Art as Diplomatic Token, *Grumpyarthistorian* (9 December 2014), http://grumpyarthistorian.blogspot.co.uk/2014/12/art-as-diplomatic-token.html.
39. Peter Aspden, 'A Diplomatic Figleaf for the Parthenon Marbles', *Financial Times* (12 December 2004).
40. A Message in Marble', *The Times* (5 December 2014).
41. Cuno, *Museum Matters*, 7.
42. Cuno, *Museum Matters*, 31.
43. Cuno, *Whose Culture?*, 27.
44. Cuno, *Who Owns Antiquity?*, p. xix.
45. Cuno, *Who Owns Antiquity?*, 123.
46. Cuno, *Who Owns Antiquity?*, p. xxxiv.
47. Tatiana Flessas, *The Ends of the Museum* (LSE Law, Society and Economy Working Papers, 14/2013; London: LSE Law, 2013).
48. Philippe de Montebello, 'And What Do You Propose Should be Done with Those Objects?', in Cuno (ed.), *Whose Culture?*, 55.
49. Cuno, *Who Owns Antiquity?*, 146.
50. Cuno, *Museum Matters*, 110.
51. Cuno, *Who Owns Antiquity?*, 147.
52. Colin Renfrew, 'Book Review', *Burlington Magazine* (November 2008), 768.
53. Quoted in Tiffany Jenkins, 'Archaeologists on the Front Line', *Spiked-Online* (13 April 2010).
54. Quoted in Jenkins, 'Archaeologists on the Front Line'.
55. Yannis Hamilakis, 'Iraq, Stewardship and "the Record": An Ethical Crisis for Archaeology', *Public Archaeology*, 3 (2003), 104–11.
56. James Cuno, 'Saving Antiquities from Islamic State', *Wall Street Journal* (21 September 2015).
57. Cuno, 'Saving Antiquities from Islamic State'.
58. Quoted in 'Greece Urges Return of Sculptures', *BBC News Online* (21 June 2009) http://news.bbc.co.uk/1/hi/entertainment/arts_and_culture/8110010.stm.
59. Christopher Hitchens, *The Parthenon Marbles: The Case for Reunification* (London: Verso Books, 2008), 24.

60. Malcolm Bell (in conversation with James Cuno), 'Who's Right? Repatriation of Cultural Property', *IIP Digital* (2 November 2010).

61. British Museum, *Annual Review 2014* (London: British Museum, 2014).

62. 'Art Expert Issues Warning Over Plan to Tour Burrell Collection', *Glasgow Herald* (5 September 2013).

63. Blake Gopnik, 'The Rush to the Box Office', *Art Newspaper* (April 2013).

64. See Derek Fincham, 'The Parthenon Sculptures and Cultural Justice', *Fordham Intellectual Property, Media & Entertainment Law Journal* (Spring 2013), 943–1016.

65. John Henry Merryman, 'The Nation and the Object', *International Journal of Cultural Property*, 3/1 (1994), 61–7.

Chapter 7. The Rise of Identity Museums

1. Robert McC. Adams, to a benefactor (quoted by W. Richard West Jr at a press conference, 25 October 1994).

2. Janet Marstine (ed.), *New Museum Theory and Practice: An Introduction* (Malden, Mass. and Oxford: Blackwell Publishing, 2006), 17.

3. Kylie Message, *New Museums and the Making of Culture* (Oxford and London: Berg, 2006), 2.

4. Quoted in Lawrence M. Small, 'A Passionate Collector', *Smithsonian Museum* (2000), http://www.smithsonianmag.com/ist/?next=/history/a-passionate-collector-33794183.

5. Quoted in Duane Blue Spruce (ed.), *Spirit of a Native Place: Building the National Museum of the American Indian* (Washington, DC: National Geographic Books, 2005), 89.

6. Jonathan King, 'North American Ethnography in the Collection of Sir Hans Sloane', in Oliver Impey and Arthur MacGregor (eds), *The Origins of Museums: The Cabinet of Curiosities in Sixteenth and Seventeenth Century Europe* (Oxford: Clarendon Press, 1985; 2nd edn, London: The House of Stratus, 2001), 319.

7. Mary Jane Lenz, 'George Gustav Heye', in Spruce (ed.), *Spirit of a Native Place*, 105.

8. George Hubbard Pepper, 'The Museum of the American Indian, Heye Foundation', *Geographical Review*, 2/6 (1916), 401–18.

9. Quoted in Roland W. *Force, Politics and the Museum of the American Indian: The Heye & the Mighty* (Honolulu: Mechas, 1999), 21.

10. Quoted in Andrew Boxer, 'Native Americans and the Federal Government', *History Review*, 64 (September 2009), http://www.historytoday.com/andrew-boxer/native-americans-and-federal-government, accessed September 2015.

11. Ira Jacknis, 'A New Thing? The NMAI in Historical and Institutional Perspective', *American Indian Quarterly*, 30/3–4 (2006), 511–42.

12. Robert Rydell, *All The World's A Fair: Visions of Empire at American International Expositions, 1876–1916* (Chicago: University of Chicago Press, 1985), 5.

13. Rydell, *All The World's A Fair*, 6.

14. Rydell, *All The World's A Fair*, 95.

15. Quoted in Spruce (ed.), *Spirit of a Native Place*, 109.

16. Quoted in Spruce (ed.), *Spirit of a Native Place*, 112.

17. *Aims and Objects of the Museum of the American Indian, Hey Foundation* (Indian Notes and Monographs, 34; New York: Museum of the American Indian, Heye Foundation, 1929).

18. Amy Lonetree, 'Continuing Dialogues: Evolving Views of the National Museum of the American Indian', *Public Historian*, 28/2 (2006), 61.

19. Janet Catherine Berlo and Aldona Jonaitis, '"Indian Country" on the National Mall', in Amy Lonetree and Amanda J. Cobb-Greetham (eds), *The National Museum of the American Indian: Critical Conversations* (Lincoln, Nebr.: University of Nebraska Press, 2008), 210–11.

20. Lissant Bolton, 'The Object in View', in Laura Lynn Peers and Alison Kay Brown (eds), *Museums and Source Communities: A Routledge Reader* (London: Routledge, 2003), 46.

21. Ruth Phillips, *Museum Pieces: Toward the Indigenization of Canadian Museums* (McGill-Queen's/Beaverbrook Canadian Foundation Studies in Art History, 7; Montreal and Ithaca, NY: McGill-Queen's University Press, 2011), 111.

22. Phillips, *Museum Pieces*, 112.

23. Phillips, *Museum Pieces*, 111.

24. Phillips, *Museum Pieces*, 111.

25. Amanda J. Cobb, 'The National Museum of the American Indian: Sharing the Gift', *American Indian Quarterly*, 29/3–4 (2005), 367.

26. Edward Rothstein, 'To Each His Own Museum, as Identity Goes on Display', *New York Times* (28 December 2010).

27. Steven Conn, *Do Museums Still Need Objects?* (Philadelphia: University of Pennsylvania Press, 2010), 39.

28. Michael F. Brown, 'Exhibiting Indigenous Heritage in the Age of Cultural Property', in James Cuno (ed.), *Whose Culture? The Promise of Museums and the Debate over Antiquities* (Princeton: Princeton University Press, 2009), 158.

29. Brown, 'Exhibiting Indigenous Heritage in the Age of Cultural Property', 159.

30. National Museum of the American Latino Commission, *To Illuminate the American Story for All: Final Report to the President and Congress of the United States* (2011).

31. 'The Thorny Path to a National Black Museum', *New York Times* (22 January 2011).

32. Robert McC. Adams, to a benefactor (quoted by W. Richard West Jr at a press conference, 25 October 1994).

Chapter 8. Atonement: Making Amends for Past Wrongs

1. Intelligence Squared debate, *The Parthenon Marbles Should be Returned to Athens* (London, 11 June 2012).
2. Elazar Barkan, 'Restitution and Amending Historical Injustices in International Morality', in John Torpey (ed.), *Politics and the Past: On Repairing Historical Injustices* (Lanham, Md.: Rowman & Littlefield, 2003), 100.
3. Richard Vernon, *Historical Redress: Must We Pay for the Past?* (London and New York: Continuum, 2012), 132.
4. Hannah Arendt, *The Origins of Totalitarianism* (New York: Harcourt Brace, 1971).
5. Edmund Burke, *Reflections on the Revolution in France* (New York: Penguin Books, 1969), 246–7.
6. Hannah Arendt, 'Preface to the First Edition', *The Origins of Totalitarianism* (New York: Harcourt, Brace, 1973), p. ix.
7. Jeffrey Olick and Brenda Coughlin, 'The Politics of Regret: Analytical Frames', in Torpey (ed.), *Politics and the Past*, 37.
8. Olick and Coughlin, 'The Politics of Regret', in Torpey (ed.), *Politics and the Past*, 45.
9. See David Lowenthal, *The Heritage Crusade and the Spoils of History* (Cambridge: Cambridge University Press, 1998); and also, *The Past is a Foreign Country* (Cambridge: Cambridge University Press, 1985).
10. David Lowenthal, 'On Arraigning Ancestors: A Critique of Historical Contrition', *North Carolina Law Review*, 87 (2009), 901–66.
11. Elazar Barkan, *The Guilt of Nations: Restitution, and Negotiating Historical Injustices* (Baltimore: Johns Hopkins University Press, 2001), 316.
12. See 'Blair "Sorrow" Over Slave Trade', on *BBC Online* news, http://news.bbc.co.uk/1/hi/6185176.stm (27 November 2006).
13. Paul Williams, *Memorial Museums: The Global Rush to Commemorate Atrocities* (Oxford: Berg, 2007).
14. John Torpey, *Making Whole What Has Been Smashed: On Reparations Politics* (Cambridge, Mass.: Harvard University Press, 2006), 16.
15. Torpey, *Making Whole What Has Been Smashed*, 1.
16. Wendy Brown, *States of Injury: Power and Freedom in Late Modernity* (Princeton: Princeton University Press, 1995), 66.
17. Barkan, *The Guilt of Nations*, p. ix.
18. Barkan, *The Guilt of Nations*, p. xvi.
19. Jean Bethke Elshtain, 'Politics and Forgiveness', in Nigel Biggar (ed.), *Burying the Past: Making Peace and Doing Justice After Civil Conflict* (Washington, DC: Georgetown University Press, 2003), 45.
20. Marina Warner, 'Sorry: The Present State of Apology', *Open Democracy* (7 November 2002).

21. Elizabeth Willis, 'The Law, Politics, and "Historical Wounds": The Dja Dja Warrung Bark Etchings Case in Australia', *International Journal of Cultural Property*, 15/1 (2008).

22. Gillian Cowlishaw, 'Collateral Damage in the History Wars', in Tess Lea, Emma Kowal, and Gillian Cowlishaw (eds), *Moving Anthropology: Critical Indigenous Studies* (Darwin: Charles Darwin University Press, 2006), 131–45.

23. Sonya Atalay, 'No Sense of the Struggle: Creating a Context for Survivance at the NMAI', *American Indian Quarterly*, 30/3–4 (2006), 601.

24. Yannis Hamilakis, *The Nation and Its Ruins: Antiquity, Archaeology, and the National Imagination in Greece* (Oxford: Oxford University Press, 2009), 243–4.

25. Alan Audi, 'A Semiotics of Cultural Property Argument', *International Journal of Cultural Property* 14/2 (May 2007), 131–56.

26. Henry Porter, 'The Greeks Gave Us the Olympics. Let Them Have Their Marbles', *The Observer* (20 May 2012).

27. Gillian K. Cowlishaw, 'Cultures of Complaint: An Ethnography of Rural Racial Rivalry', *Journal of Sociology*, 42/4 (2006), 429–45.

28. Elizabeth Willis, 'The Law, Politics, and "Historical Wounds": The Dja Dja Warrung Bark Etchings Case in Australia', *International Journal of Cultural Property*, 15/1 (2008), 49–63.

29. Dmitri M. Bondarenko, 'Benin', in Toyin Falola and Amanda Warcnock (eds), *Encyclopedia of the Middle Passage* (Westport, Conn.: Greenwood Press, 2007), 55–8.

30. Tony Judt, 'From the House of the Dead: On Modern European Memory', *New York Review of Books* (6 October 2005), 13.

31. Janna Thompson, *Taking Responsibility for the Past: Reparations and Historical Justice* (Cambridge: Polity Press; Malden, Mass: Blackwell Publishers Ltd, 2002).

Chapter 9. Burying Knowledge: The Fate of Human Remains

1. Laura Peers, *Shrunken Heads* (Oxford: Pitt Rivers Museum, 2011).

2. James Fenton, 'The Pitt Rivers Museum Oxford', *Newsletter of the Museums Ethnographers Group* (16 April 1984), 37–40.

3. Dan Hicks and Alice Stevenson, *World Archaeology at the Pitt Rivers Museum: A Characterization* (Oxford: Archaeopress, 2013), 1.

4. Quoted in Jonan Siegel, *The Emergence of the Modern Museum: An Anthology of Nineteenth-Century Sources* (Oxford: Oxford University Press, 2008), 308.

5. Quoted in 'Should Shrunken Heads Stay in Museum?', *Oxford Times* (14 February 2007).

6. Peers, *Shrunken Heads*.

7. Pitt Rivers visitor feedback form (16 August 2003); cited in Laura Peers, 'On the Treatment of Dead Enemies', in Helen Lambert and Maryon McDonald (eds), *Social Bodies* (New York and Oxford: Bergham Books, 2009), 78.

8. Quoted in 'Should Shrunken Heads Stay in Museum?'

9. Quoted in 'Should Shrunken Heads Stay in Museum?'

10. The TAC are a community-based organization set up in 1973 providing legal, heath, and cultural welfare to the Aboriginal people, and recognized by governments as the appropriate body to which to return Tasmanian Aboriginal remains.

11. *Friendly Mission: The Tasmanian Journals and Papers of George Augustus Robinson, 1829–1834*, ed. Norman James Brian Plomley (Hobart: Tasmanian Historical Research Association, 2008).

12. *Friendly Mission*, ed. Plomley.

13. Robert Anderson, quoted in TAC, 'Submission to the Working Group on Human Remains', *Human Remains Working Group Report* (London: Department for Culture, Media and Sport, 2003), 36.

14. Kennedy, 'Knowledge or Humanity', *The Guardian* (28 March 2006).

15. 'British Museum Decides to Return Two Tasmanian Aboriginal Cremation Ash Bundles', British Museum Press Release (24 March 2006).

16. DCMS, *Working Group on Human Remains Report* (London: Department of Culture, Media, and Sport, 2003).

17. DCMS, *Scoping Survey of Historic Human Remains in English Museums Undertaken on Behalf of the Ministerial Working Group on Human Remains* (London: Department of Culture, Media, and Sport, 2003).

18. 'Radiocarbon Dating of Museum Human Remains Writes Egyptian History', Natural History Museum Press Release (9 September 2013).

19. Mike Pickering and Phil Gordon, 'Repatriation: The End of the Beginning', in Des Griffen and Leon Paroissien (eds), *Understanding Museums: Australian Museums and Museology* (epublication, 2011), 3, http://www.nma.gov.au/research/understanding-museums/MPickering_PGordon_2011.html.

20. Simon Stephens, 'Maori Remains Repatriated to New Zealand', *Museums Journal* (30 October 2013).

21. Jack F. Trope and Walter R. Echo-Hawk, 'The Native American Graves Protection and Repatriation Act Background and Legislative History', in Devon A. Mihesuah (ed.), *Repatriation Reader: Who Owns Human Remains* (Lincoln, Nebr.: University of Nebraska Press, 2000), 123.

22. Simon Stephens, 'Maori Remains Repatriated to New Zealand', *Museums Journal* (30 October 2013).

23. Laura Peers, 'On the Treatment of Dead Enemies', 84.

24. Native American Graves Protection and Repatriation Act, section 2, 2.

25. Native American Graves Protection and Repatriation Act, section 7, 4.

26. Chip Colwell-Chanthaphonh, Rachel Maxson, and Jami Powell, 'The Repatriation of Culturally Unidentifiable Human Remains', *Museum Management and Curatorship*, 26/1 (2011), 36.

27. Colwell-Chanthaphonh, Maxson, and Powell, 'The Repatriation of Culturally Unidentifiable Human Remains', 27.

28. Colwell-Chanthaphonh, Maxson, and Powell, 'The Repatriation of Culturally Unidentifiable Human Remains', 27.

29. Colwell-Chanthaphonh, Maxson, and Powell, 'The Repatriation of Culturally Unidentifiable Human Remains', 29.

30. Colwell-Chanthaphonh, Maxson, and Powell, 'The Repatriation of Culturally Unidentifiable Human Remains', 37.

31. Nancy B. Rosoff, 'Integrating Native Views into Museum Procedures: Hope and Practice at the National Museum of the American Indian', in Laura Lynn Peers and Alison Kay Brown (eds), *Museums and Source Communities: A Routledge Reader* (London: Routledge, 2003), 78.

32. Elizabeth Weiss, *Reburying the Past: The Effects of Repatriation and Reburial of Scientific Inquiry* (New York: Nova Science Publishers, 2008).

33. Quoted in Elizabeth Weiss, 'The Bone Battle: The Attack on Scientific Freedom', *Liberty*, 23 (2009), 42.

34. Quoted in Weiss, 'The Bone Battle', 42.

35. Katherine Verdery, *The Political Lives of Dead Bodies: Reburial and Postsocialist Change* (New York: Columbia University Press, 1999), 28.

36. Verdery, *The Political Lives of Dead Bodies*, 29.

37. Verdery, *The Political Lives of Dead Bodies*, 31.

38. Verdery, *The Political Lives of Dead Bodies*, 51.

39. I explore this in more depth in Tiffany Jenkins, *Contesting Human Remains in Museum Collections: The Crisis of Cultural Authority* (New York: Routledge, 2010).

40. John Cove, *What The Bones Say: Tasmanian Aborigines, Science and Domination* (Ottawa: Carleton University Press, 1995).

41. Vine Deloria Jr, *Behind the Trail of Broken Treaties: An Indian Declaration of Independence* (Austin: University of Texas Press, 1985), 41.

42. Joseph Tilden Rhea, *Race Pride and the American Identity* (Cambridge, Mass.: Harvard University Press, 2001), 15.

43. Vine Deloria Jr, *Red Earth, White Lies: Native Americans and the Myths of Scientific Fact* (New York: Scribner, 1995), 19.

44. Vine Deloria Jr, *Red Earth, White Lies*, 20.

45. Vine Deloria Jr, *Red Earth, White Lies*, 6.

46. Russell Thornton, 'Repatriation as Healing the Trauma of History', in Cressida Fforde, Jane Hubert, and Paul Turnbull (eds), *The Dead And Their Possessions:*

Repatriation In Principle, Policy And Practice (New York and London: Routledge, 2004), 23.

47. Thornton, 'Repatriation as Healing the Trauma of History', 23.
48. Russell Thornton, *Studying Native America: Problems and Prospects* (Madison: University of Wisconsin Press, 1998).
49. Barbara Isaac, 'Implementation of NAGPRA: The Peabody Museum of Archaeology and Ethnology, Harvard', in Fforde, Hubert, and Turnbull (eds), *The Dead and Their Possessions*, 162.
50. Quoted in 'Memorandum submitted by the Pitt Rivers Museum', Select Committee on Culture, Media and Sport (DCMS, Appendix 49, 2000).
51. Department for Culture, Media & Sport, *Report of the Working Group on Human Remains* (London, 2003), 16.
52. Department for Culture, Media & Sport, *Report of the Working Group on Human Remains*, 101.
53. Tristram Besterman, 'Why the British Museum Should Give Back Maori Human Remains if it Wants to Take a Truly Enlightened Approach', *Museums Journal*, 108/7 (July 2008), 17.
54. Tristram Besterman, *Returning the Ancestors* (Manchester: University of Manchester Museum 2004), 4.
55. Besterman, *Returning the Ancestors*, 8.
56. Maurice Davies, 'Editorial', *Museums Journal*, 3 (March 1993), 7.
57. Moira Simpson, 'Burying the Past', *Museums Journal*, 7 (July 1994), 31.
58. Moira Simpson, *Museums and Repatriation: An Account of Contested Items in Museum Collections in the UK, with Comparative Material from Other Countries* (London: Museums Association, 1997).
59. In Tiffany Jenkins, *Contesting Human Remains in Museum Collections: The Crisis of Cultural Authority* (New York: Routledge, 2010), I analyse the rise of claims from pagan groups.
60. 'Egyptian Mummies Are Covered Up', *BBC News Online* (21 May 2008).
61. Hugh Kilmister, 'Visitor Perceptions of Ancient Egyptian Human Remains in Three United Kingdom Museums', *Papers from the Institute of Archaeology*, 14 (2003), 58.
62. Kilmister, 'Visitor Perceptions of Ancient Egyptian Human Remains in Three United Kingdom Museums', 65.

Concluding Thoughts

1. 'Zahed National Museum Set to Further Raise UAE's Profile on the World's Cultural Map', TSIC Press Release (25 November 2010).
2. 'China's Palace Museum to Become World-Class', *China US Daily* (7 July 2012).

FURTHER READING

Brown, Michael F., *Who Owns Native Culture?* (Cambridge, Mass.: Harvard University Press, 2004).

Cuno, James, *Museums Matter: In Praise of the Encyclopaedic Museum* (Chicago: University of Chicago Press, 2011).

Cuno, James (ed.), *Whose Culture? The Promise of Museums and the Debate Over Antiquities* (Princeton: Princeton University Press, 2009).

Flessas, Tatiana, *The Ends of the Museum* (LSE Law, Society and Economy Working Papers 14/2013; London: LSE Law, 2013).

Hein, Hilde S., *The Museum in Transition: A Philosophical Perspective* (Washington: Smithsonian Books, 2000).

Hitchens, Christopher, *The Parthenon Marbles: The Case for Reunification* (London: Verso Books, 2008).

Hooper-Greenhill, Eilean, *Museums and the Shaping of Knowledge* (London and New York: Routledge, 1992).

Jenkins, Tiffany, *Contesting Human Remains in Museum Collections: The Crisis of Cultural Authority* (New York: Routledge, 2010).

Lowenthal, David, 'On Arraigning Ancestors: A Critique of Historical Contrition', *North Carolina Law Review*, 87 (2009), 901–66.

Lowenthal, David, *The Past is a Foreign Country–Revisited* (Cambridge: Cambridge University Press, 2015).

McClennan, Andrew, *Inventing the Louvre: Art, Politics and the Origins of the Modern Museum in Eighteenth-Century Paris* (Berkeley and Los Angeles: University of California Press, 1999).

Miles, Margaret, *Art as Plunder: The Ancient Origins of Debate About Cultural Property* (New York and Cambridge: Cambridge University Press, 2008).

Mirza, Munira, *The Politics of Culture: The Case for Universalism* (Houndmills: Palgrave Macmillan, 2011).

Phillips, Ruth, *Museum Pieces: Toward the Indigenization of Canadian Museums* (McGill-Queen's/Beaverbrook Canadian Foundation Studies in Art History, 7; Montreal and Ithaca, NY: McGill-Queen's University Press, 2011).

St Clair, William, *Lord Elgin and The Marbles* (Oxford: Oxford University Press, 1998).

Torpey, John, *Making Whole What Has Been Smashed: On Reparations Politics* (Cambridge, Mass.: Harvard University Press, 2006).

INDEX